200 Great
Four Ingredient
Recipes

200 Great
Four Ingredient
Recipes

Joanna Farrow
& Jenny White

LORENZ BOOKS

This edition is published by Lorenz Books
Lorenz Books is an imprint of Anness Publishing Ltd
Hermes House, 88–89 Blackfriars Road, London SE1 8HA
tel. 020 7401 2077; fax 020 7633 9499
www.lorenzbooks.com; info@anness.com

© Anness Publishing Ltd 2004

UK agent: The Manning Partnership Ltd, 6 The Old Dairy, Melcombe Road,
Bath BA2 3LR; tel. 01225 478444; fax 01225 478440; sales@manning-partnership.co.uk

UK distributor: Grantham Book Services Ltd, Isaac Newton Way, Alma Park Industrial
Estate, Grantham, Lincs NG31 9SD; tel. 01476 541080; fax 01476 541061;
orders@gbs.tbs-ltd.co.uk

North American agent/distributor: National Book Network, 4501 Forbes Boulevard,
Suite 200, Lanham, MD 20706; tel. 301 459 3366; fax 301 429 5746; www.nbnbooks.com

Australian agent/distributor: Pan Macmillan Australia, Level 18, St Martins Tower,
31 Market St, Sydney, NSW 2000; tel. 1300 135 113; fax 1300 135 103;
customer.service@macmillan.com.au

New Zealand agent/distributor: David Bateman Ltd, 30 Tarndale Grove, Off Bush Road,
Albany, Auckland; tel. (09) 415 7664; fax (09) 415 8892

Publisher: Joanna Lorenz
Editorial Director: Judith Simons
Project Editor: Sarah Uttridge
Jacket and Design: Chloë Steers
Typesetting: Jonathan Harley
Illustrations: Angela Wood
Recipes: Alex Barker, Jacqueline Clark, Joanna Farrow, Brian Glover,
Jane Milton, Jennie Shapter, Marlena Spieler, Kate Whiteman
Editorial Reader: Penelope Goodare
Production Controller: Darren Price

1 3 5 7 9 10 8 6 4 2

NOTES
Bracketed terms are intended for American readers.

For all recipes, quantities are given in both metric and imperial measures and, where
appropriate, measures are also given in standard cups and spoons. Follow one set, but not a
mixture, because they are not interchangeable.

Standard spoon and cup measures are level.
1 tsp = 5ml, 1 tbsp = 15ml, 1 cup = 250ml/8fl oz

Australian standard tablespoons are 20ml. Australian readers should use 3 tsp
in place of 1 tbsp for measuring small quantities of gelatine, flour, salt, etc.

Medium (US large) eggs are used unless otherwise stated.

Contents

6 Introduction

8 The Minimalist Approach

10 Equipment

14 Minimalist Techniques

18 Fruit

20 Vegetables

22 Dairy Produce

24 Fish & Shellfish

26 Meat & Poultry

28 Herbs

30 Spices & Aromatics

34 Other Flavourings

38 Kitchen Basics

42 Short-cut Ingredients

44 Making the Basics

50 Making Simple Accompaniments

THE RECIPES

54 Breakfasts & Brunches

66 Soups

82 Snacks & Appetizers

106 Fish & Shellfish

130 Meat & Poultry

158 Vegetarian

176 Pasta & Rice

192 Salads

208 Vegetables & Side Dishes

228 Hot Desserts

246 Cold & Frozen Desserts

278 Cakes, Cookies & Bread

314 Index

INTRODUCTION

Just because a dish includes only a few ingredients, it doesn't mean you need to compromise on taste and enjoyment. Reducing the number of ingredients you use in a dish has many benefits. Not only does it make shopping easier and quicker, it also means spending less time on preparation, and it allows you to really enjoy the flavours of the few ingredients used. Fresh food tastes fantastic, so why not let the flavours of a few truly fabulous ingredients shine through rather than masking them with the taste of other ingredients?

In today's busy world, time is of the essence – and no one ever seems to have enough of it. When you're trying to cram as much as possible into a day, often the first thing that falls by the wayside is cooking. The last thing you feel like doing is spending an hour in the supermarket shopping for ingredients, then going home and preparing them before finally cooking a meal. The temptation is to grab a ready-prepared meal to heat up when you get home, or to pick up a takeaway – but sometimes, when you've had a hectic day at work or your kids have been running you ragged, what you really want is to sit down and relax with a tasty home-cooked meal. This book is devoted to helping you do just this.

The idea of making a dish that requires a huge list of ingredients can often put you off before you've even started – the shopping and preparation alone seeming like an unmanageable task. But the good news is that cooking doesn't need to be this way. It's easy to make delicious dishes using just a few ingredients – but the key to success lies in the ingredients you choose, and how you prepare and cook them.

The recipes in this book combine basic ingredients such as fruit, vegetables, meat, fish, herbs and spices, but they also make good use of ready-made or pre-prepared products such as curry pastes and pastry. Using these convenient products is a great way to save time, both on preparation and shopping, while still benefiting from the use of well-chosen, freshly cooked ingredients.

When buying basic ingredients, always try to buy the freshest, best quality ones you can to get the maximum flavour. Really fresh ingredients also have the benefit of having a higher nutritional content. If you can buy organic produce, do so. The flavour will be better and you will have the knowledge that they do not contain chemical fertilizers and pesticides. It is also a good idea to buy fruits and vegetables when they're in season. Although most are available all year round, you can really notice the difference between those that have been ripened naturally and those that have been grown out of season. Strawberries may be available in the middle of winter, but when you cut them open they are often white inside with a slightly waxy texture and none of the sweet, juicy, almost perfumed flavour of the summer fruits. There are so many fabulous ingredients at their peak in their own season that you don't have to buy unseasonal ones. Why buy tired-looking asparagus in autumn when there are plenty of mushrooms, squashes and root vegetables around – all of which can be made into delicious, varied meals.

When buying pre-prepared or ready-made ingredients such as stocks for soups, or custard to make ice cream, try to buy really good-quality, fresh varieties. When an ingredient is playing an intregral part in a dish, it needs to be well-flavoured with a good texture and consistency. If you use an inferior product with a poorer flavour, it will really show in the final dish. The same is true of flavouring ingredients such as curry pastes and spicy sauces – go for quality and you will reap the benefits.

Whether you're an experienced cook or an absolute beginner, you'll find something in this book to suit you perfectly. There are dishes for every occasion: healthy or indulgent breakfasts; warming soups; and snacks and appetizers to make when time is short. There are ideas for simple yet fabulous main courses, including chapters on vegetarian, pasta and rice dishes. There is a selection of classic and more unusual salads, as well as suggestions for making tasty vegetable side dishes. Finally, when you need a sweet treat, there are three whole chapters devoted to hot, cold and frozen desserts, and simple cakes, cookies and bread. No matter what the occasion, how much time you have, how many people you need to feed, or what you're in the mood for – you are sure to find the perfect dish within these pages.

Every recipe has an ingredients list of four items or fewer, and the only other things you will need are salt and freshly ground black pepper to season the food. In some cases flavoured oils such as garlic-, lemon-, or herb-infused olive oil are used for cooking or drizzling, so it's well worth keeping a small selection of these oils, but you can always use ordinary oil plus a little crushed garlic, chopped herbs or other flavourings if you prefer.

THE MINIMALIST APPROACH

In recent years, cooking and eating trends have changed considerably, with more emphasis on dishes that are quick and easy to prepare. This book teaches you how to really make the most of food – with simple, fabulous recipes that use only four top-quality ingredients, or fewer, enabling you to really savour the final dish. So sit back, relax and enjoy.

When you're cooking with four ingredients, each one has to be a star player. It is important to buy the best quality ingredients you can find so be selective when buying, as the better the raw materials, the more flavour the finished dish will have. Top-quality produce will also need fewer additional seasonings or flavourings to make it taste fabulous. And buying the best does not necessarily mean paying more. For example, meat from a good, traditional-style butcher is often cheaper than the better-quality types in the supermarket and it will probably have a fuller flavour. Good fish can be slightly harder to find. Be particularly choosy when buying from supermarket fish counters: avoid tired-looking specimens and remember that it is better to go for good-quality frozen fish and shellfish rather than poor-quality fresh. Farmers' market stores can be great sources of good-quality fruit and vegetables, as well as organic meat and poultry, and locally produced honey

STOCKS AND SAUCES

Ready-made stocks and sauces are infinitely useful for creating quick and easy meals and are a great way to cut down on preparation and cooking time. A basic tomato sauce can lay the foundations for hundreds of different dishes such as stews, casseroles and pasta. Simply add poultry, meat, fish, vegetables or beans and flavour with fresh herbs and spices. Sauces such as pesto are great for adding flavour, while a really great ready-made custard can be the perfect base for an ice cream. Good-quality bought sauces are readily available fresh or in jars – check out the list of ingredients on the label for some indication of the quality. A good bought liquid concentrate or fresh stock is worth keeping in the refrigerator or freezer. Remember that many bought chilled fresh products are suitable for home freezing, which is a good way of extending their shelf life. Alternatively, you can make your own supply of basic stocks and sauces and freeze them in practical, ready-to-use batches.

PRESERVED OR DRIED INGREDIENTS

Products such as sun-dried tomatoes, bottled roasted (bell) peppers and capers have a powerful taste and are useful for boosting flavour in many Mediterranean-style dishes. Dried mushrooms bring a full flavour to mushroom dishes and can be good for perking up simple soups, stews, casseroles and risottos.

STORE-CUPBOARD ESSENTIALS

Try to avoid overstocking the store cupboard (pantry). Choose good-quality extra virgin olive oil and balsamic vinegar for salad dressings and a lighter oil such as sunflower oil for cooking. A nut oil such as walnut or hazelnut is an interesting alternative to olive oil in salad dressings. One or two flavoured oils are great for adding extra taste.

Keep herb and spice supplies to a minimum as both lose their flavour comparatively quickly, particularly if exposed to light and warmth. If possible, it is better to grow or buy fresh herbs and freeze any leftovers for future use rather than stocking a cupboard full of dried herbs that have an inferior flavour. If possible, stock whole spices such as cumin and coriander and grind them as required using a mortar and pestle or in a spice grinder as ground spices tend to lose their flavour quickly. Freshly grated whole nutmeg is better than ready ground and it adds interest to potato dishes and white sauces.

As well as canned, bottled and dried goods, pre-frozen products are well worth buying: frozen prawns (shrimp) will thaw in five minutes in a colander under running cold water. The freezer can also be put to a range of other uses, from storing fresh herbs and cooked, dried beans, to extending the shelf life of nuts: these turn rancid fairly rapidly at room temperature due to their high oil content, but will freeze successfully for 3–4 months in sealed plastic bags.

Other ingredients you should always keep on hand include salt and black pepper (in a grinder), sugar, plain (all-purpose) flour and cornflour (cornstarch), plus basic staples such as pasta and rice. It is also handy to have a small selection of condiments or sauces such as soy sauce or pesto that can help to perk up or enhance the flavour of the simplest of dishes.

USING THE RECIPES

Each recipe uses no more than four ingredients, excluding salt, pepper and water. Some recipes use ready-made stock or sauce – but you can always use a home-made one if you prefer. Serving suggestions and ideas for garnishes or other decorations are included where appropriate, but these are not essential for the success of the dish. There are also suggestions for variations that offer alternative or additional flavourings and handy cook's tips that will help you achieve successful results every time

EQUIPMENT

You don't need a kitchen full of equipment to be a good cook; it is quality, not quantity, that counts, particularly when choosing essential pieces of equipment such as pans and knives. As long as you look after them, these should last for many years. This section guides you through the essential items, and suggests how you can improvise if necessary.

PANS & BAKEWARE

Always choose quality pans with a solid, heavy base because they retain heat better and are less likely to warp or buckle, and food is less likely to burn or stick. Heatproof glass lids are also useful because they allow you to keep an eye on cooking progress without having to uncover the pan repeatedly, losing heat.

PANS: SMALL, MEDIUM & LARGE

When cooking large quantities of food such as pasta or rice that need to be boiled in a large amount of water, the bigger the pan the better. It does not matter whether the pan is non-stick, but it is useful to have heatproof handles and lids so that the pan can also be used in the oven. A medium-size pan is ideal for cooking sauces and similar mixtures. Ideally, choose a non-stick pan, which will help to prevent thickened sauces sticking and burning, but you should avoid using metal implements for stirring, as they may damage the non-stick coating. The same guidelines apply to a small pan, which is ideal for preparing small quantities of food.

FRYING PAN

Select a non-stick pan that is shallow enough to allow you to easily slide a fish slice (spatula) into it. A frying pan with an ovenproof handle and lid can be put in the oven and used as a shallow casserole dish.

BAKING SHEETS

Having one or two good-quality non-stick baking sheets in the kitchen is invaluable. They can be used for a multitude of tasks, such as baking cookies and bread, or they can be placed under full dishes in the oven to catch any drips if the mixture in the dishes overflows.

ROASTING PAN

A good, heavy roasting pan is essential for roasting bigger cuts of meat and large amounts of vegetables. Choose a large pan; you will achieve better results if there is room for heat to circulate as the food cooks. Roast potatoes, for example, will not crisp well if they are crammed together in a small pan.

CUTTING & GRINDING

Chopping, slicing, cutting, peeling, grating and grinding are all essential aspects of food preparation so it's important to have the right tools for the job.

CHOPPING BOARD

Essential in every kitchen, these may be made of wood or plastic. Wooden boards tend to be heavier and more stable, but they must be thoroughly scrubbed in hot soapy water and properly dried. Plastic boards are easier to clean and more hygienic for cutting raw meat, poultry and fish.

KNIVES

When buying knives, choose the best ones you can afford. They should feel comfortable in your hand, so try several different types and practise a cutting action before you buy. You will need three different knives. A cook's knife is a good multi-purpose knife. The blade is usually about 18cm/7in long, but you may find that you prefer a slightly longer or shorter blade. A vegetable knife is a small version of the cook's knife and is used for finer cutting. A large serrated knife is essential for slicing bread, while a smaller one is useful for items such as tomatoes, which have a hard-to-cut skin.

VEGETABLE PEELERS

These may have a fixed or swivel blade. Both types will make quick work of peeling vegetables and fruit, with less waste than when using a knife.

GRATERS

These come in various shapes and sizes. Box graters have several different cutting blades and are easy to handle. Microplane graters retain their razor-sharp edges.

PEPPER MILL

Freshly ground black pepper is essential for seasoning. Look for a good pepper mill with strong blades that will not blunt easily.

LOOKING AFTER KNIVES

Although it may seem like a contradiction, the sharper the knife, the safer it is to use. It takes far more effort to use a blunt knife and this often results in accidents. Try to get into the habit of sharpening your knives regularly because the blunter they become, the more difficult they are to use and the longer it will take to sharpen them. Always wash knives carefully and dry them thoroughly to prevent them discolouring or rusting.

MEASURING EQUIPMENT

Accurate measuring equipment is essential, particularly when making breads and cakes, which usually need very precise quantities of ingredients.

WEIGHING SCALES

These are good for measuring dry ingredients. Digital scales are the most accurate but balance scales that use weights or a sliding weight are also a good choice. Spring scales with a scoop and dial are not usually as precise.

MEASURING CUPS

Suitable for dry or liquid ingredients, these standard measures usually come in a set of separate cups for different fractions or portions of a full cup.

MEASURING JUG/PITCHER

This is essential for liquids. A heatproof glass jug is useful because it allows hot liquids to be measured and it is easy to check the quantity.

MEASURING SPOONS

Table cutlery varies in size, so a set of standard measuring spoons is extremely useful for measuring small quantities.

MIXING, ROLLING & DRAINING

Bowls, spoons, whisks and strainers are all frequently used kitchen items that it would be difficult to do without.

MIXING BOWLS

You will need one large and one small bowl. Heatproof glass bowls are a good choice because they can be placed over a pan of simmering water to heat delicate sauces and to melt chocolate gently yet effectively.

WOODEN SPOONS

These are inexpensive and are essential for stirring and beating. Every kitchen should have two or three wooden spoons.

SLOTTED SPOON

This large metal or plastic spoon with draining holes is very useful for lifting food out of cooking liquid.

FISH SLICE/SPATULA

This is invaluable for lifting delicate fish fillets and other foods out of a frying pan.

ROLLING PIN

A heavy wooden or marble rolling pin is useful for rolling out pastry. If you don't have one, you may be able to improvise with a clean, dry, tall glass bottle (such as a wine bottle).

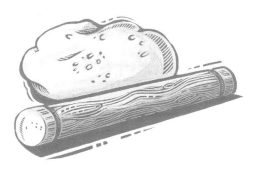

BALLOON OR ROTARY WHISK

A metal whisk is great for softly whipping cream and whisking sauces to a smooth consistency. Whisks are available in all shapes and sizes. Do not buy an enormous whisk that is difficult to use and will not fit into pans; mini-whisks are not essential – you can use a fork instead.

SIEVE

For sifting flour, icing (confectioners') sugar, cocoa and other dry ingredients, a stainless steel sieve (sifter) is essential. It can also be used for straining small quantities of cooked vegetables, pasta and rice. Wash and dry a sieve well after use to prevent it becoming clogged and damp.

COLANDER

Choose a free-standing metal colander with feet on the base. This will keep the base of the colander above the liquid that is being drained off. A free-standing design also has the advantage of leaving both hands free to empty heavy pans.

ELECTRICAL APPLIANCES

Although not essential, these can speed up food preparation.

FOOD PROCESSOR

This fabulous invention can make life a lot easier. It is perfect for processing soft and hard foods and is more versatile than a blender, which is best suited to puréeing very soft foods or liquids.

HAND-HELD ELECTRIC WHISK

A small, hand-held electric whisk or beater is very useful for making cakes, whipping cream and whisking egg whites. Choose an appliance with a powerful motor that will provide years of service.

Extra Equipment

As well as the essential items, some recipes require other equipment such as tart tins (pans) and cookie cutters. The following are some items you may find you need.

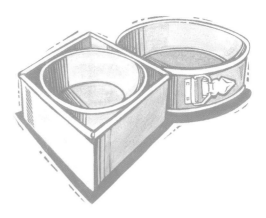

Cookie Cutters

These make quick work of cutting out pastry and cookie dough. Metal ones have a sharper cutting edge so are usually preferable to plastic ones. If you don't have cutters, you can improvise by using a sharp knife and cutting around a template, but this takes more time.

Pastry Brush

Made of bristle, with a wooden or plastic handle, this is useful for brushing food lightly with liquid – for example, brushing meat or fish with oil or marinade while grilling (broiling), or brushing pastry with beaten egg or milk.

Cake Tins/Pans

These may have loose bottoms or spring-clip sides to allow easy removal of the cake. Be sure to use the size specified in the recipe, or the cooking time will be affected.

Muffin Tins/Pans

These consist of six or twelve fairly deep cups in a tray. They can be used for baking smaller items, such as muffins, cupcakes, buns, bread rolls and deep tartlets.

Tart or Tartlet Tins/Pans

These are available with straight or fluted sides, but they are not as deep as muffin tins (pans). They come in a variety of sizes, from individual containers to very large tins. They are useful for baking all kinds of sweet and savoury tarts. Loose-bottomed tins are usually the best because the contents are easier to remove without sticking.

Skewers

These are used for kebabs and other skewered foods. Metal skewers are reusable and practical if you cook over the barbecue frequently, or cook kebabs that need lengthy cooking. Bamboo skewers are disposable and useful for foods that cook quickly. They should first be soaked in cold water for 20 minutes to stop them burning.

Palette knife/Metal Spatula

This large, flat, round-bladed, blunt knife is great for a range of tasks, such as spreading icing and fillings on cakes, lifting delicate biscuits (cookies) off baking sheets and flipping pancakes.

Griddle Pan

A good-quality, heavy griddle pan is useful for cooking meat and fish. The pan should be very hot before food is placed on it and the surface of the food should be brushed with a little oil to prevent it from sticking, rather than adding oil to the pan. The ridges leave an attractive pattern.

Wok

This traditional Asian pan is larger and deeper than a frying pan, usually with a rounded base and curved sides. A flat bottomed version is best for electric hobs. Non-stick versions are also available.

Minimalist Techniques

When cooking with a limited number of ingredients, the trick is to bring out the flavour of each one. The choice of cooking method is important because it can affect the flavour quite dramatically. Seasonings and aromatics are used to complement and bring out flavours; using them to marinate or macerate helps to intensify their relationship with the basic ingredient.

Cooking Methods to Maximize Flavour

How you cook food can make a real difference to the end result. For example, long-boiled vegetables become soggy and insipid, devoid of nutrients and flavour. In contrast, lightly steaming vegetables, baking fish wrapped in paper or foil parcels, and dry-frying spices are simple techniques that trap and enhance the natural flavour of the food. Some methods also add other flavours during cooking: for example, sprinkling smoking chips on a barbecue gives the food an extra smoky flavour.

Cooking on a Barbecue

Good-quality lumpwood charcoal will impart its characteristic smoky flavour to the food. A variety of aromatics can also be added, including hickory, oak, mesquite or applewood chips; woody herbs, such as thyme or rosemary – just the stalks will do; or shells from almonds or walnuts. Soak nutshells in cold water for about 30 minutes before adding them to the barbecue to help them smoke.

Roasting

This is a good method for cooking meat, poultry, fish and vegetables. Long, slow roasting transforms sweet vegetables such as red, orange or yellow (bell) peppers and parsnips, bringing out a rich, intense and caramelized flavour.

Grilling/Broiling

This method adds flavour by browning or charring the surface of the food. To achieve a good result the grill (broiler) must be preheated before cooking so that it is at the appropriate temperature when the food is placed under it.

Dry-frying Whole Spices

1 Heat a small frying pan over a medium heat and add the spices. Cook, stirring occasionally, until the spices give off their aroma – take care not to overdo it, however, or they will burn and the flavour will be spoilt.

2 Put the toasted spices into a mortar and roughly crush them with a pestle. (Dry-fry spices freshly, as and when you need them, rather than preparing a larger amount in advance.)

Dry-frying

Frying with no fat or oil is a useful technique for certain ingredients. Fatty meats such as bacon and pancetta release fat as the meat cooks, providing fat in which to cook the meat and any other ingredients that are added to the pan. Dry-frying whole spices, such as coriander or cumin seeds, prior to grinding, helps to enhance their taste, taking the raw edge off their flavour while making it more intense and rounded.

SHALLOW FRYING

Meat, poultry, fish and vegetables are all delicious pan-fried with a little oil or butter. They can be cooked quickly over a high heat to seal in the flavours, or slowly over a low heat to achieve tender, juicy results.

DEEP-FRYING

Meat, poultry, fish, vegetables and even fruit are delicious cooked in hot oil. It is a very quick method and gives rich results. The outside of the food is sealed almost as soon as it hits the oil, forming a crisp exterior that encloses the flavour and juices of the ingredients. Most foods need to be dipped in a protective coating such as batter or breadcrumbs before frying. Never add too much food at once to the oil – this lowers the temperature, giving soggy, greasy results.

STEAMING

This healthy cooking method is excellent for foods such as vegetables and fish. The natural flavours and nutrients of the food are retained, giving moist, tasty results.

MICROWAVING

Vegetables can be cooked successfully in a microwave. The result is similar to steaming, and traps all the flavour and nutrients. Before cooking, place the vegetables in a suitable covered container with a little water, then cook on full power.

BAKING IN PARCELS

Traditionally known as cooking *en papillotte*, this cooking method is a form of steaming. It is perfectly suited to foods such as fish and vegetables. The food is wrapped in baking parchment or foil to make a neat parcel, then baked. The steam and juices from the food are trapped within the parcel as it cooks, capturing the full flavour. Be sure to fold or crumple the edges of the parcel well to ensure that all the steam and juices are retained.

SIMPLE WAYS OF INTRODUCING FLAVOUR

As well as selecting the cooking method best suited to the ingredients, there are several quick and simple methods of adding flavour using herbs, spices and aromatics. Match the seasoning to the ingredient and go for simple techniques such as marinating, stuffing or coating with a dry spice rub, all of which will complement and help to intensify the flavours.

FLAVOURS FOR FISH

Classic aromatics used for flavouring fish and shellfish include lemon, lime, parsley, dill, fennel and bay leaves. These flavours all have a fresh, intense quality that complements the delicate taste of fish and shellfish without overpowering it. All work well added before, during or after cooking.

- To flavour whole fish, such as trout or mackerel, stuff a few lemon slices and some fresh parsley or basil into the body cavity before cooking. Season with plenty of salt and freshly ground black pepper, then wrap the fish in foil or baking parchment, ensuring the parcel is well sealed. Place in an ovenproof dish or on a baking tray; bake until cooked through.

- To marinate chunky fillets of fish, such as cod or salmon, arrange the fish fillets in a dish in a single layer. Drizzle the fish with olive oil, then sprinkle over a little crushed garlic and grated lime rind and squeeze over the lime juice. Cover the dish in clear film (plastic wrap) and leave to marinate in the refrigerator for at least 30 minutes. Grill (broil) lightly until the fish is just cooked through.

- To make an unusual marinade for salmon, arrange the fillets in a single layer in an ovenproof dish. Drizzle the fillets with a little light olive oil and add a split vanilla pod. Cover and leave to marinate in the refrigerator for 2 hours before cooking in the oven.

PEPPING UP MEAT & POULTRY

Meat and poultry suit both delicate and punchy seasonings. Dry rubs, marinades and sticky glazes are all perfect ways to introduce flavour into the meat and poultry. Marinating the tougher cuts of meat, such as stewing steak, also helps to tenderize it.

- To make a fragrant Cajun spice rub for pork chops, steaks and chicken, mix together 5ml/1 tsp each of dried thyme, dried oregano, finely crushed black peppercorns, salt, crushed cumin seeds and hot paprika. Rub into the raw meat or poultry, leave in a cool place for 1–2 hours, then cook over a barbecue or roast until cooked through.

- To marinate red meat, such as beef, lamb or venison, prepare a mixture of two-thirds red wine to one-third olive oil in a shallow non-metallic dish. Stir in some chopped garlic and bruised fresh rosemary sprigs. Add the meat and turn to ensure it is thoroughly coated in the marinade. Cover and chill for at least 2 hours or overnight before cooking.

- To make a mild-spiced sticky mustard glaze for chicken, pork or red meat, mix 45ml/3 tbsp each of Dijon mustard, clear honey and demerara sugar, 2.5ml/½ tsp chilli powder, 1.5ml/¼ tsp ground cloves, and salt and freshly ground black pepper. Cook the poultry or meat over the barbecue or under the grill (broiler) and brush it with the mustard glaze about 10 minutes before the end of the cooking time.

VIBRANT VEGETABLES

Most fresh vegetables have a subtle flavour that needs to be brought out and enhanced. When using delicate cooking methods such as steaming and stir-frying, go for light, fresh flavourings that will enhance the taste of the vegetables without overpowering them. When using more robust cooking methods, such as roasting, choose richer flavours such as garlic and spices.

- To make delicately fragrant, Asian-style steamed vegetables, add a bruised stalk of lemon grass and/or a few kaffir lime leaves to the steaming water, then cook vegetables such as pak choi (bok choy) over the water until they are just tender. Alternatively, place the same aromatics in the steamer, directly under the vegetables, and then steam as before until just tender.

- To add a rich flavour to stir-fried vegetables, add a splash of sesame oil just before the end of cooking time. (Do not use more than about 5ml/1 tsp because sesame oil has a very strong flavour and can be overpowering.)
- To enhance the taste of naturally sweet vegetables, such as parsnips and carrots, glaze them with honey and mustard before roasting. Mix together 30ml/ 2 tbsp wholegrain mustard and 45ml/ 3 tbsp clear honey, and season with salt and freshly ground black pepper. Brush the glaze over the prepared vegetables to coat completely, then roast until they are sweet and tender.
- It is worth buying onions in different sizes, so that you will always have the right amount. Whole onions keep well, but leftover chopped onion will rapidly taint everything in the refrigerator.
- Cooking vegetables without peeling, when possible, speeds up preparation time and helps to preserve key nutrients. However, peeling may remove some of the pesticide residues on non-organic fruit and vegetables.

FRAGRANT RICE AND GRAINS

Classic accompaniments, such as rice and couscous, can be enhanced by the addition of simple flavourings. Adding herbs, spices and aromatics can help to liven up the subtle flavour of the rice and grains. Remember to choose flavourings that will complement the dish that the rice or grains will be served with.

- To make exotic fragrant rice to serve with Asian-style stir-fries and braised dishes, add a whole star anise or a few cardamom pods to a pan of rice before cooking. The rice will absorb the flavour of the spice during cooking.

- To make zesty herb rice or couscous, heat a little chopped fresh tarragon and grated lemon rind in olive oil or melted butter until warm, then drizzle the flavoured oil (or butter) and herbs over freshly cooked rice or couscous. Serve immediately.
- To make simple herb rice or couscous, fork chopped fresh herbs through the cooked grains and drizzle over a little oil just before serving.
- To give rice an exotic golden colour, add a pinch of turmeric to the cooking water. Only a small amount is needed.
- Cook rice in home-made or bought fresh stock for extra flavour. Alternatively, use leftover vegetable cooking water, or canned tomato juice, diluted with an equal quantity of water.

STORING COOKED RICE
It is well worth cooking extra rice and using the rest another day. Leftover cooked rice will keep in the refrigerator for up to a week in a covered container. It can also be frozen for up to 6 months. To reheat, put in a pan with a little water and cover. Heat gently for a few minutes, stirring frequently, until the water has evaporated and the rice is hot.

Fruit

Widely used in both sweet and savoury dishes, fruit can be used either as a main ingredient or as a flavouring to complement and enhance the taste of other ingredients. The many different varieties offer the cook ample opportunity to create fabulous dishes – whether it's cod fillets with lime juice, lamb and apricot or a sumptuous dessert made with summer berries.

Orchard Fruit

This family includes apples, pears and quinces, which, depending on the variety, are in season from early summer to late autumn. Choose firm, unblemished fruit and store in a cool, dry place.

Apples

There are two main categories of apples – eating and cooking. Eating apples have sweet flesh and taste good raw. Many can also be used for cooking; they remain firm, which makes them ideal for pan-frying and for making open tarts. Cooking apples have a tart flavour and are too sharp to eat raw. When they are cooked, their flesh breaks down and becomes pulpy, making them ideal for sauces and purées.

Pears

Most commercially available pears are dessert fruits, which are just as good for eating as they are for cooking. They can be pan-fried or used in tarts and pies. They are also excellent poached, especially in a wine syrup.

Quinces

Related to the pear, quinces have hard, sour flesh. Cooking and sweetening brings out their delicious, scented flavour. Although they can be hard to find, they are worth buying when available, and are often used in jellies and sauces.

Stone Fruit

Peaches, nectarines, plums, apricots and cherries all belong to this family of fruit, which contain a stone (pit) in the middle. Most stone fruits are at their best through the summer months but some, such as plums, are best through the autumn. Choose firm, smooth-skinned fruit without any blemishes and store in a cool, dry place. Eat raw, at room temperature, or cook.

Soft Fruit

These delicate fruits, which include strawberries, raspberries, blackberries, blackcurrants, redcurrants and white currants, need careful handling and storing. Choose brightly coloured fruit and check for signs of mould or overripeness. Store in the refrigerator for up to 2 days.

Citrus Fruit

Oranges, lemons, limes, grapefruit, mandarins and satsumas are popular citrus fruits, and there are also hybrids such as clementines. The lemon is probably the most versatile member of the citrus family, with many uses in both savoury and sweet cooking. Citrus fruits are available all year round, with satsumas and clementines at their best in winter. Choose plump fruit that feels heavy. The skin should be bright and not shrivelled. Buy unwaxed fruit when using the rind in a recipe, or scrub the fruit well before use.

Exotic Fruit

Once expensive and rarely available, these wonderful fruits are now widely available in supermarkets throughout the year. Eat them fresh or use them in recipes.

Mangoes

There are many varieties of this sweet, fragrant, juicy fruit, which are delicious eaten on their own with a squeeze of lime juice, or used in recipes. Choose mangoes that have a fragrant smell, even through the skin, and give slightly when gently squeezed. Store in a cool place, but not the refrigerator, for up to a week.

Pineapple

These sweet, tangy, juicy fruits are delicious in fruit salads and desserts. When choosing a pineapple, pull off one of the green leaves at the top – if it comes away easily, the pineapple should be ripe enough to eat. Store pineapples in a cool place, but not the refrigerator, for up to a week.

Bananas

These popular fruits are ripe when the skin is yellow with a few specks. Avoid storing bananas in the refrigerator.

Kiwi Fruit

The pale green flesh of kiwi fruit is full of sweet-sharp flavour that goes well with other fruit in salads and is good in various desserts and savoury cooking. Kiwi fruit are rich in vitamin C. Choose fruit with smooth, plump skin and store in the refrigerator for up to 4 days.

Passion Fruit

These small, round fruits have a tough, wrinkled purple-brown skin. A passion fruit should feel heavy if it is nice and juicy. Store in the refrigerator.

Other Fruit

A few fruits don't fit into any particular group, but are still delicious and versatile.

Rhubarb

Technically not a fruit, but treated as one, tart, pink rhubarb is used in pies, tarts, crumbles and mousses. It is available from early spring to midsummer. Pale, finer-textured pink forced rhubarb is available in winter. Choose crisp, firm stalks and store in the refrigerator.

Melons

Charentais, Ogen, cantaloupe, Galia and honeydew are all dessert melons, in season from summer to winter. Slice, remove the seeds and enjoy. Watermelons have crisp, juicy flesh, studded with dark seeds. Serve chilled, from summer to autumn.

Figs

With their dense, sweet red flesh, fresh figs are delicious raw or cooked in savoury or sweet dishes, and are available in summer. Handle figs carefully and store in the refrigerator for up to 2 days.

Grapes

At their best in late summer, grapes are excellent with cheese, in fruit salads, or combined with savoury ingredients in salads.

VEGETABLES

Used in salads and savoury dishes, vegetables are delicious served as the main ingredient in a side dish, or as a flavouring ingredient within a main dish. Take your time when choosing vegetables, selecting healthy-looking specimens that are in season for maximum flavour – you'll really notice the difference.

ROOT VEGETABLES & POTATOES
These vegetables include carrots, parsnips, beetroot (beets), swedes (rutabagas) and turnips and many varieties of potato. They can be roasted, boiled, steamed or deep-fried. Choose firm vegetables with unblemished skins; avoid withered specimens and green-tinged potatoes, or ones with shoots. (If potatoes turn green, cut off and discard the green part – it is harmful if eaten.) Store in a cool, dark place for up to 2 weeks. Scrub them well if cooking them in their skins.

CABBAGE
Regardless of variety, cabbage has a distinct flavour and can be steamed, stir-fried or boiled. The white and red varieties are tight-leafed and ideal for shredding, and can be enjoyed raw in salads such as coleslaw. Green cabbage can be loose or close-leafed, smooth or crinkly and is best cooked. Store in the refrigerator for up to 10 days.

BROCCOLI
With a delicious flavour and crisp texture, broccoli and purple sprouting broccoli can be boiled, steamed and stir-fried. Choose specimens with bright green heads that have no sign of yellowing. Store in the refrigerator and use within 4–5 days. It is better to buy broccoli loose, as pre-packed broccoli will deteriorate more quickly.

CAULIFLOWER
Good cut into florets and served raw with dips, cauliflower can also be boiled or steamed, and is delicious coated in cheese sauce. To ensure even cooking, remove the hard central core, or cut into florets. Choose densely packed heads, avoiding specimens with any black spots, and store in the refrigerator for 5–10 days.

TOMATOES
There are numerous varieties of tomatoes, including cherry, plum and beefsteak. They are eaten raw or cooked. Choose plump, bright-red specimens, ideally on the vine, and store in the refrigerator for 5–8 days.

AUBERGINES/EGGPLANTS
These can be fried, stewed, brushed with oil and grilled (broiled), or stuffed and baked. Choose firm, plump, smooth-skinned specimens and store in the refrigerator, where they will keep for 5–8 days.

PEPPERS/BELL PEPPERS
These may be red, yellow, orange or green; the green are unripened, and are less sweet. Peppers can be grilled, roasted, fried and stewed. Choose firm, unblemished ones and store in the refrigerator for 5–8 days.

CHILLIES
There are many types of chilli, all with a different taste and heat. Generally the bigger the chilli, the milder it is; green chillies tend to be hotter than red ones.

SALAD LEAVES
There are many types of lettuce and other salad leaves. They are delicate but most will keep for a few days in the refrigerator. Prepare salad leaves at the last minute.

SPINACH
Tender young spinach leaves are tasty raw. Mature spinach leaves can be fried, boiled or steamed until just wilted. Store in the refrigerator for 2–3 days, and wash well.

LEAFY ASIAN VEGETABLES
Asian vegetables, such as pak choi (bok choy), can be used raw in salads or cooked. Prepare as cabbage or spinach.

THE ONION FAMILY
This includes onions, shallots, spring onions (scallions), leeks and garlic. Roast for a rich, sweet flavour. Choose firm, unblemished specimens. Store onions in a cool, dry place for up to 2 weeks; store leeks and spring onions in the refrigerator for 2–3 days.

GREEN BEANS
Many varieties of green beans are available throughout the year. Choose firm, fresh-looking beans with a bright green colour; avoid yellowish ones. Store in the refrigerator for up to 5 days.

PEAS
Fresh peas are generally only available in their pods in the summer. Only buy really fresh ones because their natural sugar content quickly turns to starch, giving them a mealy texture.

CORN
Large corn cobs are good boiled and served with butter, while baby corn are better added to stir-fries. Buy only the freshest specimens; stale vegetables can be starchy.

SQUASHES
These include courgettes (zucchini); butternut, acorn and spaghetti squashes; pumpkins and marrows (large zucchini). Except for courgettes and marrows all need peeling and seeding before use. They can be cut up and boiled or baked whole. Select smooth, unblemished vegetables. Store in a cool place for 1 week; store courgettes in the refrigerator for 4–5 days.

MUSHROOMS
There are many types of edible wild fungi or mushrooms. Wild mushrooms are seasonal and are generally found in late summer, autumn and winter. Chestnut mushrooms are a good alternative; they have more flavour than most cultivated mushrooms. Shiitake mushrooms are full-flavoured and delicious in Chinese- and Asian-style dishes. Choose firm, fleshy specimens and store them in paper bags in a cool place.

DAIRY PRODUCE

Milk and milk products, such as yogurt, butter and cheese, are widely used in cooking and can add a delicious richness to many sweet and savoury dishes. Strong-tasting cheeses, such as Gorgonzola or Parmesan, not only contribute a wonderful texture, but also add real bite to many savoury dishes.

MILK

Full-fat (whole) milk and lower-fat semi-skimmed and skimmed milk are pasteurized and available fresh or in long-life cartons. Buttermilk is a by-product of the butter-making process and is often used in baking.

CREAM

Double (heavy) cream has a high fat content and can be poured, whipped and heated without curdling. Whipping cream has a lower fat content and can be whipped to give a lighter, less firm texture. Single (light) cream has a lower fat content still and cannot be whipped; it is used for pouring. Clotted cream is very thick and has the highest fat content. Sour cream has the same fat content as single cream, but it is cultured, giving it a thick texture and slightly sour, fresh taste.

YOGURT

Varying in fat content, yogurt may be set or runny, with a thin or creamy texture. All except Greek (US strained plain) yogurt tends to curdle when heated.

BUTTER

There are two main types of butter – salted and unsalted (sweet). Unsalted is better for baking cakes and cookies.

EGGS

Widely used in sweet and savoury cooking, eggs are incredibly versatile. Hens' eggs are the most commonly used, and can be boiled, poached, fried and scrambled, as well as made into omelettes or baked with a range of ingredients, such as fresh herbs and vegetables. They are also important in cake-baking. It is worth buying the best you can afford – hens reared in better conditions produce better-tasting eggs. Test for freshness by placing in a bowl of cold water: a fresh egg will remain horizontal; a stale one will tilt to a vertical position in the water.

HARD CHEESES

Good for cooking, these firm, tasty cheeses should have a dry rind, and will keep in the refrigerator, wrapped in baking parchment, for up to 2 weeks. Cheddar is available in many mild and strong varieties. Its high fat content and good melting properties make it great for sauces. Parmesan is a dry Italian cheese with a full, strong flavour. Only cheeses stamped with "Parmigiano Reggiano" come from the area around Parma. Swiss Gruyère has a dry texture and nutty flavour, and is good for melting.

SEMI-HARD CHEESES

These vary in softness. Fontina is a deep golden Italian cheese with a pale brown rind and lots of holes. It melts fairly well but is not good for sauces. A salty Greek cheese, Halloumi has a firm, rubbery texture, and is perfect for grilling (broiling). Choose semi-hard cheeses that feel springy and have firm rinds. Wrap in waxed paper and store in the refrigerator for 1–2 weeks.

BLUE CHEESES

These strong, often sharp, cheeses usually melt well and are especially good for cooking and flavouring sauces. Blue Stilton is a strong, sharp cheese, which melts well into sauces and complements chicken and more robust meats. The perfect Stilton should have the blue mould spreading out to the rind. Gorgonzola is an Italian cheese with a rich, piquant flavour and a firm but creamy texture. It melts smoothly and can be used in a wide range of dishes. Also Italian, Dolcelatte has a mild flavour and a soft, creamy texture. It is good with summer fruit and is used in cooking.

SOFT & FRESH CHEESES

These mild, unripened cheeses include mozzarella, traditionally made from buffalo milk, which has a soft, elastic texture and a mild milky flavour. It is good melted and is used in many Italian dishes, especially pizza. Feta is a white, firm Greek sheep milk cheese that has a crumbly texture and a sharp, salty flavour. It is not ideal for general cooking as it does not melt easily, but it is excellent in salads. Creamy, mild mascarpone has a high fat content and can be used in both sweet and savoury recipes, as can ricotta, a soft, delicately flavoured white cheese. All of these cheeses should smell fresh when bought. Cover, and store in the refrigerator for up to 1 week.

LOW-FAT CHEESES

A few traditional hard cheeses, such as Parmesan and Single Gloucester, were once made with skimmed milk (the cream was skimmed off to use for cooking or to make butter), but full-fat milk was used for most. Today, with the growing obsession with low-fat foods, increasing numbers of cheeses are being made in low-fat versions. The fat, however, is what gives the cheese its texture and depth of flavour. Consequently, low-fat versions of traditional cheeses tend to lack both body and texture. It is far better to use a smaller amount of a traditional cheese than a large quantity of a bland, low-fat substitute. Some soft cheeses have a lower percentage of fat than harder cheeses.

WHITE RIND CHEESES

These creamy cheeses, with a firm, white mould rind, are delicious used in salads or cooked. French Brie is one of the best. Its flavour can be mild or, when ripe, extremely strong, tangy and creamy. It can be grilled (broiled), baked, or coated in breadcrumbs and deep-fried. Firm goat's cheese is excellent for slicing and melting; one of the most popular types is shaped in a log, often sold sliced into a white ring. Soft goat's cheese, without the rind, tastes milder.

Fish & Shellfish

Full of flavour and quick to cook, fish and shellfish are delicious cooked simply. Always buy really fresh specimens: look for bright-eyed fish with plump flesh, undamaged skin and a faint aroma of the sea. Choose heavy lobsters and crabs. Good fishmongers will scale, cut and fillet the fish for you. Cover and store it towards the bottom of the refrigerator, and use within a day of purchase.

Oily Fish

The rich flesh of oily fish is extremely tasty and very good for you. Oily fish are rich in omega 3 fatty acids, which are an essential part of a healthy diet.

Anchovies & Sardines

When available fresh, anchovies and sardines are delicious grilled (broiled), with lemon juice. Good-quality salted anchovies are versatile and delicious in pasta sauces.

Mackerel

These fish have iridescent skin and quite firm, brownish flesh. They can be baked whole, wrapped in baking parchment with lemon and herbs, or marinated and grilled.

Salmon

A versatile fish, salmon is excellent poached, grilled or wrapped in foil and baked in the oven. Wild salmon is more expensive than farmed, but far better in taste and nutritional value.

Rich, Meaty Fish

Fish in this group are firm and have a meaty texture. Some have a mild flavour, while others, such as tuna, are more robust.

Monkfish

Tasty baked, pan-fried and grilled, this fish is usually sold prepared as monkfish tails, which have a firm, meaty texture and a delicate flavour. Ask the fishmonger to remove all traces of skin and membrane, as this turns very rubbery on cooking.

Sea Bass

This is an expensive fish but its flavour is well worth the cost. Try fillets pan-fried in a little butter and served with lime juice.

Tuna

Fresh tuna is now more widely available – bluefin is the most prized, followed by yellowfin. It is best served rare. Steaks are best pan-fried for 1–2 minutes each side.

Swordfish

Pink-tinged, meaty swordfish is excellent cooked over a barbecue, but be sure not to overcook it because the flesh becomes dry.

Red Mullet

An attractive fish, red mullet has a yellow stripe and fine, delicious white flesh. Pan-fry the fillets with the skin on; serve with mashed potato.

WHITE FISH

These fish have a firm yet delicate white flesh, excellent cooked simply with subtle or piquant flavouring.

COD

Large cod fillet has a firm texture and an almost milky quality to its flesh.

PLAICE/FLOUNDER

Cooked whole or as fillets, this fish can be fried, grilled, steamed or baked. It is often slightly bland, so add a piquant sauce or herbs and olive oil to perk it up.

HADDOCK

This flaky fish can be used instead of cod or in recipes calling for white fish. Smoked haddock is delicious, but avoid the bright yellow dyed variety and go for the paler, undyed version instead.

SKATE

This fish has a hard, cartilaginous skeleton and no bones. It is sold as flat wings. Piquant capers are a perfect companion. Skate is available most of the year but it is best in autumn and winter.

EXTRACTING MEAT FROM A COOKED CRAB

1 *Lay the crab on its back and twist off the legs and claws. Use a hammer to break open the claws and legs, and pick out the meat.*
2 *There is a flap or opening on the body – carefully lift this up and twist it off, gently pulling the crab out of its shell.*
3 *Discard the gills from the side of the body and spoon out the brown meat from the main body section and from the shell.*

SHELLFISH

There are several different types of shellfish. Molluscs have either one or two shells. Once dead, they deteriorate rapidly and can cause food poisoning. Because of this, they must always be fresh and cooked alive. Crustaceans, including crabs, lobsters and prawns (shrimp), have a protective shell that is shed occasionally as the creature grows. Store shellfish in the refrigerator and always use them within 1–2 days of purchase.

MUSSELS

Sweet, mild-tasting mussels need to be cleaned thoroughly before cooking. Wash or scrub in cold water and pull off any black hairs (the beard) protruding from the shell. Tap any open mussels on a work surface and discard any that do not close straight away, along with any broken shells. When cooked, discard any mussels that have remained closed.

CRAB

These crustaceans are cooked live by placing in cold water and gradually bringing to the boil. However, crab is also available ready-cooked. A crab yields a small amount of meat for its size, so make sure you allow about 500g/1¼lb weight of whole crab per person.

PRAWNS/SHRIMP

There are many types of prawns of different sizes, cooked or raw, in the shell, or peeled. They are delicious pan-fried with chopped garlic and chilli. To peel prawns, hold the head in one hand and pull off the tail shell with the other. Hold the body and pull off the head, body shell and claws. Remove the black vein running along the back with the point of a knife or a skewer.

Meat & Poultry

If possible, buy organic meat and poultry. It is better to eat less meat of better quality than a larger quantity of cheaper meat. Animals and birds that have been raised in a good environment and fed on quality feed produce better-tasting meat than mass-reared, unhappy livestock. When you are cooking with only a few ingredients, each one needs to have an excellent flavour and texture.

Pork

Comparatively inexpensive, pork is a very versatile meat. It is generally tender and has an excellent flavour.

Shoulder, Leg & Loin

The shoulder or leg is the best cut for roasting. To make good crackling, ensure that the rind is thoroughly dry and rub it generously with sea salt. Loin or shoulder chops are suited to pan-frying or braising.

Pork Tenderloin

A lean, long piece of meat, the tenderloin can dry out during cooking. Wrap it in bacon to keep it moist before roasting.

Belly

Usually quite fatty, belly pork is good roasted and braised. It is especially tasty with Asian flavourings.

Spare Ribs

Meaty pork ribs can be delicious marinated and then roasted or cooked on a barbecue with a sticky glaze.

Bacon

Available smoked or unsmoked. If possible, buy dry-cured bacon. Streaky (fatty) bacon has a higher percentage of fat than back bacon, and can be cooked to a crisp-fried texture. Back bacon has larger rashers (strips) and larger lean areas.

Gammon

This salty, smoky meat is available in a whole piece or as steaks. Whole gammon may need soaking to reduce the salt. Steaks can be pan-fried or grilled (broiled).

Pancetta

Traditional Italian cured bacon, pancetta comes either in rashers (strips) or cut into dice. It can be pan-fried.

Prosciutto

This dry-cured ham is eaten raw, cut into very thin slices. It can also be cooked, usually as a topping on dishes or to enclose other ingredients before grilling or roasting.

Beef

Well-flavoured and versatile, beef is good for stewing, roasting, grilling, pan-frying and stir-frying.

Fillet/Beef Tenderloin, Forerib, Topside & Silverside/Pot Roast

These are best roasted. To make the most of the flavour, serve medium, not well-done.

STEAKS

Sirloin, T-bone, porterhouse, fillet (beef tenderloin) and sirloin are best pan-fried over a high heat.

SHIN OR LEG/SHANK, CHUCK & BRISKET

These cuts can be quite tough and are best stewed slowly to tenderize them and bring out their excellent flavour.

MINCED/GROUND MEAT

This is a very versatile ingredient for meat sauces, chilli con carne, meatballs, pasta, samosas, pies and many other dishes.

LAMB

Delicious in roasts and superb grilled, pan-fried and stewed, lamb is one of the best-loved of all meats.

BEST END OF NECK, LEG, SHOULDER & SADDLE

These are the best cuts for roasting. Best end of neck can be cut into chops. Shoulder contains more fat than leg and has an excellent flavour. Spring lamb tastes best.

CHUMP CHOPS & LEG STEAKS

These have a full flavour and can be either grilled (broiled) or pan-fried.

SAUSAGES & OFFAL/ VARIETY MEATS

Offal refers to all offcuts from the carcass but in everyday use: the term usually means liver and kidneys.

SAUSAGES

There are many types of fresh sausage from around the world. Depending on the type, they are fried, grilled or baked.

CARVING A ROAST CHICKEN

1 Leave the bird to rest for 10 minutes, then remove the legs. Cut the joints to make thighs and drumstick portions.
2 Remove the wings, then gently carve the meat off the breasts, working down on either side of the breastbone.

LIVER

Pigs', lambs' or calves' liver has a strong flavour and is good pan-fried, with bacon and onions served with mashed potato.

KIDNEYS

Lambs' kidneys are lighter in flavour than pigs'. They should be halved and the central core discarded before they are pan-fried or used in stews and pies.

POULTRY & GAME BIRDS

Many people prefer the lighter flavour of poultry and game birds to that of red meat.

CHICKEN

Buy organic or free-range chicken. Choose smooth-skinned, unblemished, plump birds. Poussins (baby chickens) can either be roasted, or spatchcocked and then cooked over the barbecue.

DUCK

Duck can be very fatty, with little meat, but some farmed birds are leaner. An average duck will serve two or three people. Duck breasts and legs are a good choice.

PHEASANT

One pheasant will serve two. The breast meat is fairly dry and needs constant basting during roasting. Choose pheasants that are no older than six months; older birds are tough.

HERBS

Invaluable in a huge number of sweet and savoury recipes, herbs add flavour and colour to many dishes. Fresh herbs are widely available and their flavour is superior to that of dried herbs. Many are easy to grow yourself at home – either in the garden or in a pot on the windowsill. You can grow them from seed, or buy them already growing in pots from supermarkets and garden centres.

ROBUST HERBS

These strong-tasting, often pungent herbs are good with meat and well-flavoured dishes. Use in moderation.

BAY LEAVES

These shiny, aromatic leaves can be added to meat dishes, roasts, casseroles and stews before cooking, and removed before serving, as they are too tough to eat. They keep their flavour well when dried, and are an essential part of a bouquet garni.

ROSEMARY

This pungent herb is delicious with lamb – insert a few sprigs into slits in the skin of a leg of lamb and the flavour will really penetrate the meat during roasting. For other recipes, use the whole leaves or chop them finely.

THYME

One of the traditional herbs used in a bouquet garni, thyme has small leaves and some types have woody stems. It has a strong, pungent flavour. Add whole sprigs to meat dishes or strip the leaves and use them in pasta sauces.

LAVENDER

This can be used sparingly to complement chicken dishes and also in sweet recipes such as drinks and desserts. The stalks and leaves can be used as well as the flowers.

SAGE

Peppery-tasting sage has large, slightly furry leaves. It is a great companion for pork and is excellent with potatoes and also in tomato and garlic pasta dishes. Ravioli served with a little melted butter and warmed sage leaves is particularly delicious. Use in moderation because its flavour can be overpowering if used in excess.

CHIVES

Long slender chives have a distinct onion-like flavour. Chives are best snipped with scissors. They are good in potato salads and egg and dairy dishes.

OREGANO & MARJORAM

These two closely related herbs have a distinctive flavour that is excellent in tomato-based sauces and with other vegetables, and also in chicken, cheese and egg dishes. Oregano dries more successfully than most herbs.

FREEZING HERBS

This is a great way of preserving fresh herbs because it retains their natural flavour. Use in cooked dishes only. Chop the herbs and place about one tablespoonful in each compartment of an ice cube tray. Pour over water to cover and freeze. To use, simply add a herb ice cube to the pan and stir.

DELICATE HERBS

These softer-leafed herbs tend not to require long cooking to bring out their flavours Use in salads or add towards the end of cooking time.

BASIL

Widely used in Italian dishes, basil has delicate leaves and should be added at the end of cooking. It has a slightly aniseed flavour that goes well with chicken, fish, all types of vegetables and pasta. It is one of the main ingredients of pesto.

CORIANDER/CILANTRO

The deep, almost woody flavour of coriander is superb in spicy dishes. It is good in Thai-style soups and curries, meat and egg dishes, as well as more robustly flavoured fish dishes.

PARSLEY

Flat or curly leafed, parsley is one of the most versatile herbs and adds flavour to a wide range of savoury dishes. The flat-leafed variety has a stronger flavour and it can be used as an ingredient in its own right to make soup.

MINT

There are many different varieties of mint, including apple mint and spearmint. It goes well with lamb, desserts and drinks.

TARRAGON

This fragrant herb has a strong aniseed flavour and is most often paired with chicken and fish.

CHERVIL

This pretty herb has a mild aniseed flavour that makes a successful addition to fish, chicken, cheese and creamy savoury dishes. It is also good in salads.

MAKING A BOUQUET GARNI

This classic flavouring for stews, casseroles and soups is very easy to make. Using a piece of string, tie together a fresh bay leaf and a sprig each of parsley and thyme. Alternatively, tie the herbs in a square of muslin (cheesecloth).

FRAGRANT HERBS

These distinctive herbs have a strong, aromatic scent and flavour and suit many different kinds of dishes.

KAFFIR LIME LEAVES

These dark green leaves are used to impart a citrus flavour to many South-east Asian soups and curries. Add the leaves whole, torn or finely shredded.

LEMON BALM

With a distinctive lemon flavour and fragrance, this herb complements all ingredients that go well with citrus fruit or juice. Lemon balm makes a good addition to fish, chicken and vegetable dishes as well as sweet drinks and desserts. Use in moderation, as it can be overpowering.

DILL

This pretty, feathery herb has a distinctive flavour that is perfect with fish, chicken and egg dishes. It also goes very well with potatoes, courgettes (zucchini) and cucumber. It should be added to dishes just before serving because its mild flavour diminishes with cooking.

FENNEL

Similar to dill in appearance, the aniseed flavour of fennel works well with fish. Fennel butter makes an excellent glaze for vegetables.

Spices & Aromatics

These flavourings play a very important role when cooking with a limited number of ingredients, adding a warmth and roundness of flavour to simple dishes. It is difficult to have every spice to hand, but a few key spices will be enough to create culinary magic. Black pepper is essential in every kitchen; cumin seeds, coriander seeds, dried chillies and turmeric are also good basics.

Dried Spices

Store spices in airtight jars or containers in a cool, dark place. If you can, buy small quantities that will be used up fairly quickly because the flavours of spices diminish with age. Check the use-by dates of spices and force yourself to throw away any spices that are old or no longer fragrant; there is little point in using old, tasteless spices to flavour food because the results will not be satisfactory.

Salt

Probably the most important of all seasonings, salt is an essential ingredient in almost every cuisine and is undoubtedly the most widely used ingredient throughout the whole world. It has been used for many years, not only to flavour and bring out the taste of foods, but to preserve them as well. Cured fish and meat, such as salt cod, prosciutto, salt beef and bacon, are preserved in salt to draw out moisture and prevent them from decomposing.

The type of salt used is important – rock salt and sea salt do not have added chemicals, which are often found in table salt (added to help it pour smoothly). Rock salt is available in crystal form and can be ground in a mill. Sea salt has a strong taste and it is used in smaller amounts. It is available in flakes, crystals or finely ground.

Pepper

Black pepper is one of the most commonly used spices. It should always be freshly ground because, once ground, it loses its flavour quickly. It is used in almost all savoury recipes and can also be used to bring out the taste of fruit such as pineapple and strawberries. Green peppercorns have a mild flavour. They are available dried or preserved in brine and are excellent for flavouring pâtés and meat dishes. White pepper is hotter than green, but less aromatic than black.

Chilli Flakes

Crushed dried red chillies can be added to, or sprinkled over, all kinds of dishes – from stir-fries and grilled (broiled) meats to pasta sauces and pizza. They can be added to salad dressings for an extra kick.

Cayenne Pepper

This fiery, piquant spice is made from dried hot red chillies, so use sparingly. It is excellent in cheese dishes and creamy soups and sauces.

PAPRIKA

An essential seasoning for Hungarian goulash and used in many Spanish dishes, paprika is available in mild and hot forms. It has a slightly sweet flavour.

TURMERIC

Made from dried turmeric root, the ground spice is bright yellow with a peppery, slightly earthy flavour. It is used in many classic Indian recipes. Turmeric can be used as a cheaper alternative to saffron for its ability to turn dishes a golden yellow colour, although the flavour is not the same.

CHILLI POWDER

Useful for adding a kick to many foods, from Mexican dishes to pasta sauces, this varies from mild to fierce. Use cautiously.

MUSTARD SEEDS

These may be black, brown or white. They are used to make the condiment mustard and are also used as a flavouring in cooking. Black mustard seeds are added to Indian dishes, for their crunchy texture as well as flavour. Try adding a few mustard seeds to bread dough to give it a spicy kick.

CUMIN

This warm, pungent spice is widely used in Indian and North African cooking. Cumin works well with meats and a variety of vegetables, particularly robust-tasting sweet potatoes, squashes and cabbage.

CARAWAY SEEDS

These small dark seeds have a fennel-like flavour. They are very versatile and make a lively addition to savoury breads and sweet cakes, while also complementing strongly flavoured sausage dishes and vegetables such as cabbage.

FENNEL SEEDS

These pretty little green seeds have a sweet, aniseed-like flavour that pairs well with chicken and robust fish dishes. They also taste good in breads.

CORIANDER

Available whole or ground, this warm, aromatic spice is delicious with most meats, particularly lamb. Ground coriander and cumin combine to make an excellent and simple spice rub.

GREEN CARDAMOM

This fragrant spice is widely used in Indian and North African cooking to flavour both sweet and savoury dishes. The pods enclose little seeds that are easily scraped out and can be crushed in a mortar with a pestle.

GINGER

The ground, dried spice is particularly useful for baking. For a fresher flavour in savoury recipes and drinks, it is best to use aromatic fresh root ginger.

NUTMEG

This large aromatic seed has a rich, woody flavour, which adds a warmth to milk, egg and cream dishes and enhances the flavour of spinach. Nutmeg is available ready ground, but the flavour is far better when the spice is freshly grated. Try sprinkling a little grated nutmeg over milk-based soups before serving.

MACE

This spice is the casing of the nutmeg – it has a similar flavour but is slightly milder. Mace is great for flavouring butter for savoury dishes, but nutmeg can be used instead if it is unavailable.

CINNAMON

This warm spice is available in sticks and ground into powder and has many uses in savoury and sweet recipes. Add sticks to stews, casseroles and other liquid dishes, then remove them before serving. Use ground cinnamon in baking, desserts and hot and cold drinks.

STAR ANISE

This pretty, star-shaped spice has a strong aniseed flavour. It is widely used in Chinese and Asian cooking and goes very well with pork and chicken. It is also good for flavouring rice – simply add a single star anise to the cooking water. It can also be used to enliven the flavour of sweet dishes such as ice creams and jellies.

ALLSPICE

This berry has a warm, slightly cinnamon-clove flavour. It is more readily available in its ground form and can be used in both savoury and sweet cooking. It goes particularly well in warming winter recipes and in rich fruit cake.

CLOVES

Available whole or ground, these dried flower buds are used in savoury and sweet dishes. They can be quite bitter on their own, but the heat of cooking tempers their flavour. Ham is particularly tasty studded with whole cloves before baking, while the ground spice is suitable for cakes and cookies. Ground cloves have a strong flavour, so use sparingly.

VANILLA

Pure, or natural vanilla essence (extract) is distilled from vanilla pods (beans) and is a useful alternative to using the pods and seeds themselves. It tends to have a far better flavour than vanilla flavour essence, which uses a synthetic substitute for vanilla and can be quite overpowering.

SESAME SEEDS

These small, oil-rich seeds have a sweet, rich flavour, which can be brought out by roasting or frying them in butter. They make a delicious addition to salads, fish and poultry dishes and breads, and are tasty stirred into mashed potatoes. Roasted sesame seeds keep well in a screw-top jar.

FRESH SPICES & AROMATICS

These wonderful flavourings are widely used in many dishes, to which they add a rich, round, aromatic taste.

FRESH ROOT GINGER

This pale-brown root should be peeled and then sliced, shredded, finely chopped or grated as required. It is used in curries, stir-fries, and grilled (broiled) and braised dishes. Store ginger in the refrigerator for up to 6 weeks. Preserved and crystallized stem ginger can be used in sweet dishes.

GALANGAL

Similar in appearance to fresh root ginger, galangal is used in Thai and Indonesian cooking. Treat as for fresh root ginger, but store for a maximum of 3 weeks.

LEMON GRASS

This woody pale green stalk is excellent with fish and chicken, and can be used to flavour sweet dishes. Bruise the bulbous end of the stalk and add whole to curries and soups, or finely slice or chop the end of the stalk and stir into the dish.

GARLIC

A member of the onion family and therefore often regarded as a vegetable, garlic also deserves mention as an aromatic for its role in flavouring all kinds of savoury dishes. The potency of garlic depends on how it has been prepared. Crushed garlic gives the most powerful flavour, while finely chopping, shredding or slicing gives a slightly milder result. Use garlic to flavour dressings or dips, or use whole, peeled cloves to flavour oils or vinegars.

READY-MADE SPICE MIXES

There is an excellent selection of ready-made spice mixes available that make great short-cut flavouring ingredients for a wide range of savoury dishes.

HARISSA

This North African spice paste is made of chillies, garlic, coriander, caraway, olive oil and other spices. It is delicious with oily fish as well as meat.

CHERMOULA

This is another useful North African spice paste, which includes coriander, parsley, chilli and saffron.

CAJUN SEASONING

This spice mixture made of black and white pepper, garlic, cumin and paprika is good for rubbing into meat before cooking over a barbecue or grilling (broiling).

JERK SEASONING

This Caribbean spice blend is made of dry spices and goes well with chicken and pork.

CURRY POWDER & PASTE

A blend of different ground Indian spices, curry powders vary enormously, from mild to very hot.

GARAM MASALA

This Indian mixture of ground roasted spices is usually made from cumin, coriander, cardamom and black pepper. Ready-mixed garam masala is widely available, although the flavour is better when the spices are freshly roasted and ground just before they are needed.

CHINESE FIVE-SPICE

This is a mixture of ground spices, including anise pepper, cassia, fennel seeds, star anise and cloves. It is used in Chinese cooking, particularly to season pork and chicken dishes. Chinese five-spice is a powerful mixture and should be used sparingly.

OTHER FLAVOURINGS

As well as herbs, spices and aromatics, there are a number of other important basic flavourings. Chocolate, and sweeteners such as sugar and honey are mainly used in sweet dishes, but small amounts are sometimes added to savoury ones. Savoury sauces and condiments, such as soy sauce, enhance the taste of savoury ingredients, and alcohol is widely used in sweet and savoury cooking.

SUGARS & SWEETNERS

Refined and raw sugars and sweet spreads such as honey and marmalade can all be used to sweeten and flavour.

GRANULATED SUGAR

This refined white sugar has large crystals. It is used for sweetening drinks and everyday cooking; it can also be used as a crunchy cookie or cake topping, or stirred into crumble mixtures for extra texture.

CASTER/SUPERFINE SUGAR

This fine-grained white sugar is most frequently used in baking. It has a fine texture which means it is particularly well suited to making cakes and cookies.

ICING/CONFECTIONERS' SUGAR

The finest of all the refined sugars, this sugar has a light, powdery texture. It is used for making icing and sweetening flavoured creams. It is also good for dusting on cakes, desserts and cookies as a decoration.

DEMERARA SUGAR

This golden sugar consists of large crystals with a rich, slightly honeyish flavour. It adds a crunchy texture to cookies.

BROWN SUGARS

These dark, unrefined sugars have a rich, caramel flavour. There are different types including light and dark muscovado (brown) sugar and dark brown molasses sugar. The darker the sugar, the more intense its flavour. Always check you are buying unrefined sugar because "brown" sugars are often actually white sugar that has been coloured after refining.

GOLDEN/LIGHT CORN SYRUP

This versatile syrup is delicious as a spread, glaze or baking ingredient. Use in place of other liquid sweeteners, such as honey or molasses, in equal amounts.

HONEY

Clear honey is used to flavour desserts, cakes and cookies as well as savoury dressings. It is a good base for barbecue sauces and glazes for chicken or meat.

MARMALADE

Most commonly served as a sweet spread, marmalade can also make an interesting ingredient. Try orange marmalade as the base for a quick sauce for duck.

MAPLE SYRUP

Pure maple syrup is a nutritious sweetener with many uses. Avoid cheaper versions, which may be adulterated with corn syrup, flavourings, colour and preservatives.

FLAVOURINGS

Various different ingredients are added to dishes to add extra flavour or to enhance those already present.

CHOCOLATE

There are many different types of chocolate, each with its own unique flavour. For cooking, chocolate with at least 70 per cent cocoa solids will give the best flavour. Children often prefer the milder taste of milk chocolate. White chocolate has a low cocoa solids content and is sweet with a very mild flavour. Chocolate spread is also a useful ingredient. It can be melted and stirred into ice cream, custard or drinks, or used in many desserts.

COFFEE

To achieve a strong coffee flavour, use good- quality espresso. You do not need an espresso machine for this because espresso coffee is sold for use in cafetières or filter machines. Make a double-strength brew to flavour desserts, sauces, cakes and cookies.

REDCURRANT JELLY

The tangy flavour of this clear red jelly goes very well with both hot and cold meats, and lamb in particular. It is also good with Brie.

ALMOND ESSENCE/EXTRACT

This distinctive-tasting flavouring is perfect for cakes, cookies and desserts, and is also used for flavouring cream that will be served with fruit desserts.

ALCOHOL

Wine, spirits, beer and cider add body to both sweet and savoury dishes. Wines and spirits can be used to perk up cooked dishes and to macerate fruits and enliven desserts.

BEER & CIDER

Both beer and cider are excellent for making stews and casseroles.

WINE

Fruity red wines can be used to enrich meat dishes, tomato sauces and gravies. Dry white wine can be incorporated into fish or chicken dishes. Sweet white wines and sparkling wines can be used to make jellies and sweet sauces.

PORT

Ruby port can be added to sauces for red meats – but bear in mind that it is richer and sweeter than red wine, so use it more sparingly. Port is also suitable for macerating summer fruits.

SHERRY & MARSALA

These fortified wines can be used in savoury and sweet recipes.

SPIRITS

Use rum and brandy for flavouring meat sauces, ice creams and cakes. Clear spirits, such as vodka and gin, can be used for sorbets; add vodka to tomato-based pasta dishes and fish dishes to give an extra kick. Irish cream liqueurs are good for desserts.

MAKING TOMATO KETCHUP

This tastes much better than the commercial kind and uses up tomatoes if you grow your own and have a glut. Chop 2.75kg/6lb tomatoes into quarters and put in a preserving pan with 25g/1oz salt and 600ml/1 pint/2½ cups vinegar. Simmer until the tomatoes are soft, then strain through coarse muslin (cheesecloth). Return the pureé to the pan, add 225g/8oz sugar and simmer until the ketchup starts to thicken. Add 2.5ml/½ tsp each of allspice, ground cloves, cinnamon and cayenne. Pour into bottles.

SAUCES & CONDIMENTS

Not only are sauces and condiments perfect for serving with main dishes at the table, they are also ideal for adding extra flavour and bite to simple dishes during the cooking process.

MUSTARD

There are many different kinds of mustard. Wholegrain mustard, containing whole mustard seeds, has a sweet, fruity taste and makes a mild, flavourful salad dressing. French Dijon mustard has a fairly sharp, piquant flavour which complements red meat and makes a sharply flavoured dressing. English mustard comes as a dry powder or ready prepared and is excellent added to cheese dishes, or used to enliven bland, creamy sauces. It has a hotter flavour than the other types.

TOMATO PURÉE/PASTE

This concentrated purée is made from tomatoes, salt and citric acid and is available in tubes or in small cans. Tomato pureé is great for adding flavour, and sometimes body, to sauces and stews.

PASSATA/BOTTLED STRAINED TOMATOES

This Italian product, made of sieved tomatoes, has a fairly thin consistency and makes a good base for a tomato sauce.

TOMATO KETCHUP

Add a splash of this strong table condiment to tomato sauces for a sweet-sour flavour.

WORCESTERSHIRE SAUCE

This thin, brown, very spicy sauce brings a piquant flavour to casseroles, stews and soups. It can also be used in cheese dishes.

BLACK BEAN SAUCE

Made from a mixture of puréed salted black beans with soy sauce, sugar and spice, this sauce is used in Chinese and Asian dishes. It is usually blended into stir-fries.

SWEET CHILLI SAUCE

You can add this sweet, spicy dipping sauce to stir-fries and braised chicken dishes, and it can be used as a glaze for chicken or prawns (shrimp) before grilling (broiling) or cooking over a barbecue.

SOY SAUCE

Made from fermented soy beans, soy sauce is salty and adds a rich, rounded flavour to Asian-style stir-fries, glazes and sauces.

TERIYAKI MARINADE

This Japanese marinade has a sweet, salty flavour. Use it to marinate meat, chicken and fish before frying; the leftover marinade will cook down to make a delicious sauce.

TABASCO SAUCE

This chilli sauce is very hot, so should be used sparingly. It is good for enlivening cheese dishes and is also used in a number of cocktails to produce a spicy flavour.

OYSTER SAUCE
Add this thick Chinese sauce with a sweet, meaty taste to stir-fries and braised dishes.

PESTO
Use fresh pesto, made with basil, garlic, pine nuts and Parmesan cheese, on pasta or to flavour sauces, soups, stews and dressings. There are also variations such as red pesto, made with roasted red (bell) peppers.

MAYONNAISE
If you need to use bottled mayonnaise, choose the best brand you can afford. Add other ingredients, such as garlic, gherkins or mustard, to suit the main dish.

TAHINI
This sesame spread can be found in larger supermarkets and health food stores, and is used in dips, such as hummus. The darker version is made from whole sesame seeds.

HOISIN SAUCE
Occasionally known as Peking sauce, this is a thick, reddish-brown sauce often used in Chinese cooking. It is a mixture of garlic, soya beans (soybeans), chillies and spices.

PRESERVED FRUIT & NUTS
Fruit and nuts that have been dried or preserved in salt, vinegar or oil are invaluable as flavouring ingredients.

PRESERVED LEMONS
A classic ingredient of North African cooking, the lemons are preserved whole or in large pieces in a mixture of salt and spices. The chopped peel is usually added to chicken dishes to add an intense, sharp, citrus flavour.

DRIED FRUIT
Dried apricots, prunes, figs, currants, sultanas (golden raisins) and raisins can be added to savoury dishes and meat stews to impart a rich, sweet flavour. They are also good for adding flavour and body to sweet desserts, cakes and cookies.

NUTS
Almonds, walnuts, pine nuts and others are useful for adding to savoury dishes such as salads, vegetable dishes, pastes and dips, as well as desserts and baking.

PEANUT BUTTER
This nutty spread is excellent for making a speedy satay sauce and adding to bought cookies. Peanuts, like all nuts, are highly nutritious but they are also particularly high in fat.

COCONUT MILK
Thin, creamy coconut milk is made from pulped coconut and is widely used in Thai and Asian cooking, particularly in curries and soups.

CREAMED COCONUT
Sold in blocks, this is dissolved in water to make coconut milk or cream.

DESICCATED/DRY UNSWEETENED SHREDDED COCONUT
This substitute for raw grated coconut is added to curries, and is widely used in baking.

KITCHEN BASICS

Keep a good supply of basic essentials and you will be able to cook almost anything at any time. The following are some useful ingredients that will be invaluable in every kitchen. Try to remember to check your stocks regularly and be vigilant about throwing away out-of-date ingredients and replacing them with fresh ones.

FLOUR

This is an essential ingredient in every kitchen. There are many different types, which serve many purposes in both sweet and savoury cooking – from baking cakes to thickening gravy and making cheese and other sauces.

WHEAT FLOURS

Plain (all-purpose) flour can be used in most recipes, including sauces. Self-raising (self-rising) flour has a raising agent added and is useful for cakes and other baking recipes. Wholemeal (whole-wheat) flour is available as plain or self-raising. Strong bread flour contains more gluten than plain flour, giving the springy texture required for breads.

GLUTEN-FREE FLOURS

For those with an intolerance of gluten, which is found in wheat and other grains, gluten-free flour is an invaluable ingredient. It is widely available from most large supermarkets and health food stores.

CORNFLOUR/CORNSTARCH

This very fine white flour is useful for thickening sauces and stabilizing egg mixtures, such as custard, to prevent them curdling. A little cornflour is first blended with cold water or another liquid to make a smooth, runny paste, which is then stirred into a hot sauce, soup or stew and boiled until it thickens.

RAISING AGENTS

Self-raising flour contains raising agents, normally baking powder, which give a light texture to cakes and cookies. You can add baking powder to plain flour to achieve the same result.

OILS

Essential both for cooking and adding flavour, there are many different types of oil, all of which have their own individual character and use in the kitchen. Every cook should have a bottle of oil to be used for cooking, and also a range of more interesting oils for drizzling and flavouring.

OLIVE OIL

Extra virgin olive oil has the best, most pronounced flavour and is also the most expensive type. It is best reserved for condiments or for making salad dressings. Ordinary olive oil is better used in cooking. Light olive oil is paler and milder in flavour than ordinary olive oil and is therefore ideal for making more lightly flavoured salad dressings.

GROUNDNUT/PEANUT OIL

This virtually flavourless oil is used for frying, baking and making salad dressings, such as mayonnaise. It is very stable so it can be heated to the high temperatures required for deep and stir-frying.

Corn Oil

Golden-coloured corn oil is versatile, despite its fairly strong flavour, and can be used in most types of cooking.

Vegetable Oil

This is a blend of oils, usually including corn oil and other vegetable oils. It is quite flavourless, inexpensive and useful in most types of cooking.

Sesame Oil

Both sesame and toasted sesame seed oils have strong flavours and should be used sparingly when cooking. Sesame oil is added to Chinese food before serving.

Hazelnut & Walnut Oils

Both are quite strongly flavoured and useful as dressings rather than for cooking. They are delicious drizzled over cooked fish, poultry or vegetables, or used to give salad dressings an unusual tang.

Flavoured Oils

There are many types and brands of flavoured oils. Look out for those using a good-quality olive oil as the base.

Chilli Oil

This is available in various styles – it adds a pleasing spicy kick to all sorts of dishes such as pasta, fish and salads. Add a drizzle just before serving the food. It can also be used as a dipping sauce.

Garlic Oil

This is a good alternative to fresh garlic. It has a fairly pronounced flavour so it should be used in moderation.

Lemon-infused Oil

This is excellent with fish, chicken and pasta, and also for salad dressings.

Pasta & Noodles

These are invaluable standby ingredients that can be used as the base of many hot and cold dishes.

Pasta

There is a wide variety of pasta in all shapes and sizes. Egg pasta is enriched with egg yolks and it has a richer flavour than plain pasta. Green pasta derives its colour from the addition of spinach. Wholewheat pasta is also widely available. Large shapes and tubes are good with thick or chunky sauces, or in salads, and long thin pasta is better with smooth sauces. Cook pasta at a rolling boil in plenty of salted water.

Egg Noodles

Made from wheat flour and eggs, these may be thick, medium or thin. Use them for stir-fries or as an accompaniment to Chinese and Asian dishes.

Rice Noodles

These translucent white noodles are a good alternative to wheat noodles – particularly for those on a gluten-free diet. They are available as broad flat or thin noodles that can be added to stir-fries and soups as well as used cold as the base for salads. Rice noodles are easy to prepare because they don't need to be cooked. Simply soak in boiling water for about 5 minutes, then stir-fry, add to soups or allow to cool, then toss with salad ingredients.

Couscous & Polenta

Like pasta and noodles, couscous and polenta can be served as an accompaniment or can act as the base of many dishes. They have a mild flavour, and go particularly well with strongly flavoured ingredients.

Couscous

Made from durum wheat, couscous is often regarded as a type of pasta. Traditional couscous needed long steaming before serving, but the majority of brands available in supermarkets today are "instant" and need only brief soaking in water. It is the classic accompaniment to Moroccan tagines, but also goes well with all kinds of meat, fish and vegetable stews. It makes an excellent base for salads.

Polenta

This is made from finely ground cornmeal. It is cooked with water and served either soft (rather like mashed potato) or left to set and then cut into pieces that can be grilled (broiled) or fried. Both quick-cook and ready-made polenta are available in most supermarkets and can be made into simple, hearty dishes. You can buy polenta that takes 40–45 minutes to cook or a much quicker version that can be cooked in less than 5 minutes. It is best served with flavourful ingredients.

Rice

This versatile grain can be served as an accompaniment, or form the base of both sweet and savoury dishes. Most types of rice are available in both white and brown (wholegrain) versions; brown rice has a nuttier flavour and slightly chewy texture.

Long-grain Rice

The narrow grains of white rice cook to a light, fluffy texture. Generally served as an accompaniment to main dishes, long-grain rice is also used in stir-fries and salads.

Short-grain Rice

There are several types of short, stubby, polished rice such as pudding rice and sushi rice. These usually have a high starch content and cook into tender grains that cling together and can be shaped easily.

Thai Jasmine Rice

This white, slightly sticky rice has a scented flavour. It is delicious served with Thai curries or in stir-fries.

Risotto Rice

This rice has medium-length polished grains. The grains can absorb a great deal of liquid while still retaining their shape. There are several types of risotto rice, including the popular arborio and carnaroli. When cooking risotto rice, it is imperative to stir it regularly. Liquid or stock should be added periodically throughout cooking.

Basmati Rice

The grains of basmati rice are long and slender and, during cooking, become even longer, which partly accounts for its wonderful fluffy texture. This rice is widely used in Indian cooking and is excellent in almost any savoury rice dish or served with curries.

Vegetables, Beans & Lentils

Dried, canned and bottled vegetables, beans and lentils can be used as the basis for all kinds of dishes.

Canned Tomatoes

Available chopped or whole, canned tomatoes are an essential item in every kitchen. They are very versatile and can be used to make an incredible variety of sauces, pasta dishes, pizza toppings, soups and stews. Look out for canned Italian pomodorino tomatoes in a thick juice; they make a superbly rich sauce.

Dried Mushrooms

Wild mushrooms that have been dried, such as porcini and morels, are a useful alternative to fresh, seasonal wild mushrooms, which are not always available. They add a rich flavour to pasta dishes and casseroles. Soak them in boiling water for about 30 minutes before use.

Bottled Antipasti

Red (bell) peppers, aubergines (eggplants), mushrooms and artichoke hearts preserved in olive oil with garlic and herbs are a classic Italian appetizer and can also make a tasty addition to salads and pasta dishes.

Olives

Black and green, olives bring a rich flavour to salads and pasta dishes. The difference in colour in olives is not a matter of type, but simply when the olive is picked. Green olives are picked when immature and have a sharper flavour and crunchier texture than black olives, which have been ripened on the tree. Olives also make a quick and easy appetizer when served with salami and fresh bread.

Dried Pulses

Pulses such as flageolet beans, chickpeas, red kidney beans, cannellini beans and butter (lima) beans have a long shelf-life in their dried form but take a while to prepare, requiring soaking and long boiling. If you wish to use them, save time by cooking them in bulk and freezing some for future use. The cooking time for dried pulses is at least halved by using a pressure cooker.

Canned Pulses

The canned alternatives to dried pulses are very useful when you are short of time. They simply need to be rinsed in cold water, and can then be used straight away in hot dishes or incorporated into salads. Cans of mixed pulses are available, but try to avoid the varieties that are packed in a synthetic-flavoured dressing or that include overcooked green beans.

Red Lentils

Compared to most dried beans, the small, bright orange pulses known as red lentils have a relatively short cooking time of 20–30 minutes, with no need for soaking, and are ideal for making a quick and tasty Indian-style dhal. They are also excellent for thickening soups and casseroles and for making croquettes.

Short-cut Ingredients

There are some useful products available that can help you save valuable time in the kitchen. These ingredients are usually pre-prepared in some way, taking the time and effort out of preparation. They provide a quick base for dishes so you will need fewer ingredients and can spend less time on shopping and cooking, and more time relaxing and eating.

Pastry
Making pastry is time-consuming, but ready-made pastry is widely available in supermarkets and can make quick work of tarts, pies and filled pastries, allowing you to concentrate your efforts on the filling. Shortcrust, sweet shortcrust, puff and filo pastry can all be purchased frozen or chilled and ready to use. Some pastries even come ready-rolled so that all you have to do is open the packet, cut, fold and fill the pastry, and then bake it until crisp and golden.

Cookie Dough
Cartons of chocolate chip cookie dough can be useful for many sweet recipes. It can be shaped and baked to make plain cookies, and these can then be coated with a topping or sandwiched together with a chocolate filling or ice cream to make a decadent treat. The dough can also be rolled thinly and used to line muffin tins (pans) to make a crisp cookie cup to fill with ice cream for dessert. Bitesize pieces of the cookie dough can be stirred into a vanilla ice cream mix to make cookie dough ice cream.

Marzipan
Good-quality marzipan is widely available. It is perfect for decorating cakes, but it can be used in many other ways as well. Try rolling it out thinly and using it as a tart base under fruit, or chop it into small pieces and add to cookies and cakes.

Custard
Fresh ready-made custard is great served hot as an accompaniment to desserts, but it also makes a useful base for ice creams, sauces and soufflés.

Frozen Fruit
Mixed frozen fruit has already been prepared, ready for making into desserts and sauces. It is available all year round, which means that you can enjoy the sweet taste of summer fruits during the winter when they are out of season. Frozen fruit is often cheaper than fresh.

Batter Mixes
Simply combine these with an egg and water and use to make pancakes or to coat foods such as fish, vegetables or fruit before deep-frying.

CAKE MIXES

With the simple addition of an egg and water, these easy-to-use mixes can be turned into a freshly baked cake in no time at all. Sprinkling the cake mixture with chopped nuts before baking, or sandwiching the cake with cream and fresh summer fruits once it has cooled, can transform these simple mixes into a delicious indulgent treat for enjoying with a cup of tea or coffee, or an impressive dessert for a special occasion.

CAKES & COOKIES

Store-bought cakes and cookies can often be used as the base for simple desserts. Delicious dark chocolate brownies can be combined with cream and macerated fruit to create a rich, indulgent dessert, or blended with milk and ice cream to make a decadent milkshake. Broken ginger cookies or sponge fingers can be used as the base for many creamy desserts, such as trifle.

PIZZA BASE MIXES

You can buy ready-baked pizza bases, but these can often be rather cardboard-like. Uncooked dough mixes tend to be far more authentic and take very little effort to use.

PASTA SAUCES

Both bottled and fresh pasta sauces are widely available in supermarkets. Several simple sauces are available, such as tomato or tomato and herb, which are useful for tossing with pasta, spreading over a pizza base or as the base for a quick soup. Ready-made cheese sauces are also versatile – not only are they good for serving with pasta, but also for topping vegetable gratins, or combining with whisked egg whites and some extra grated cheese to make a quick and simple soufflé.

RICE MIXES

It is now possible to buy rice mixes for cooking in the microwave. These come in a variety of flavours, including mushroom and pilau, and are extremely useful as the base for quick rice dishes such as kedgeree. Good-quality mixes for risotto are another worthwhile investment. The best contain no artificial additives, and can be simply boiled, and ready in a matter of minutes. .

BAGS OF MIXED SALAD

You can save time on selecting and preparing a variety of leaves and also save some space in the refrigerator by buying bags of mixed salad. For maximum flavour, choose a bag that includes some strong-tasting items, such as rocket (arugula).

STIR-FRY VEGETABLES

These packs make preparing a stir-fry even quicker. The ones that contain a range of Chinese vegetables, such as bamboo shoots and water chestnuts, are particularly useful.

MEXICAN INGREDIENTS

Ready-made flour and corn tortillas, as well as taco shells, are great for wrapping or filling with chicken, beef or salad to make fabulous Mexican dishes such as enchiladas and fajitas.

MAKING THE BASICS

Having a few ready-made basics, such as stocks, pasta sauces and flavoured oils, can really help with everyday cooking. They can all be bought ready-made, but are easy to make at home. Stocks take time to prepare, but can be frozen for several months. Flavoured oils are easy to make and keep in the same way as ordinary oils so it's well worth having a few on hand.

FLAVOURED OILS

All these flavourings make rich-tasting oils that are perfect for drizzling, making salad dressings and cooking.

GARLIC OIL

Add several whole garlic cloves to a bottle of olive oil and leave for about 2–3 weeks. Strain the oil into a clean bottle and store in a cool, dark place.

HERB-INFUSED OIL

Half-fill a jar with washed and dried fresh herbs, such as rosemary or basil. Pour over olive oil to cover, then seal the jar and place in a cool, dark place for 3 days. Strain the herb-flavoured oil into a clean jar or bottle and discard the herbs.

LEMON OR LIME OIL

Finely pare the rind from 1 lemon or lime, place on kitchen paper, and leave to dry for 1 day. Add the dried rind to a bottle of olive oil and leave to stand for up to 3 days. Strain the flavoured oil into a clean jar or bottle and discard the rind.

CHILLI OIL

Add several dried chillies to a bottle of olive oil and leave for about 2 weeks before using. If the flavour is not sufficiently pronounced after this time, leave the chillies in the oil to infuse for another week. The bottle gives a very decorative effect.

STOCK

You cannot beat the flavour of good home-made stock. To freeze, pour the cooled stock into 600ml/1 pint/2½ cup containers and freeze for up to 2 months.

CHICKEN STOCK

Put a 1.3kg/3lb chicken carcass into a large pan with 2 peeled and quartered onions, 2 halved carrots, 2 roughly chopped celery sticks, 1 bouquet garni, 1 peeled garlic clove and 5 black peppercorns. Add 1.2 litres/2 pints/5 cups cold water to cover the chicken and vegetables and then bring to the boil. Reduce the heat, cover and simmer for 4–5 hours. Strain the stock through a sieve lined with kitchen paper and leave to cool.

VEGETABLE STOCK

Put 900g/2lb chopped vegetables, including onions, leeks, tomatoes, carrots, parsnips and cabbage, in a large pan. Pour in 1.5 litres/2½ pints/6¼ cups water. Bring to the boil and simmer for 30 minutes, then strain.

Dark Beef Stock

Preheat the oven to 230°C/450°F/Gas 8. Put 1.3kg/3lb beef bones in a roasting pan and roast for 40 minutes, until browned, turning occasionally. Transfer to a large pan with 2 roughly chopped carrots, 2 quartered onions, 3 roughly chopped celery sticks, 2 chopped tomatoes, 1 bouquet garni, 6 black peppercorns and 5ml/1 tsp salt. Cover with water and cook as for chicken stock.

Fish Stock

Put 2 chopped onions, 1.3kg/3lb fish bones and heads, 300ml/½ pint/l¼ cups white wine, 5 black peppercorns and 1 bouquet garni in a large pan. Pour in 2 litres/3½ pints/9 cups water. Bring to the boil and simmer for 20 minutes, then strain the stock and leave to cool.

Marinades

These strong-tasting mixes are perfect for adding flavour to meat, poultry, fish and vegetables. Most ingredients should be left to marinate for at least 30 minutes.

Ginger & Soy Marinade

This is perfect for use with chicken and beef. Peel and grate a 2.5cm/1in piece of fresh root ginger and peel and finely chop a large garlic clove. In a small bowl, whisk together 60ml/4 tbsp olive oil and 75ml/5 tbsp dark soy sauce. Season with pepper and stir in the ginger and garlic.

Rosemary & Garlic Marinade

This is ideal for robust fish, lamb and chicken. Roughly chop the leaves from 3 fresh rosemary sprigs. Crush 2 garlic cloves and whisk together with the chopped rosemary, 75ml/5 tbsp olive oil and the juice of 1 lemon.

Lemon Grass & Lime Marinade

Use with fish and chicken. Finely chop 1 lemon grass stalk. Whisk together the grated rind and juice of 1 lime with 75ml/5 tbsp olive oil and the lemon grass. Season.

Red Wine & Bay Marinade

This is ideal for red meat, particularly tougher cuts. Whisk together 150ml/¼ pint/⅔ cup red wine, 1 chopped garlic clove, 2 torn fresh bay leaves and 45ml/3 tbsp olive oil. Season with black pepper.

Dressings

Freshly made dressings are delicious drizzled over salads but are also tasty served with cooked vegetables and simply cooked fish, meat and poultry. You can make these dressings a few hours in advance and store them in a sealed container in the refrigerator until ready to use. Give them a quick whisk before drizzling over the food.

Honey & Wholegrain Mustard Dressing

Drizzle this sweet, peppery dressing over leafy salads, fish, chicken and red meat dishes or toss with warm new potatoes. Whisk together 15ml/1 tbsp wholegrain mustard, 30ml/2 tbsp white wine vinegar, 15ml/1 tbsp honey and 75ml/5 tbsp extra virgin olive oil and season to taste.

EASY TOMATO SAUCE

Toss with pasta, use on a pizza base or serve with chicken or fish. Heat 15ml/1 tbsp olive oil in large a pan, add 1 chopped onion and fry for 3–4 minutes until soft. Add 1 chopped garlic clove and cook for about 1 minute more. Pour in 400g/14oz chopped canned tomatoes and stir in 15ml/1 tbsp tomato purée (paste). Add 30ml/2 tbsp dried oregano and simmer for about 15 minutes, until thickened. Season.

MUSTARD CHEESE SAUCE

Toss with boiled vegetables or baked white fish. Melt 25g/1oz/2 tbsp butter in a medium pan and stir in 25g/1oz/¼ cup plain (all-purpose) flour. Cook, stirring, for 2 minutes. Remove the pan from the heat and stir in 5ml/1 tsp prepared English mustard, then gradually add 200ml/7fl oz/scant 1 cup milk, stirring to avoid lumps. (If the sauce becomes lumpy, whisk until smooth.) Return to the heat and bring to the boil, then boil, stirring constantly, for 2–3 minutes, until thickened. Remove from the heat and stir in 115g/4oz/1 cup grated Cheddar. Season to taste.

ORANGE & TARRAGON DRESSING

Serve this fresh, tangy dressing with salads and grilled (broiled) fish. Whisk together the rind and juice of 1 large orange with 45ml/3 tbsp olive oil and 15ml/1 tbsp chopped fresh tarragon. Season to taste.

TOASTED CORIANDER & CUMIN DRESSING

Drizzle this warm, spicy dressing over grilled chicken, lamb or beef. Heat a small frying pan and sprinkle in 15ml/1 tbsp each of coriander and cumin seeds. Dry-fry until the seeds release their aromas and start to pop, then crush the seeds using a mortar and pestle. Add 45ml/3 tbsp olive oil, whisk to combine, then leave it to infuse for 20 minutes. Season to taste.

QUICK SATAY SAUCE

Serve with grilled (broiled) chicken, beef or prawns (shrimp), or toss with egg noodles. Put 30ml/2 tbsp crunchy peanut butter in a pan and stir in 150ml/¼ pint/⅔ cup coconut milk, 45ml/3 tbsp hot water, a pinch of chilli powder and 30ml/2 tbsp light soy sauce. Simmer gently for 1 minute.

SAVOURY SAUCES

Hot and cold savoury sauces lie at the heart of many dishes or can be the finishing touch that makes a meal – tomato sauce tossed with pasta, cheese sauce poured over a vegetable gratin, apple sauce to accompany pork, or a spoonful of mayonnaise with poached salmon. This section covers a range of basic sauces, as well as a few more unusual ones, to ensure that even the simplest meal need never be dull.

APPLE SAUCE

Serve with pork. Peel, core and slice 450g/1lb cooking apples and place in a pan. Add a splash of water, 15ml/1 tbsp caster (superfine) sugar and a few whole cloves. Cook the apples over a gentle heat, stirring occasionally, until the fruit becomes pulpy.

QUICK CRANBERRY SAUCE

Serve with roast chicken or turkey. Put 225g/8oz/2 cups cranberries in a pan with 75g/3oz/scant ½ cup light muscovado sugar, 45ml/3 tbsp port and 45ml/3 tbsp orange juice. Bring to the boil, then simmer, uncovered, for 10 minutes, or until the cranberries are tender. Stir occasionally.

TRADITIONAL PESTO

Toss with pasta, stir into mashed potatoes or plain boiled rice, or use to flavour sauces and dressings. Put 50g/2oz fresh basil leaves in a food processor and blend to a paste with 25g/1oz/¼ cup toasted pine nuts and 2 peeled garlic cloves. With the water still running, drizzle in 120ml/4fl oz/½ cup extra virgin olive oil until the mixture is smooth. Spoon the pesto into a bowl and stir in 25g/1oz/⅓ cup freshly grated Parmesan cheese. Season to taste with salt and freshly ground black pepper.

PARSLEY & WALNUT PESTO

Put 50g/2oz fresh parsley leaves in a food processor and blend to a paste with 25g/1oz/¼ cup walnuts and 2 peeled garlic cloves. Drizzle in 120ml/4fl oz/½ cup extra virgin olive oil until the mixture is smooth. Spoon the pesto into a bowl and stir in 25g/1oz/⅓ cup freshly grated Parmesan cheese. Season to taste.

ROCKET PESTO

Put 50g/2oz fresh rocket (arugula) leaves into a food processor and blend to a paste with 25g/1oz/¼ cup toasted pine nuts and 2 peeled garlic cloves. With the motor still running, drizzle in 120ml/4fl oz/½ cup extra virgin olive oil until the mixture is smooth. Spoon the pesto into a bowl and stir in 25g/1oz/⅓ cup freshly grated Parmesan cheese. Season to taste.

WHITE WINE SAUCE

Boil 300 ml/½ pint/1¼ cups each of milk and white wine with 2 bay leaves or a bouquet garni, remove from the heat, cover and leave to stand for 1 hour, then remove the herbs. Melt 25g/1oz/2tbsp butter, add 25g/1oz/¼ cup flour and cook gently, stirring, for 2 minutes. Remove from the heat and gradually whisk in the wine mixture, then bring to the boil and cook, stirring constantly, for 2–3 minutes, until thickened. Season to taste.

MAYONNAISE

Put 2 egg yolks, 10ml/2 tsp lemon juice, 5ml/1 tsp Dijon mustard and some salt and ground black pepper in a food processor. Process briefly to combine, then, with the motor running, drizzle in, very gradually at first, about 350ml/12fl oz/1½ cups olive oil. The mayonnaise will become thick and pale. Scrape the mayonnaise into a bowl.

FLAVOURINGS FOR MAYONNAISE

Aioli is good with piping hot chips (French fries). Follow the recipe for plain mayonnaise, and add 2 peeled garlic cloves to the food processor with the egg yolks. For lemon mayonnaise add the grated rind of 1 lemon with the egg yolks. For herb mayonnaise, finely chop a handful of fresh herbs, such as basil, coriander (cilantro) and tarragon, then stir into the mayonnaise.

SAVOURY DIPS

These richly flavoured dips are delicious served with tortilla chips, crudités or small savoury crackers, but can also be served as an accompaniment to grilled (broiled) or poached chicken and fish. The creamy dips also make flavourful dressings for salads; you may need to thin them slightly with a squeeze of lemon juice or a little cold water.

BLUE CHEESE DIP

This sharp, tangy mixture is best served with crunchy crudités. Put 200ml/7fl oz/ scant 1 cup crème fraîche in a large bowl and add 115g/4oz/1 cup crumbled blue cheese, such as Stilton. Stir well until the mixture is smooth and creamy. Season with salt and freshly ground black pepper and fold in 30ml/2 tbsp chopped fresh chives.

SOUR CREAM & CHIVE DIP

This tasty dip is a classic combination: it goes particularly well with crudités and savoury crackers. Put 200ml/7fl oz/scant 1 cup sour cream in a bowl and add 30ml/ 2 tbsp chopped fresh chives and a pinch of caster (superfine) sugar. Stir well to mix, then season with salt and plenty of freshly ground black pepper to taste.

AVOCADO & CUMIN SALSA

Serve this spicy Mexican-style salsa with tortilla chips; they're the perfect shape for scooping up the chunky salsa. Peel, stone (pit) and roughly chop 1 ripe avocado. Transfer to a bowl and gently stir in 1 finely chopped fresh red chilli, 15ml/ 1 tbsp toasted crushed cumin seeds, 1 chopped ripe tomato, the juice of 1 lime, 45ml/3 tbsp olive oil and 30ml/2 tbsp chopped fresh coriander (cilantro). Season and serve.

GRAVY

This classic sauce for roast poultry and meat is quick and easy to make. Remove the cooked poultry or meat from the roasting pan, transfer to a serving platter, cover with foil and leave to rest. Spoon off all but about 30ml/2 tbsp of the cooking fat and juices, leaving the sediment in the pan. Place the pan over a low heat and add a splash of white wine for poultry or red wine for meat, stirring in any sediment from the roasting pan. Stir in 30ml/2 tbsp plain (all-purpose) flour and mix to a paste. Remove from the heat and gradually pour in 450ml/¾ pint/scant 2 cups stock. Return to the heat and then stir over a medium heat until the gravy comes to the boil. Simmer for 2–3 minutes, until thickened. Adjust the seasoning and serve.

SWEET SAUCES

These luscious sauces are perfect spooned over ice cream and other desserts.

RASPBERRY AND VANILLA SAUCE

Scrape the seeds from a vanilla pod (bean) into a food processor. Add 200g/7oz/ 1 cup raspberries and 30ml/2 tbsp icing (confectioners') sugar. Process to a purée, adding water to thin, if necessary.

CUSTARD

Heat 300ml/½ pint/1¼ cups milk with a vanilla pod (bean) until just boiling, remove from the heat, cover and leave for 10 minutes, then strain. Beat 3 egg yolks with 15ml/1tbsp caster (superfine) sugar in a bowl. Gradually add the milk, whisking constantly. Reheat gently in a clean pan and cook, stirring, until slightly thickened, then remove from the heat. (If it curdles, plunge the base of the pan in cold water, whisk in 15ml/1tbsp cornflour (cornstarch) until smooth, then reheat). If using as a base for ice cream or other recipes, more sugar may be needed.

CHOCOLATE FUDGE SAUCE

Put 175ml/6fl oz/¾ cup double (heavy) cream in a pan with 45ml/3 tbsp golden (light corn) syrup, 200g/7oz/scant 1 cup light muscovado (brown) sugar and a pinch of salt. Heat gently, stirring, until the sugar has dissolved. Add 75g/3oz/½ cup chopped plain (semisweet) chocolate and stir until melted. Simmer the sauce gently for about 20 minutes, stirring occasionally, until thickened. Cover and place over a pan of simmering water.

FLAVOURED CREAMS

Fresh cream is always delicious, and these ideas for flavouring it will make it even more luxurious.

ROSEMARY AND ALMOND CREAM

Pour 300ml/½ pint/1¼ cups double (heavy) cream into a pan and add 2 fresh rosemary sprigs. Heat until it is just about to boil, then remove from the heat and leave to stand for 20 minutes. Discard the rosemary. Pour into a bowl and chill. Whip into soft peaks and stir in 30ml/2 tbsp chopped toasted almonds.

RUM & CINNAMON CREAM

This cream goes well with coffee, chocolate and fruit. Put 300ml/½ pint/1¼ cups double (heavy) cream in a pan and add 1 cinnamon stick. Heat the mixture until just about to boil, then remove the pan from the heat and leave it to stand for about 20 minutes. Strain through a fine sieve; place in the refrigerator until cold. Whip the cold cream until it stands in soft peaks, then stir in 30ml/2 tbsp rum and 15ml/1 tbsp icing (confectioners') sugar.

CARDAMOM CREAM

This subtle, aromatic cream is delicious served with fruit salads, compotes, tarts and pies. It goes particularly well with tropical fruits, such as mango. Pour 300ml/½ pint/1¼ cups double (heavy) cream into a pan and add 3 green cardamom pods. Heat the mixture gently until just about to boil, then remove the pan from the heat and leave to stand for about 20 minutes. Strain the cream through a fine sieve and place in the refrigerator until cold. Whip the cold cream until it stands in soft peaks.

PRALINE CREAM

1 Put 115g/4oz/½ cup sugar and 75ml/ 5 tbsp water in a small, heavy pan. Stir over a gentle heat until dissolved, then boil (not stirring) until golden.

2 Remove from the heat, stir in 50g/2oz/ ⅓ cup whole blanched almonds and pour on to a lightly oiled baking sheet. Leave until hard.

3 Break into smaller pieces and put in a food processor. Process for about 1 minute until finely chopped.

4 In a large bowl, whip 300ml/½ pint/ 1¼ cups double (heavy) cream into soft peaks. Stir in the praline and serve.

Making Simple Accompaniments

When you've made a delicious main meal, you need to serve it with equally tasty accompaniments. The following section is full of simple, speedy ideas for fabulous side dishes – from creamy mashed potatoes, fragrant rice and spicy noodles to Italian-style polenta and simple, healthy vegetables.

Potatoes

Just about any main dish goes well with potatoes. They can be cooked simply – boiled, steamed, fried or baked – but they are even better mashed with milk and butter to make creamy mashed potatoes.

Perfect Mashed Potatoes

Peel 675g/1½lb floury potatoes and cut them into large chunks. Place in a pan of salted boiling water. Return to the boil, then simmer for 15–20 minutes, or until completely tender. Drain the potatoes and return to the pan. Leave over a low heat for a couple of minutes. Take the pan off the heat and mash the potatoes until smooth. Beat in 45–60ml/3–4 tbsp warm milk and about 15g/½oz/1tbsp butter, until creamy, then season to taste with plenty of ground black pepper.

Pesto Mash

Make mashed potatoes as described above, then stir in 30ml/2 tbsp pesto sauce until it is thoroughly combined.

Mustard Mash

Make mashed potatoes as above, then stir in 15–30ml/1–2 tbsp wholegrain mustard.

Cheese and Parsley Mash

Make mashed potatoes as above, then stir in 30ml/2 tbsp freshly grated Cheddar and 15ml/1 tbsp chopped fresh flatleaf parsley.

Apple & Thyme Mash

Serve with pork. Make mashed potatoes as instructed above. Heat 25g/1oz/2 tbsp butter in a pan and add 2 peeled, cored and sliced eating apples. Fry for 4–5 minutes, turning frequently. Roughly mash, then fold into the potatoes, with 15ml/1 tbsp fresh thyme leaves.

Crushed Potatoes with Parsley and Lemon

Cook 675g/1½lb new potatoes in salted boiling water for 15–20 minutes, until tender. Drain the potatoes and crush roughly, using a fork. Stir in 30ml/2 tbsp extra virgin olive oil, the grated rind and juice of 1 lemon and 30ml/2 tbsp chopped fresh flatleaf parsley. Season to taste.

Crushed Potatoes with Cheese and Pine Nuts

Make crushed potatoes as above, omitting the lemon, then stir in 30ml/2 tbsp each of grated Cheddar and toasted pine nuts.

Crushed Potatoes with Garlic & Basil

Cook 675g/1½lb new potatoes in a pan of boiling salted water for 15–20 minutes until tender. Drain and crush roughly, using the back of a fork. Stir in 30ml/2 tbsp extra virgin olive oil, 2 finely chopped garlic cloves and a handful of torn basil leaves until well combined. Season to taste.

Rice

This versatile grain can be served simply – either boiled or steamed – or can be flavoured or stir-fried with different ingredients to make a tasty, exciting accompaniment to curries, stir-fries, stews and grilled (broiled) meat or fish.

Easy Egg-Fried Rice

Cook 115g/4oz/generous ½ cup long-grain rice in a large pan of boiling water for 10–12 minutes, until tender. Drain well and refresh under cold running water. Heat 30ml/2 tbsp sunflower oil in a large frying pan and add 1 finely chopped garlic clove. Cook for 1 minute, then add the rice and stir-fry for a further minute. Push the rice to the side of the pan and pour 1 beaten egg into the pan. Cook the egg until set, then break up with a fork and stir into the rice. Add soy sauce to taste, and mix well.

Star Anise & Cinnamon Rice

Add 225g/8oz/ 1 cup basmati rice to a large pan of salted boiling water. Return to the boil, then reduce the heat and add a cinnamon stick and 2 star anise. Simmer gently for 10–15 minutes, until tender. Drain, removing the spices before serving.

Coconut Rice

Put 225g/8oz/generous 1 cup basmati rice in a pan and pour in a 400ml/14oz can coconut milk. Cover with water, add some salt and bring to the boil. Simmer for 12 minutes, until tender, then drain.

Coriander & Spring Onion Rice

Cook 225g/8oz/1 cup basmati rice in salted boiling water for about 12 minutes, until tender. Drain the rice well and return to the pan. Stir in 3 sliced spring onions (scallions) and 1 chopped bunch of fresh coriander (cilantro). Serve immediately.

Noodles

There are many different types of noodles, all of which are quick to cook and make the perfect accompaniment to Chinese- and Asian-style stir-fries and curries. Serve on their own, or toss with simple flavourings.

Soy & Sesame Egg Noodles

Cook a 250g/9oz packet of egg noodles according to the instructions on the packet. Drain well and place in a large bowl. Drizzle over 30ml/2 tbsp dark soy sauce and 10ml/2 tsp sesame oil, then stir in 15ml/1 tbsp toasted sesame seeds. Serve hot or cold.

Peanut Noodles

Cook a 250g/9oz packet of egg noodles. Heat 15ml/1 tbsp sunflower oil in a wok and add 30ml/2 tbsp crunchy peanut butter. Add a splash of cold water and a dash of soy sauce and stir the mixture over a gentle heat until thoroughly combined. Add the noodles to the pan and toss to coat with the peanut mixture. Sprinkle with fresh coriander (cilantro) and serve.

Chilli & Spring Onion Noodles

Soak 115g/4oz flat rice noodles in cold water for 30 minutes, until softened. Drain well. Heat 30ml/2 tbsp olive oil in a wok or large frying pan. Add 2 finely chopped garlic cloves and 1 seeded and finely chopped red chilli and fry these gently for 2 minutes. Add a bunch of sliced spring onions (scallions) to the pan. Cook for a minute or so, then stir in the rice noodles. Season before serving.

POLENTA

This classic Italian dish made from cornmeal makes an easy yet delicious accompaniment to many dishes and is a useful alternative to the usual potatoes, bread or pasta. It can be served in two ways – either soft, or set and cut into wedges and grilled (broiled) or fried. Soft polenta is rather like mashed potatoes, while the grilled or fried variety has a much firmer texture and lovely crisp shell. Both types can be enjoyed plain, or flavoured with other ingredients such as cheese, herbs and spices. Traditional polenta requires lengthy boiling and constant attention during cooking, but the quick-cook varieties, which are widely available in most large supermarkets, give excellent results and are much simpler and quicker to prepare.

SOFT POLENTA

Cook 225g/8oz/2 cups quick-cook polenta according to the instructions on the packet. As soon as it is cooked, stir in about 50g/2oz/¼ cup butter. Season and serve.

MAKING POLENTA

1 Pour 1 litre/1¾ pints/4 cups water into a heavy pan and bring to the boil. Remove the pan from the heat.

2 In a steady stream, gradually add 185g/6½oz/1¼ cups instant polenta, whisking to prevent lumps forming.

3 Return the pan to the heat and cook, stirring constantly with a wooden spoon, until the polenta is thick and creamy and starts to come away from the sides of the pan – this will take only a few minutes.

4 Season with salt and pepper, add a little butter and mix thoroughly.

SOFT POLENTA WITH PARMESAN & SAGE

Cook 225g/8oz/2 cups quick-cook polenta. As soon as the polenta is cooked, stir in 115g/4oz/1⅓ cups freshly grated Parmesan cheese and a handful of chopped fresh sage. Stir in 25g/1oz/2tbsp butter and season to taste before serving.

SOFT POLENTA WITH CHEDDAR CHEESE & THYME

Cook 225g/8oz/2 cups quick-cook polenta according to the instructions on the packet. As soon as it is cooked, stir in 50g/2oz/½ cup grated Cheddar cheese and 30ml/2 tbsp chopped fresh thyme until well combined. Stir 25g/1oz/2tbsp butter into the cheesy polenta and season to taste.

FRIED CHILLI POLENTA TRIANGLES

Cook 225g/8oz/2 cups quick-cook polenta. Stir in 5ml/1 tsp dried chilli flakes, add more seasoning if necessary, and spread the mixture out on an oiled baking sheet to a thickness of about 1cm/½in. Leave the polenta until cold and set, then chill for 20 minutes. Turn the polenta out on to a board and cut it into large squares, then cut each square into 2 triangles. Heat 30ml/2 tbsp olive oil in a large frying pan. Fry the triangles in the olive oil for 2–3 minutes on each side, until golden, then lift out and drain on kitchen paper before serving.

GRILLED POLENTA WITH GORGONZOLA

Cook 225g/8oz/2 cups quick-cook polenta according to the instructions on the packet. Check the seasoning, adding more if necessary, and spread the mixture out on an oiled baking sheet to a thickness of about 1cm/½in. Leave until cold and completely set, then chill for about 20 minutes. Turn the polenta out on to a board and cut it into large squares, then cut each square into 2 triangles. Pre-heat the grill (broiler) and arrange the polenta triangles on the grill pan. Cook for about 5 minutes, or until golden brown, then turn over and top with slivers of Gorgonzola. Grill for a further 5 minutes, or until bubbling.

SIMPLE VEGETABLE DISHES

Fresh vegetables are delicious cooked on their own but can also be stir-fried with other ingredients. This can be a great way to add flavour and create colourful, enticing and healthy vegetable dishes.

STIR-FRIED CABBAGE WITH HAZELNUTS

Heat 30ml/2 tbsp sunflower oil in a wok or large frying pan and add 4 chopped rashers (strips) smoked streaky (fatty) bacon. Stir-fry for about 3 minutes, or until the bacon starts to turn golden, then add ½ shredded green cabbage to the pan. Stir-fry for 3–4 minutes, until the cabbage is just tender. Season and stir in 25g/1oz/¼ cup roughly chopped toasted hazelnuts.

CREAMY BRUSSELS SPROUTS

Heat 15ml/1 tbsp sunflower oil in a wok or large frying pan. Add 1 chopped garlic clove and stir-fry for about 30 seconds. Shred 450g/1lb Brussels sprouts and add to the pan. Stir-fry for 3–4 minutes, until just tender. Season and stir in 30ml/2 tbsp crème fraîche. Warm through and serve.

HONEY-FRIED PARSNIPS & CELERIAC

Peel 250g/8oz parsnips and 115g/4oz celeriac. Cut both into matchsticks. Heat 30ml/2 tbsp olive oil in a wok or large frying pan and add the vegetables. Fry over a gentle heat for 6–7 minutes, stirring occasionally, until golden and tender. Season, then stir in 15ml/1 tbsp clear honey. Serve after 1 minute.

FLAVOURED BREADS

Bread is the perfect ready-made side dish. Look out for part-baked breads that you can finish off in the oven – this way you can enjoy the taste of fresh bread in just a few minutes.

ITALIAN BREADS

Ciabatta, a long, oval bread with a chewy texture, is often available in ready-to-bake form. Look out for ciabatta with sun-dried tomatoes or olives. Focaccia is made with olive oil and is softer. It is available plain or flavoured with fresh rosemary and garlic.

INDIAN BREADS

Traditionally cooked in a clay oven, naan is easy to find in supermarkets and is a delicious accompaniment to any curry dish. It is available either plain or flavoured with spices. Chapati, a flatbread, is a lighter alternative. The small, round breads can be slightly more difficult to find but are well worth searching for.

BREAKFASTS & BRUNCHES

No one wants the bother of lots of ingredients and lengthy preparation for their very first meal of the day. This collection of wonderfully simple yet delicious dishes has been created with convenience in mind. Whether you want a healthy, refreshing Honey and Watermelon Tonic for breakfast, a fibre-packed Crunchy Oat Cereal or a deliciously indulgent serving of Eggs Benedict for a lazy weekend brunch, you're sure to find the perfect recipe here to set you up for the day ahead.

CRUNCHY OAT CEREAL

Serve this tasty cereal simply with milk or, for a real treat, with yogurt and fresh fruit such as raspberries or blueberries. Oats are a traditional breakfast food, and this delicious recipe makes a welcome change from porridge or muesli.

SERVES 6

INGREDIENTS
200g/7oz/1¾ cups jumbo rolled oats
150g/5oz/1¼ cups pecan nuts, roughly chopped
90ml/6 tbsp maple syrup
75g/3oz/6 tbsp butter, melted

1 Preheat the oven to 160°C/325°F/Gas 3. Mix all the ingredients together and spread on to a large baking tray.

2 Bake for 30–35 minutes, or until golden and crunchy. Leave to cool, then break up into clumps and serve.

COOK'S TIPS
- *This cereal will keep in an airtight container for up to two weeks. Store in a cool, dry place.*
- *You can use other types of nuts if you prefer. Try roughly chopped almonds or hazelnuts instead of pecan nuts, or use a mixture.*

CHOCOLATE BRIOCHE SANDWICHES

This luxury breakfast sandwich is a bit of a twist on the classic pain au chocolat *and beats a boring slice of toast any day. The pale green pistachio nuts work really well with the chocolate spread, adding a satisfying crunch as well as a contrast in colour.*

SERVES 4

INGREDIENTS
8 thick brioche bread slices
120ml/8 tbsp chocolate spread
30ml/2 tbsp shelled pistachio nuts, finely chopped

1 Toast the brioche slices until golden on both sides. Spread four of the slices thickly with the chocolate spread and sprinkle over the chopped pistachio nuts in an even layer.

2 Place the remaining brioche slices on top of the chocolate and nuts and press down gently. Using a sharp knife, cut the sandwiches in half diagonally and serve immediately.

APRICOT TURNOVERS

These sweet and succulent pastries are delicious served with a big cup of milky coffee for a late breakfast or mid-morning treat. They're also excellent made with different fruit conserves, such as strawberry, blackcurrant or plum.

SERVES 4

INGREDIENTS
225g/8oz ready-made puff pastry, thawed if frozen
60ml/4 tbsp apricot conserve
30ml/2 tbsp icing (confectioners') sugar

1 Preheat the oven to 190°C/375°F/Gas 5. Roll out the pastry on a lightly floured surface to a 25cm/10in square. Using a sharp knife, cut the pastry into four 13cm/5in squares.

2 Place a tablespoon of the apricot conserve in the middle of each square of pastry. Using a pastry brush, brush the edges of the pastry with a little cold water and fold each square over to form a triangle. Gently press the edges together to seal.

3 Carefully transfer the turnovers to a baking sheet and bake for 15–20 minutes, or until risen and golden. Using a metal spatula, remove the pastries to a wire rack to cool, then dust generously with icing sugar and serve.

Warm Pancakes with Pears

If you can find them, use Williams pears for this recipe because they are juicier than most other varieties. For a really indulgent breakfast, top the pancakes with a generous spoonful of crème fraîche or fromage frais.

SERVES 4

INGREDIENTS
8 ready-made pancakes
50g/2oz/¼ cup butter
4 ripe pears, peeled, cored and thickly sliced
30ml/2 tbsp light muscovado (brown) sugar

1 Preheat the oven to 150°C/330°F/Gas 2. Tightly wrap the pancakes in foil and place in the oven to warm through.

2 Meanwhile, heat the butter in a large frying pan and add the pears. Fry for 2–3 minutes, until the undersides are golden. Turn the pears over and sprinkle with sugar. Cook for a further 2–3 minutes, or until the sugar dissolves and the pan juices become sticky.

3 Remove the pancakes from the oven and take them out of the foil. Divide the caramelized pears among the pancakes, placing them in one quarter. Fold each pancake in half over the filling, then into quarters, and place two folded pancakes on each plate. Drizzle over any remaining juices and serve immediately.

VARIATION
In place of caramelized pears, you could fill the pancakes with soft fresh fruits, such as strawberries, raspberries or blackberries, sprinkled with a little caster (superfine) sugar, if you like.

CROQUE-MONSIEUR

This classic French toastie is delicious served at any time of day, but with a foaming cup of milky coffee it makes a particularly enjoyable Sunday brunch. This is quite a filling dish, just the thing to keep you going until suppertime.

SERVES 4

INGREDIENTS
8 white bread slices
a little softened butter
4 large lean ham slices
175g/6oz Gruyère cheese, thinly sliced

1 Preheat the grill (broiler). Arrange the bread on the grill rack and toast four slices on both sides and the other four slices on one side only.

2 Butter the slices of bread that have been toasted on both sides and top with the ham, then the cheese, and season with plenty of ground black pepper.

3 Lay the remaining, half-toasted bread slices on top of the cheese, with the untoasted side uppermost. Grill the tops of the sandwiches until golden brown, then cut them in half using a sharp knife and serve immediately.

VARIATIONS
Gruyère is traditionally used for croque-monsieur, but you could use mild Cheddar instead. Prosciutto and Gorgonzola, served with a smear of mustard, also make a delicious alternative to the classic ham and Gruyère combination.

EGGS BENEDICT

Use a good-quality bought hollandaise sauce for this recipe because it will make all the difference to the end result. Eggs Benedict are delicious served on half a toasted English muffin. Organic eggs have a superior flavour to eggs from battery hens.

SERVES 4

INGREDIENTS
4 large (US extra large) eggs
4 lean ham slices
60ml/4 tbsp hollandaise sauce

1 Pour cold water into a medium pan to a depth of about 5cm/2in and bring to a gentle simmer. Crack two eggs into the pan and bring back to the simmer. Simmer for 2–3 minutes, until the white is set, but the yolk is still soft.

2 Meanwhile, arrange the ham slices on four serving plates (or on top of four toasted, buttered muffin halves if using). Remove the eggs from the pan using a slotted spoon and place on top of the ham on two of the plates. Cook the remaining eggs in the same way.

3 Spoon the hollandaise sauce over the eggs, sprinkle with salt and pepper and serve immediately.

EGGY BREAD

Thickly sliced stale white bread is usually used for eggy bread, but the slightly dry texture of panettone makes a great alternative. Serve with a selection of fresh summer fruits such as strawberries, raspberries and blackcurrants.

SERVES 4

INGREDIENTS
2 large (US extra large) eggs
4 large panettone slices or 4 slices of thick white bread
50g/2oz/¼ cup butter or 30ml/2tbsp sunflower oil
30ml/2 tbsp caster (superfine) sugar

1 Break the eggs into a bowl and beat with a fork, then pour them into a shallow dish. Dip the panettone slices in the beaten egg, turning them to coat evenly.

2 Heat the butter or oil in a large non-stick frying pan and add the panettone slices. (You will probably have to do this in batches, depending on the size of the pan.) Fry the panettone slices over a medium heat for 2–3 minutes on each side, until golden brown.

3 Remove the panettone slices from the pan and drain on kitchen paper. Cut the slices in half diagonally and dust with the sugar. Serve immediately.

SCOTCH PANCAKES

Also known as drop scones, Scotch pancakes are available in most supermarkets.
The combination of really crisp bacon and maple syrup with the warmed pancakes
makes an irresistible breakfast or brunch dish.

SERVES 4

INGREDIENTS
8 ready-made Scotch pancakes
8 dry-cured smoked back (lean) bacon rashers (strips)
30ml/2 tbsp maple syrup

1 Preheat the oven to 150°C/330°F/Gas 2. Wrap the pancakes in a sheet of foil and place them in the oven to warm through.

2 Meanwhile, preheat the grill (broiler) and arrange the bacon on a grill pan. Grill (broil) for 3–4 minutes on each side, until crisp.

3 Divide the warmed pancakes between four warmed serving plates and top with the grilled bacon rashers. Drizzle with the maple syrup and serve immediately.

VARIATION
Raisin varieties of Scotch pancakes are also readily
available and work equally well in this recipe.

HONEY & WATERMELON TONIC

This refreshing juice will help to cool the body, calm the digestion and cleanse the system, and may even have aphrodisiac qualities. On hot days add ice cubes to keep the juice cool. The distinctive pinkish-red flesh of the watermelon gives this tonic a beautiful hue – decorate with fresh mint leaves to provide a stunning colour contrast.

SERVES 4

INGREDIENTS
1 watermelon
1 litre/1¾ pints/4 cups chilled still mineral water
juice of 2 limes
clear honey, to taste

1 Cut the watermelon flesh into chunks, cutting away the skin. Place in a large bowl, pour the chilled water over and leave to stand for 10 minutes.

2 Pour the mixture into a large strainer set over a bowl. Using a wooden spoon, press gently on the fruit to extract all the liquid.

3 Stir in the lime juice and sweeten to taste with honey. Pour into tall glasses and serve.

NEW YORK EGG CREAM

No one knows precisely why this legendary drink is called egg cream, but some say it was a witty way of describing richness at a time when no one could afford to put both expensive eggs and cream together in a drink. Use really creamy milk for a luxurious taste. Dust a little cocoa powder over the top before serving, if you like.

SERVES 1

INGREDIENTS
45–60ml/3–4 tbsp good-quality chocolate syrup
120ml/4fl oz/½ cup chilled milk
175ml/6fl oz/¾ cup chilled sparkling mineral water

1 Carefully pour the chocolate syrup into the bottom of a tall glass avoiding dripping any on the inside of the glass.

2 Pour the chilled milk into the glass on to the chocolate syrup.

3 Gradually pour the chilled sparkling mineral water into the glass, skim off any foam that rises to the top of the glass and carefully continue to add the remaining chilled sparkling mineral water. Stir well before drinking.

COOK'S TIP
An authentic egg cream is made with an old-fashioned seltzer dispenser that you press and spritz. In any case, you can use soda water (club soda) rather than mineral water, if you like.

SOUPS

Soup is one of the most versatile dishes around and can be served as an appetizer or a complete light meal. From Simple Cream of Onion Soup and Pea Soup with Garlic to the more exotic Squash Soup with Tomato Salsa, and the tasty Three-delicacy Soup they are all incredibly straightforward to make and only need a few ingredients and flavourings to create fabulous, mouthwatering results.

SIMPLE CREAM OF ONION SOUP

This wonderfully soothing soup has a deep, buttery flavour that is achieved with the minimum of fuss. It makes delicious comfort food to warm you up on a cold day. For the best flavour, use home-made stock if you happen to have it, or buy fresh stock from the supermarket – this is much better than stock cubes.

SERVES 4

INGREDIENTS
115g/4oz/½ cup unsalted (sweet) butter
1kg/2¼lb yellow onions, sliced
1 litre/1¾ pints/4 cups good chicken or vegetable stock
150ml/¼ pint/⅔ cup double (heavy) cream

COOK'S TIP
Some crisp croûtons or chopped chives will complement the smooth soup when sprinkled over just before serving.

---

1 Melt 75g/3oz/6 tbsp of the unsalted butter in a large, heavy pan. Set about 200g/7oz of the onions aside and add the rest to the pan. Stir to coat in the butter, then cover and cook very gently for about 30 minutes. The onions should be very soft and tender, but not browned.

2 Add the chicken or vegetable stock, 5ml/1 tsp salt and freshly ground black pepper to taste. Bring to the boil, reduce the heat and simmer gently for 5 minutes, then remove the pan from the heat.

3 Leave the soup to cool, then process it in a blender or food processor. Return the soup to the rinsed pan.

4 Meanwhile, melt the remaining butter in another pan and cook the remaining onions over a low heat, covered, until soft but not browned. Uncover and continue to cook the onions gently until they turn golden yellow.

5 Add the cream to the soup and reheat it gently until hot, but do not allow it to boil. Taste and adjust the seasoning.

6 Add the buttery onions and stir for 1–2 minutes, then ladle the soup into bowls. Serve the soup immediately.

PEA SOUP WITH GARLIC

If you keep a bag of peas in the freezer, you can rustle up this delicious soup in minutes. It has a wonderfully sweet taste and smooth texture, and is just right served with crusty bread and garnished with a little chopped mint.

SERVES 4

INGREDIENTS
25g/1oz/2 tbsp butter
1 garlic clove, crushed
900g/2lb/8 cups frozen peas
1.2 litres/2 pints/5 cups chicken stock

1 Heat the butter in a large pan and add the garlic. Fry gently for 2–3 minutes, until softened, then add the peas. Cook for 1–2 minutes more, then pour in the chicken stock.

2 Bring the soup to the boil, then reduce the heat to a simmer. Cover the pan and cook for 5–6 minutes, until the peas are tender. Leave to cool slightly, then transfer the mixture to a food processor and process until smooth (you may have to do this in two batches).

3 Return the soup to the pan and heat through gently but do not allow to boil. Season with salt and pepper to taste.

VARIATIONS
- *You can use fresh peas in place of frozen for this recipe, but they will take a little longer to cook.*
- *If you don't like the taste of garlic, you could substitute 3 or 4 spring onions (scallions).*

CURRIED CAULIFLOWER SOUP

This spicy, creamy soup is perfect for lunch on a cold winter's day served with crusty bread and garnished with fresh herbs. You can also make broccoli soup in the same way, using the same weight of broccoli in place of the cauliflower.

SERVES 4

INGREDIENTS
750ml/1¼ pints/3 cups milk
1 large cauliflower
15ml/1 tbsp garam masala

1 Pour the milk into a large pan and place over a medium heat. Cut the cauliflower into florets and add to the milk with the garam masala. Season with salt and ground black pepper.

2 Bring the milk to the boil, then reduce the heat, partially cover the pan with a lid and simmer for about 20 minutes, or until the cauliflower is tender.

3 Let the mixture cool for a few minutes, then transfer to a food processor and process until smooth (you may have to do this in two batches). Return the purée to the pan and heat through gently, checking and adjusting the seasoning. Serve immediately.

Avocado Soup

This delicious soup has a fresh, delicate flavour and a wonderful colour. For added zest, add a generous squeeze of lime juice or spoon 15ml/1 tbsp salsa into the soup just before serving. Choose ripe avocados for this soup – they should feel soft when gently pressed. Keep very firm avocados at room temperature for 3–4 days until they soften. To speed ripening, place in a paper bag with a ripe banana.

SERVES 4

INGREDIENTS
2 large ripe avocados
300ml/½ pint/1¼ cups sour cream
1 litre/1¾ pints/4 cups well-flavoured chicken stock
small bunch of fresh coriander (cilantro)

1 Cut the avocados in half, remove the peel and lift out the stones (pits). Chop the flesh coarsely and place it in a food processor with 45–60ml/3–4 tbsp of the sour cream. Process until smooth.

2 Heat the chicken stock in a pan. When it is hot, but still below simmering point, stir in the rest of the cream with salt to taste.

3 Gradually stir the avocado mixture into the hot stock. Heat gently but do not let the mixture approach boiling point.

4 Chop the coriander. Ladle the soup into individual heated bowls and sprinkle each portion with chopped coriander and black pepper. Serve immediately.

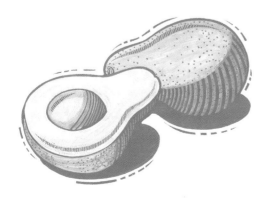

Potato & Garlic Broth

Roasted garlic takes on a mellow, sweet flavour that is subtle, not overpowering, in this delicious vegetarian soup. Choose floury potatoes for this soup, such as Maris Piper, Estima, Cara or King Edward – they will give the soup a delicious velvety texture. Serve the broth piping hot with melted Cheddar or Gruyère cheese on French bread, as the perfect winter warmer.

Serves 4

Ingredients
2 small or 1 large whole head of garlic (about 20 cloves)
4 medium potatoes (about 500g/1¼lb in total), diced
1.75 litres/3 pints/7½ cups good-quality hot vegetable stock
chopped flat leaf parsley, to garnish

1 Preheat the oven to 190°C/375°F/Gas 5. Place the unpeeled garlic bulbs or bulb in a small roasting pan and bake for 30 minutes until soft in the centre.

2 Meanwhile, par-boil the potatoes in a large pan of lightly salted boiling water for 10 minutes.

3 Bring the stock to the boil in another pan. Drain the potatoes and add them to the stock.

4 Squeeze the garlic pulp into the soup, reserving a few whole cloves, stir and season to taste. Simmer for 15 minutes and serve topped with whole garlic cloves and parsley.

SQUASH SOUP WITH TOMATO SALSA

Creamy butternut squash makes good soup with very few additional ingredients.
Select a really good bought tomato salsa for this soup and add a sprinkling of
chopped fresh oregano or marjoram as a garnish.

SERVES 4–5

INGREDIENTS
1 large butternut squash or small pumpkin, halved and seeded
75ml/5 tbsp garlic-flavoured olive oil
2 onions, chopped
60–120ml/4–8 tbsp tomato salsa

1 Preheat the oven to 220°C/425°F/Gas 7. Place the butternut squash or pumpkin on a baking sheet, brush with some of the oil and roast for 25 minutes. Reduce the temperature to 190°C/375°F/Gas 5 and cook for 20–25 minutes more, or until the squash is tender.

2 Heat the remaining oil in a large, heavy pan and cook the chopped onions over a low heat for about 10 minutes, or until softened.

3 Meanwhile, scoop the squash out of its skin, adding it to the pan. Pour in 1.2 litres/2 pints/5 cups water and stir in 5ml/1 tsp salt and plenty of black pepper. Bring to the boil, cover and simmer for 10 minutes.

4 Cool the soup slightly, then process it in a blender or food processor to a smooth purée. Alternatively, press the soup through a fine strainer with the back of a spoon. Reheat without boiling, then ladle it into warmed bowls. Top each serving with a spoonful of salsa and serve.

TUSCAN BEAN SOUP

Cavolo nero is a dark green cabbage with a nutty flavour from Tuscany and southern Italy. It is ideal for this traditional recipe. It is available in most large supermarkets, but if you can't get it, use Savoy cabbage instead. Serve with ciabatta bread.

SERVES 4

INGREDIENTS
2 × 400g/14oz cans chopped tomatoes with herbs
250g/9oz cavolo nero leaves
400g/14oz can cannellini beans
60ml/4 tbsp extra virgin olive oil

1 Pour the tomatoes into a large pan and add a can of cold water. Season with salt and pepper and bring to the boil, then reduce the heat to a simmer.

2 Roughly shred the cabbage leaves and add them to the pan. Partially cover the pan and simmer gently for about 15 minutes, or until the cabbage is tender.

3 Drain and rinse the cannellini beans, add to the pan and warm through for a few minutes. Check and adjust the seasoning, then ladle the soup into bowls, drizzle with a little olive oil and serve.

Butter Bean, Sun-dried Tomato & Pesto Soup

This soup is so quick and easy to make: the key is to use a good-quality home-made or bought fresh stock for the best result. The pesto and sun-dried tomatos give it a rich, minestrone-like flavour.

Serves 4

Ingredients

900ml/1½ pints/3¾ cups chicken or vegetable stock
2 × 400g/14oz cans butter (lima) beans, drained and rinsed
60ml/4 tbsp sun-dried tomato purée (paste)
75ml/5 tbsp pesto

1 Put the stock in a pan with the butter beans and bring just to the boil. Reduce the heat and stir in the tomato purée and pesto. Cook gently for 5 minutes.

2 Transfer six ladlefuls of the soup to a blender or food processor, scooping up plenty of the beans. Process until smooth, then return the purée to the pan.

3 Heat gently, stirring frequently, for 5 minutes, then season if necessary. Ladle into four warmed soup bowls and serve with warm crusty bread.

Cappelletti in Chicken Broth with Parmesan

This soup is traditionally served in northern Italy on Santo Stefano (St Stephen's Day, the day after Christmas) and on New Year's Day as a change from all the special celebration food. Cappelletti are little stuffed pasta shapes that resemble hats.

SERVES 4

INGREDIENTS
1.2 litres/2 pints/5 cups chicken stock
90–115g/3½–4oz/1 cup fresh or dried cappelletti
about 45ml/3 tbsp finely chopped fresh flat leaf parsley (optional)
about 30ml/2 tbsp freshly grated Parmesan cheese

1 Pour the chicken stock into a large pan and bring to the boil. Add a little seasoning to taste, then drop in the pasta.

2 Stir well and bring back to the boil. Lower the heat to a simmer and cook according to the instructions on the packet, until the pasta is *al dente*, that is, tender but still firm to the bite.

3 Swirl in the finely chopped fresh flat leaf parsley, if using, then taste and adjust the seasoning, if necessary. Ladle into four warmed soup plates, then sprinkle with the freshly grated Parmesan cheese and serve immediately.

COOK'S TIP
In place of home-made stock use two 300g/11oz cans of condensed beef consommé, adding water as instructed, or chilled commercial stock.

TINY PASTA IN BROTH

This traditional Italian soup is ideal for a light supper served with ciabatta bread and also makes a delicious first course for an al fresco meal. Use a richly flavoured home-made or bought fresh stock.

SERVES 4

INGREDIENTS
1.2 litres/2 pints/5 cups beef stock
75g/3oz/³⁄₄ cup dried tiny soup pasta
2 pieces bottled roasted red (bell) pepper, about 50g/2oz
coarsely shaved Parmesan cheese

1 Bring the beef stock to the boil in a large pan. Add seasoning to taste, then drop in the dried soup pasta. Stir well and bring the stock back to the boil.

2 Reduce the heat so that the soup simmers and cook for 7–8 minutes, or according to the packet instructions, until the pasta is *al dente*, that is, tender but still firm to the bite.

3 Drain the pieces of roasted pepper and dice them finely. Place them in the base of four warmed soup plates. Taste the soup for seasoning before ladling it into the soup plates. Serve immediately, topped with shavings of Parmesan.

COOK'S TIP
A wide variety of different types of pastina or soup pasta are available, including stellette (stars), anellini (tiny thin rounds), risoni (rice-shaped) and farfalline (little butterflies). Choose just one shape or a combination of varieties for an interesting result.

Stilton and Watercress Soup

A good creamy Stilton and plenty of peppery watercress bring maximum flavour to this rich, smooth soup, which is superlative in small portions. Serve it with warmed crusty bread, or a selection of crackers and oatcakes.

SERVES 4–6

INGREDIENTS
600ml/1 pint/2½ cups chicken or vegetable stock
225g/8oz watercress or rocket (arugula)
150g/5oz Stilton or other blue cheese
150ml/¼ pint/⅔ cup single (light) cream

1 Pour the stock into a pan and bring almost to the boil. Remove and discard any very large stalks from the watercress or rocket. Add the watercress to the pan and simmer gently for 2–3 minutes, until tender.

2 Crumble the cheese into the pan and simmer for 1 minute more, until the cheese has started to melt. Process the soup in a blender or food processor, in batches if necessary, until very smooth. Return the soup to the pan.

3 Stir in the cream and check the seasoning. The soup will probably not need any extra salt, as the blue cheese is already quite salty. Heat the soup gently, without boiling, then ladle it into warm bowls.

Jalapeño-style Soup

Chicken, chilli and avocado combine to make this simple but unusual soup. When using canned chillies, it is important to rinse them thoroughly before adding them to the soup so as to remove the flavour of the pickling liquid.

Serves 6

Ingredients
1.5 litres/2½ pints/6¼ cups chicken stock
2 cooked chicken breast fillets, skinned and cut into large strips
1 drained canned chipotle or jalapeño chilli, rinsed
1 avocado

1 Heat the stock in a large pan and add the chicken and chilli. Simmer over a very gentle heat for 5 minutes to heat the chicken through and release the flavour from the chilli.

2 Cut the avocado in half, remove the stone (pit) and peel off the skin. Slice the avocado flesh neatly lengthways.

3 Using a slotted spoon, remove the chilli from the stock and discard it. Pour the soup into heated serving bowls, distributing the chicken evenly among them.

4 Carefully add a few avocado slices to each bowl and serve immediately

THREE-DELICACY SOUP

This delicious soup combines the three ingredients of chicken, ham and prawns. For extra flavour, sprinkle with finely chopped chives or your favourite herbs.

SERVES 4

INGREDIENTS
115g/4oz chicken breast fillet
115g/4oz honey-roast ham
115g/4oz peeled prawns (shrimp)
700ml/1¼ pints/3 cups chicken stock

1 Thinly slice the chicken breast and ham into small pieces. If the prawns are large, cut them in half lengthways.

2 In a wok or saucepan, bring the stock to a rolling boil, add the chicken, ham and prawns. Bring back to the boil, add salt to taste and simmer for 1 minute.

3 Ladle into individual soup bowls and serve immediately.

COOK'S TIP
Fresh, uncooked prawns impart the best flavour. If these are not available, you can use ready-cooked prawns. They must be added towards the end of cooking, to prevent over-cooking.

SNACKS & APPETIZERS

When you want a simple snack to keep you going for a few hours, or a little something to whet the appetite before a main meal – think simplicity. From mouthwatering dips to spicy Chilli Prawn Skewers and Curried Lamb Samosas, this chapter is packed with simple, fuss-free ideas that you won't be able to resist. Serve golden, melt-in-the-mouth Parmesan Tuiles or Gruyère and Basil Tortillas with drinks, or enjoy Chinese Crab Wontons as an appetizer.

Spanish Salted Almonds

Served with a glass of chilled dry sherry, these delicious salted nuts make a perfect tapas dish or pre-dinner snack. Sea salt does not have any of the added chemicals that are often found in table salt, and has a stronger taste.

Serves 4–6

INGREDIENTS
1 egg white
200g/7oz/generous 1 cup shelled unblanched almonds
a good handful of flaked sea salt

1 Preheat the oven to 200°C/400°F/Gas 6. Whisk the egg white in a bowl until it forms stiff peaks.

2 Add the almonds to the egg white, and stir until the nuts are thoroughly coated. Pour the mixture on to a baking sheet and spread out evenly in a single layer.

3 Sprinkle the salt over the almonds and bake for about 15 minutes, or until the egg white and salt are crusty. Leave to cool completely, then serve in bowls with a selection of other nibbles, dips and pâtés.

Gruyère & Basil Tortillas

These simple fried tortilla wedges make a great late-night snack with sweet chilli sauce. If you have a few slices of ham or salami in the refrigerator, add these to the tortillas as well. A mild Cheddar cheese could be used in place of Gruyère.

SERVES 2

INGREDIENTS
15ml/1 tbsp olive oil
2 soft flour tortillas
115g/4oz Gruyère cheese, thinly sliced
a handful of fresh basil leaves
15ml/1 tbsp olive oil

1 Heat the oil in a frying pan, over a medium heat. Add one of the tortillas, arrange the Gruyère cheese slices and basil leaves on top and season with salt and pepper.

2 Place the remaining tortilla on top to make a sandwich and flip the whole thing over with a metal spatula. Cook for a few minutes, until the underneath is golden brown.

3 Slide the tortilla sandwich on to a chopping board or plate and cut into wedges. Serve immediately.

POLENTA CHIPS

These tasty Parmesan-flavoured batons are best served warm straight from the oven, with a spicy, tangy dip. A bowl of Thai chilli dipping sauce or a creamy, chilli-spiked guacamole are perfect for dipping them into.

MAKES ABOUT 80

INGREDIENTS
375g/13oz/3¼ cups instant polenta
150g/5oz/1½ cups freshly grated Parmesan cheese
90g/3½oz/7 tbsp butter
olive oil, for brushing

1 Put 1.5 litres/2½ pints/6¼ cups water into a large, heavy pan and bring to the boil. Reduce the heat, add 10ml/2tsp salt and pour in the polenta in a steady stream, stirring constantly with a wooden spoon. Cook over a low heat for about 5 minutes, stirring, until the mixture thickens and comes away from the sides of the pan.

2 Remove the pan from the heat and add the cheese and butter. Season to taste. Stir well until the mixture is smooth. Pour on to a smooth surface, such as a marble slab or a baking sheet.

3 Using a metal spatula, spread out the polenta to a thickness of 2cm/¾in and shape into a rectangle. Leave to stand for at least 30 minutes until cold. Meanwhile preheat the oven to 200°C/400°F/Gas 6 and lightly oil two or three baking sheets.

4 Cut the polenta slab in half, then carefully cut into even-size strips. Bake for 40–50 minutes, or until dark golden brown and crunchy, turning from time to time. Serve warm.

PARMESAN TUILES

These delicate lacy tuiles look very impressive and make splendid nibbles for a party,
but they couldn't be easier to make. Believe it or not, they use only a single ingredient
– Parmesan cheese. Being hard and dry, Parmesan can be grated into longish strands.

MAKES 8–10

INGREDIENTS
115g/4oz Parmesan cheese

1 Preheat the oven to 200°C/400°F/Gas 6. Line two baking sheets with baking
parchment. Grate the cheese using a fine grater, pulling it down slowly to make
long strands.

2 Spread the grated cheese in 7.5–9cm/3–3½in rounds on the baking parchment,
forking it into shape. Do not spread the cheese too thickly; it should just cover
the parchment. Bake for 5–7 minutes, or until bubbling and golden brown.

3 Leave the tuiles on the baking sheet for about 30 seconds and then carefully
transfer them, using a metal spatula, to a wire rack to cool completely.
Alternatively, drape over a rolling pin to make a curved shape.

COOK'S TIP
Tuiles can be made into little cup shapes by draping
over an upturned egg cup. These little cups can be
filled to make tasty treats to serve with drinks. Try a
little cream cheese flavoured with herbs.

PEPERONATA

This richly flavoured spicy tomato and sweet red pepper dip is perfect served with crisp Italian-style bread sticks – enjoy it with drinks or as a snack while watching television. It also makes a tasty relish served with grilled chicken and fish dishes. It is delicious served hot, cold or at room temperature and can be stored in the refrigerator for several days.

SERVES 4

INGREDIENTS
60ml/4 tbsp garlic-infused olive oil
2 large red (bell) peppers, halved, seeded and sliced
pinch dried chilli flakes
400g/14oz can pomodorino tomatoes

1 Heat the oil in a large pan over a low heat and add the sliced peppers. Cook very gently, stirring occasionally, for 3–4 minutes.

2 Add the chilli flakes to the pan and cook for 1 minute, then pour the tomatoes into the pan and season to taste. Cook gently for 50 minutes to 1 hour, stirring occasionally.

COOK'S TIP
Long, slow cooking helps to bring out the sweetness of the peppers and tomatoes, so don't be tempted to cheat on the cooking time by cooking over a higher heat.

ARTICHOKE & CUMIN DIP

This dip is so easy to make and is unbelievably tasty. Serve with olives, hummus and wedges of pitta bread to make a summery snack selection. Grilled artichokes bottled in oil have a fabulous flavour and can be used instead of canned artichokes. You can also vary the flavourings – try adding chilli powder in place of the cumin and add a handful of basil leaves to the artichokes before blending.

SERVES 4

INGREDIENTS
2 × 400g/14oz cans artichoke hearts, drained
2 garlic cloves, peeled
2.5ml/½ tsp ground cumin
olive oil

1 Put the artichoke hearts in a food processor with the garlic and ground cumin, and a generous drizzle of olive oil. Process to a smooth purée and season with salt and ground black pepper to taste.

2 Spoon the purée into a serving bowl and serve with an extra drizzle of olive oil swirled on the top and slices of warm pitta bread for dipping.

HUMMUS

This classic Middle Eastern chickpea dip is flavoured with garlic and tahini (sesame seed paste). A little ground cumin can also be added, and olive oil can be stirred in to enrich the hummus, if you like. It is delicious served with wedges of toasted pitta bread or with crudités such as carrot and celery sticks.

SERVES 4–6

INGREDIENTS
400g/14oz can chickpeas, drained
60ml/4 tbsp tahini
2–3 garlic cloves, chopped
juice of ½–1 lemon

1 Using a potato masher or fork, coarsely mash the chickpeas in a mixing bowl. If you like a smoother purée, process the chickpeas in a food processor or blender until a smooth paste is formed.

2 Mix the tahini into the bowl of chickpeas, then stir in the chopped garlic cloves and lemon juice. Season to taste with freshly ground black pepper and salt, and if needed, add a little water. Serve the hummus at room temperature.

VARIATION
Process 2 roasted red (bell) peppers with the chickpeas, then continue as described above. Serve the hummus sprinkled with lightly toasted pine nuts and paprika mixed with olive oil.

Eggs Mimosa

Mimosa describes the fine yellow and white egg in this dish, which looks very similar to the flower of the same name. The eggs taste delicious when garnished with black pepper and basil leaves. Egg yolk can also be used as a garnish for a variety of other savoury dishes, such as sauces, soups and rice dishes.

Makes 20

Ingredients

12 eggs, *hard-boiled and peeled*
2 ripe avocados, *halved and stoned (pitted)*
1 garlic clove, *crushed*
15ml/1 tbsp olive oil

1 Reserve two of the hard-boiled eggs and halve the remainder. Remove the yolks with a teaspoon and blend them in a food processor or blender with the avocados, garlic and oil, adding freshly ground black pepper and salt to taste. Spoon or pipe the mixture into the halved egg whites using a piping (pastry) bag with a 1cm/½in or pipe star nozzle.

2 Press the remaining egg whites through a sieve (strainer) and sprinkle over the filled eggs. Press through the yolks and arrange on top. Arrange the filled egg halves on a serving platter.

CHOPPED EGG & ONIONS

This is one of the oldest dishes in Jewish culinary history. It is delicious served sprinkled with chopped fresh parsley and onion rings on crackers, piled on toast, or used as a sandwich or bagel filling. Serve chopped egg and onion as part of a buffet with a selection of different dips and toppings.

SERVES 4–6

INGREDIENTS

10 eggs

8 spring onions (scallions) and/or 1 yellow or white onion, very finely chopped, plus extra to garnish

60–90ml/4–6 tbsp mayonnaise or rendered chicken fat

mild French wholegrain mustard, to taste (optional if using mayonnaise)

1 Put the eggs in a pan and cover with cold water. Bring the water to the boil and when it boils, reduce the heat and simmer over a low heat for 10 minutes.

2 Remove the eggs with a slotted spoon, place in a strainer and hold under cold running water. When cool, remove the shells from the eggs and discard. Dry the eggs on a clean dishtowel and chop coarsely.

3 Place the chopped eggs in a large bowl, add the onions, season generously with salt and black pepper and mix well. Add enough mayonnaise or chicken fat to bind the mixture together. Stir in the mustard, if using, and chill before serving.

COOK'S TIP
The amount of rendered chicken fat or mayonnaise required will depend on how much onion you use in this dish. Add spoonfuls gradually until you have the desired consistency.

BAKED EGGS WITH LEEKS

This simple but elegant appetizer is perfect for last-minute entertaining. Garnish the baked eggs with crisp, fried fresh sage leaves and serve with warm, fresh crusty bread for a special meal. Small- to medium-sized leeks (less than 2.5cm/1in in diameter) are best for this dish as they are more tender than large ones.

SERVES 4

INGREDIENTS
15g/½oz/1 tbsp butter, plus extra for greasing
225g/8oz small leeks, thinly sliced
75–90ml/5–6 tbsp whipping cream
4 eggs

1 Preheat the oven to 190°C/375°F/Gas 5. Generously butter the base and sides of four ramekins.

2 Melt the butter in a frying pan and cook the leeks over a medium heat, stirring frequently, for 3–5 minutes, until softened, but not browned.

3 Add 45ml/3 tbsp of the cream and cook over a low heat for 5 minutes, until the leeks are very soft and the cream has thickened a little. Season to taste.

4 Place the ramekins in a small roasting pan and divide the leeks among them. Break an egg into each, spoon over the remaining cream and season.

5 Pour boiling water into the roasting pan to come about halfway up the sides of the ramekins. Bake in the preheated oven for about 10 minutes, until just set. Serve piping hot.

ISRAELI CHEESE WITH OLIVES

In Israel, mild white cheeses spiked with seasonings, such as this one that is flavoured with piquant green olives, are served with drinks and little crackers or toast. It is also good served for brunch – spread generously on chunks of fresh, crusty bread.

SERVES 4

INGREDIENTS
200g/7oz soft white (farmer's) cheese
65g/2½oz feta cheese, preferably sheep's milk, lightly crumbled
30 pitted green olives, some chopped, the rest halved or quartered
3 large pinches of fresh thyme leaves, plus extra to garnish

1 Place the soft white cheese in a mixing bowl and stir with the back of a spoon or a fork until soft and smooth. Add the crumbled feta cheese and stir the two cheeses together until they are thoroughly combined.

2 Add the chopped and halved or quartered olives and the pinches of fresh thyme to the cheese mixture and mix thoroughly.

3 Spoon the mixture into a bowl, sprinkle with thyme and serve with crackers, toast, chunks of bread or bagels.

YOGURT CHEESE IN OLIVE OIL

In Greece, sheep's yogurt is hung in muslin to drain off the whey before being patted into balls of soft cheese. Here the cheese is bottled in extra virgin olive oil with dried chillies and fresh herbs to make a wonderful gourmet gift or aromatic appetizer.

FILLS TWO 450G/1LB JARS

INGREDIENTS
1 litre/1¾ pints/4 cups Greek (US strained plain) sheep's yogurt
10ml/2 tsp crushed dried chillies or chilli powder
30ml/2 tbsp chopped fresh herbs, such as rosemary, thyme or oregano
about 300ml/½pint/1¼ cups extra virgin olive oil, preferably garlic-flavoured

1 Sterilize a 30cm/12in square of muslin (cheesecloth) by soaking it in boiling water. Drain and lay it over a large plate. Season the yogurt generously with salt and place it on the centre of the muslin. Bring up the sides of the muslin and tie firmly with string.

2 Hang the bag over a large bowl to catch the whey. Leave for 2–3 days until the yogurt stops dripping.

3 Sterilize two 450g/1lb glass preserving or jam jars by heating them in the oven at 150°C/300°F/Gas 2 for 15 minutes.

4 Mix the crushed dried chillies and herbs. Take teaspoonfuls of the cheese and roll into balls with your hands. Lower into the jars, sprinkling each layer with the herb mixture.

5 Pour the oil over the cheese until completely covered. Store in the refrigerator for up to 3 weeks. To serve, spoon the cheese out of the jars with a little of the flavoured olive oil and spread on slices of lightly toasted bread.

Walnut & Goat's Cheese Bruschetta

The combination of toasted walnuts and melting goat's cheese is lovely in this simple appetizer, served with a pile of salad leaves. Toasting the walnuts helps to bring out their flavour. Walnut bread is readily available in most large supermarkets and makes an interesting alternative to ordinary crusty bread.

SERVES 4

INGREDIENTS
50g/2oz/½ cup walnut pieces
4 thick slices walnut bread
120ml/4fl oz/½ cup French dressing
200g/7oz chèvre or other semi-soft goat's cheese

1 Preheat the grill (broiler). Lightly toast the walnut pieces, then remove and set aside. Put the walnut bread on a foil-lined grill rack and toast on one side. Turn the slices over and drizzle each with 15ml/1 tbsp of the French dressing.

2 Cut the goat's cheese into 12 slices and place three on each piece of bread. Grill (broil) for about 3 minutes, until the cheese is melting and beginning to brown.

3 Transfer the bruschetta to serving plates, sprinkle with the toasted walnuts and drizzle with the remaining French dressing. Serve the bruschetta immediately with salad leaves.

COOK'S TIP
Use slices from a slender loaf, so that the portions are not too wide. If you can buy only a large loaf, cut the slices in half to make neat, chunky pieces.

RED ONION & OLIVE PISSALADIÈRE

For a taste of the Mediterranean, try this French-style pizza. Cook the sliced red onions slowly until they are caramelized and sweet before piling them into the pastry cases. To prepare the recipe in advance, pile the cooled onions on to the pastry round and chill the pissaladière until you are ready to bake it.

SERVES 6

INGREDIENTS
75ml/5 tbsp extra virgin olive oil
500g/1¼lb small red onions, thinly sliced
500g/1¼lb puff pastry, thawed if frozen
75g/3oz/¾cup small pitted black olives

1 Preheat the oven to 220°C/425°F/Gas 7. Heat the oil in a large, heavy frying pan and cook the onions gently, stirring frequently, for 15–20 minutes, until they are soft and golden. Season to taste.

2 Roll out the pastry thinly on a floured surface. Cut out a 33cm/13in round and transfer it to a lightly dampened baking sheet.

3 Spread the onions over the pastry in an even layer to within 1cm/½in of the edge. Sprinkle the olives on top. Bake the tart for 20–25 minutes, until the pastry is risen and deep golden. Cut into wedges and serve warm.

Marinated Anchovies

These tiny fish tend to lose their freshness very quickly, so marinating them in garlic and lemon juice is the perfect way to enjoy them. It is probably the simplest way of preparing these fish, because it requires no cooking.

Serves 4

Ingredients
225g/8oz fresh anchovies, heads and tails removed, and split open along the belly
juice of 3 lemons
2 garlic cloves, finely chopped
30ml/2 tbsp extra virgin olive oil

1 Turn the anchovies on to their bellies, and press down along their spine with your thumb. Using the tip of a small knife, carefully remove the backbones from the fish. Arrange the anchovies skin side down in a single layer on a plate.

2 Squeeze two-thirds of the lemon juice over the fish and sprinkle them with salt. Cover and leave to stand for 1–24 hours, basting occasionally with the juices, until the flesh is white and no longer translucent.

3 Transfer the anchovies to a serving plate and drizzle with the olive oil and the remaining lemon juice. Sprinkle the fish with the chopped garlic, then cover with clear film (plastic wrap) and chill until ready to serve.

Cook's Tips
* *Serve the anchovies sprinkled with parsley for a decorative finish.*
* *Use flaked sea salt rather than ordinary salt because it has no added chemicals and a stronger taste.*

CHILLI PRAWN SKEWERS

Try to get the freshest prawns you can to use for this recipe. If you buy whole prawns, you will need to remove the heads and shells, leaving the tail section intact. Serve the prawn skewers with extra lime wedges.

SERVES 4

16 giant raw prawns (shrimp), shelled with the tail section left intact
1 lime, cut into 8 wedges
60ml/4 tbsp sweet chilli sauce

1 Place eight bamboo skewers in cold water and leave to soak for at least 10 minutes, then preheat the grill (broiler) to high.

2 Thread a prawn on to each skewer, then a lime wedge, then another prawn. Brush the sweet chilli sauce over the prawns and lime wedges.

3 Arrange the skewers on a baking sheet and grill (broil) them for about 2 minutes, turning them once, until cooked through. Serve immediately, handing round more chilli sauce for dipping.

CHINESE CRAB WONTONS

Serve these mouthwatering parcels as part of a dim sum selection or with a bowl of soy sauce for dipping, as a first course for a Chinese meal. They are also perfect for serving as snacks with drinks at parties as they can be prepared in advance, then steamed at the last minute. Wonton wrappers are available in most Asian food stores and need to be soaked in cold water for a few minutes before use.

SERVES 4

INGREDIENTS
50g/2oz/⅓ cup drained, canned water chestnuts
115g/4oz/generous ½ cup fresh or canned white crab meat
12 wonton wrappers

1 Finely chop the water chestnuts, mix them with the crab meat and season with salt and pepper.

2 Place about a teaspoonful of the mixture along the centre of each wonton wrapper. Roll up the wontons, tucking in the sides as you go to form a neat parcel.

3 Fill the bottom part of a steamer with boiling water and place the wontons, seam down, in the steamer basket. Sit the basket on top of the water and cover with a tight-fitting lid. Steam for 5–8 minutes, or until the wonton wrappers are tender. Serve hot or warm.

CRISP FRIED WHITEBAIT

This must be one of the simplest of all classic fish dishes and it is absolutely delicious served with lemon wedges and some thinly sliced brown bread and butter. If you prefer, serve the whitebait with a simple lemon and herb dip – mix 150ml/¼ pint/ ⅔ cup natural (plain) yogurt with the grated rind of one lemon and 45ml/3 tbsp chopped fresh herbs, such as parsley. Serve chilled.

SERVES 4

INGREDIENTS
oil, for deep-frying
150ml/½ pint/⅔ cup milk
115g/4oz/1 cup plain (all-purpose) flour
450g/1lb whitebait

1 Pour the oil into a large pan or deep-fryer. Put the milk in a shallow bowl and spoon the flour into a paper bag. Season the flour well with salt and pepper.

2 Dip a handful of the whitebait into the bowl of milk, drain them well, then put them into the paper bag. Shake gently to coat them evenly in the seasoned flour, then transfer to a plate. Repeat until all the fish have been coated. This is the easiest method of flouring whitebait before frying, but don't add too many at once to the bag, or they will stick together.

3 Heat the oil to 190°C/375°F or until a cube of stale bread, dropped into the oil, browns in about 20 seconds. Add a batch of whitebait, preferably in a frying basket, and deep-fry for 2–3 minutes, until crisp and golden brown. Drain and keep hot while you cook the rest. Serve very hot.

COOK'S TIP
Most whitebait are sold frozen. Thaw them before use and dry them thoroughly on kitchen paper before dipping in the milk.

Bacon-rolled Mushrooms

The Japanese name for this dish is Obimaki enoki: *an obi (belt or sash) is made from bacon and wrapped around enokitake mushrooms before they are grilled. The strong, smoky flavour of the bacon complements the subtle flavour of mushrooms.*

SERVES 4

INGREDIENTS
450g/1lb fresh enokitake mushrooms
6 rindless smoked streaky (fatty) bacon rashers (strips)
4 lemon wedges

1 Cut off the root part of each enokitake cluster 2cm/¾in from the end. Do not separate the stems. Cut the bacon rashers in half lengthways.

2 Divide the enokitake into 12 equal bunches. Take one bunch, then place the middle of the enokitake near the edge of one bacon rasher, with 2.5–4cm/1–1½in of enokitake protruding at each end.

3 Carefully roll up the bunch of enokitake in the bacon. Tuck any straying short stems into the bacon and slide the bacon slightly upwards at each roll to cover about 4cm/1½in of the enokitake. Secure the end of the bacon roll with a cocktail stick (toothpick). Repeat with the remaining ingredients to make 11 more rolls.

4 Preheat the grill (broiler) to high. Place the enokitake rolls on an oiled wire rack. Grill (broil) both sides until the bacon is crisp and the enokitake start to char. This takes 10–13 minutes.

5 Remove the enokitake rolls and place on a board. Using a fork and knife, chop each roll in half in the middle of the bacon belt. Arrange the top part of the enokitake roll standing upright, the bottom part lying down next to it. Add a wedge of lemon to each portion and serve.

CHILLI-SPICED CHICKEN WINGS

These spicy, fried chicken wings are always the perfect snack for parties and go incredibly well with cold beer! If you want an even more fiery version, use cayenne pepper in place of the chilli powder. Serve with a fresh tomato and onion salsa dip.

SERVES 4

INGREDIENTS
12 chicken wings
30ml/2 tbsp plain (all-purpose) flour
15ml/1 tbsp chilli powder
sunflower oil, for deep-frying

1 Pat the chicken wings dry with kitchen paper. Mix the flour, chilli powder and salt to taste and put into a large plastic bag. Add the chicken wings, seal the bag and shake well to coat the chicken wings in the seasoned flour.

2 Preheat the oven to a low temperature. Heat enough sunflower oil for deep-frying in a large pan and add the chicken wings, three or four at a time. Fry for 8–10 minutes, or until the wings are golden and cooked through.

3 Remove the chicken wings with a slotted spoon and drain on kitchen paper. Keep warm in the oven. Repeat with the remaining wings and serve hot.

VARIATION
To make a milder version that will be a hit with kids, use sweet paprika in place of the chilli powder.

Vietnamese Spring Rolls

You will often find these little spring rolls on the menu in Vietnamese restaurants, where they are called "rice paper rolls". Serve them with a chilli dipping sauce and garnish with sprigs of fresh herbs.

Serves 4

Ingredients
15ml/1 tbsp sunflower oil
350g/12oz/1½ cups minced (ground) pork
30ml/2 tbsp oyster sauce
8 rice-paper roll wrappers

1 Heat the oil in a frying pan and add the pork. Fry for 5–6 minutes, or until browned. Season well with salt and pepper, stir in the oyster sauce and remove from the heat. Leave to cool.

2 Lay the rice paper wrappers on a clean work surface. Place one-eighth of the pork mixture down one edge of each wrapper. Roll up the wrappers, tucking in the ends as you go to form a roll, and then serve immediately.

CURRIED LAMB SAMOSAS

Filo pastry is perfect for making samosas. Once you've mastered folding them, you'll be amazed how quick they are to make and serve as tasty appetizers. Throughout Asia, samosas are sold by street vendors and eaten at any time of day.

MAKES 12

INGREDIENTS
25g/1oz/2 tbsp butter
225g/8oz/1 cup minced (ground) lamb
30ml/2 tbsp mild curry paste
12 filo pastry sheets

1 Heat a little of the butter in a large pan and add the lamb. Fry for 5–6 minutes, stirring occasionally, until browned. Stir in the curry paste and cook for 1–2 minutes. Season and set aside. Preheat the oven to 190°C/375°F/Gas 5.

2 Melt the remaining butter in a pan. Cut the pastry sheets in half lengthways. Brush one strip of pastry with butter, then lay another strip on top and brush with more butter.

3 Place a spoonful of lamb in the corner of the strip and fold over to form a triangle at one end. Keep folding over in the same way to form a triangular package. Brush with butter and place on a baking sheet. Repeat using the remaining pastry. Bake for 15–20 minutes until golden. Serve hot.

COOK'S TIP
Prepare samosas in advance if you like and simply fry quickly to reheat them before serving. Alternatively, serve cold.

FISH & SHELLFISH

The delicate taste of fish and shellfish is perfectly suited to subtle, simple flavourings such as fresh herbs, citrus juice and succulent tomatoes. The fabulous recipes in this chapter make the most of these ingredients to achieve truly wonderful dishes, such as Grilled Hake with Lemon & Chilli, Marinated Smoked Salmon with Lime & Coriander and Smoked Haddock Fillets with Quick Parsley Sauce.

POACHED FISH IN SPICY TOMATO SAUCE

A selection of white fish fillets are used in this Middle-Eastern dish – cod, haddock, hake or halibut are all good. Serve the fish with flat breads, such as pitta, and a spicy tomato relish. It is also good with couscous or rice and a green salad with a refreshing lemon juice dressing.

SERVES 8

INGREDIENTS
600ml/1 pint/2½ cups fresh tomato sauce
2.5–5ml/½–1 tsp harissa
60ml/4 tbsp chopped fresh coriander (cilantro) leaves
1.5kg/3¼lb mixed white fish fillets, cut into chunks

1 Heat the tomato sauce with the harissa and coriander in a large pan. Add seasoning to taste and bring to the boil.

2 Remove the pan from the heat and add the fish to the hot sauce. Return to the heat and bring the sauce to the boil again. Reduce the heat and simmer very gently for about 5 minutes, or until the fish is tender. (Test with a fork: if the flesh flakes easily, then it is cooked.)

3 Taste the sauce and adjust the seasoning, adding more harissa if necessary. Serve hot or warm.

COOK'S TIP
Harissa is a chilli paste spiced with cumin, garlic and coriander. It is fiery and should be used with care until you are familiar with the flavour. Start by adding a small amount and then add more after tasting the sauce.

Baked Whole Fish with Tomato & Pine Nuts

Whole fish marinated in lemon juice and cooked with pine nuts in a spicy tomato sauce is a speciality of Jewish cooking, particularly as a festival treat for Rosh Hashanah, the Jewish New Year. The fish may be cooked and served with head and tail on, as here, or if you like, with these removed.

SERVES 6–8

INGREDIENTS
1.2kg/2½lb fish, such as snapper, cleaned, with head and tail left on
juice of 2 lemons
65g/2½oz/scant ¾ cup pine nuts, toasted
350ml/12fl oz/1½ cups spicy tomato sauce

1 Prick the fish all over with a fork and rub with 2.5ml/½ tsp salt. Put the fish in a large dish and pour over the lemon juice. Leave to stand for 2 hours.

2 Preheat the oven to 180°C/350°F/Gas 4. Sprinkle half of the pine nuts over the base of an ovenproof dish, top with half of the sauce, then add the fish and its marinade. Add the remaining tomato sauce and pine nuts.

3 Cover the ovenproof dish tightly with a lid or foil and bake in the preheated oven for 30 minutes, or until the fish is tender. Serve the fish immediately, straight from the dish.

FILO-WRAPPED FISH WITH TOMATO SAUCE

Select a chunky variety of tomato sauce for this simple but delicious recipe. When working with filo pastry, keep it covered with a damp dishtowel, as once it's exposed to air it dries out quickly and is difficult to handle.

SERVES 3–4

INGREDIENTS
about 130g/4½oz filo pastry (6–8 large sheets)
about 30ml/2 tbsp olive oil, for brushing
450g/1lb salmon or cod steaks or fillets
550ml/18fl oz/2½ cups fresh tomato sauce

1 Preheat the oven to 200°C/400°F/Gas 6. Take a sheet of filo pastry, brush with a little olive oil and cover with a second sheet of pastry. Place a piece of fish on top of the pastry, towards the bottom edge, then top with 1–2 spoonfuls of the tomato sauce, spreading it in an even layer.

2 Roll the fish in the pastry, taking care to enclose the filling completely. Brush with olive oil. Arrange on a baking sheet and repeat with the remaining fish and pastry. You should have about half the sauce left, to serve with the fish.

3 Bake for 10–15 minutes, or until golden. Meanwhile, reheat the remaining sauce. Serve immediately.

ROAST COD WRAPPED IN PROSCIUTTO

Wrapping chunky fillets of cod in wafer-thin slices of prosciutto keeps the fish succulent and moist, at the same time adding flavour and visual impact. Serve with baby new potatoes and a herb salad for a stylish supper or lunch dish.

SERVES 4

INGREDIENTS
2 thick skinless cod fillets, each weighing about 375g/13oz
75ml/5 tbsp extra virgin olive oil
75g/3oz prosciutto, thinly sliced
400g/14oz tomatoes, on the vine

1 Preheat the oven to 220°C/425°F/Gas 7. Pat the fish dry on kitchen paper and remove any stray bones. Season lightly on both sides with salt and pepper.

2 Place one fillet in an ovenproof dish and drizzle 15ml/1 tbsp of the oil over it. Cover with the second fillet, laying the thick end on top of the thin end of the lower fillet to create an even shape. Lay the ham over the fish, overlapping the slices to cover the fish in an even layer. Tuck the ends of the ham under the fish and tie it in place at intervals with fine string.

3 Using kitchen scissors, snip the tomato vines into four portions and add to the dish. Drizzle the tomatoes and ham with the remaining oil and season lightly. Roast for about 35 minutes, until the tomatoes are tender and lightly coloured and the fish is cooked through. Test the fish by piercing one end of the parcel with the tip of a sharp knife to check that it flakes easily.

4 Slice the fish and transfer the portions to warm plates, adding the tomatoes. Spoon over the cooking juices from the dish and serve immediately.

Cod & Spinach Parcels

The best way to serve this dish is to slice each parcel into about four and reveal the meaty large flakes of white fish contrasting with the green spinach. Drizzle the sauce from the roasting pan over the slices.

SERVES 4

INGREDIENTS
4 × 175g/6oz pieces of thick cod fillet, skinned
225g/8oz large spinach leaves
2.5g/½ tsp freshly grated nutmeg
45ml/3 tbsp white wine

1 Preheat the oven to 180°C/350°F/Gas 4. Season the fish well with salt and freshly ground black pepper.

2 Blanch the spinach leaves in boiling water for a minute and then refresh them under cold running water.

3 Pat the spinach leaves dry on absorbent kitchen paper.

4 Wrap the spinach around each fish fillet. Sprinkle with nutmeg. Place in a roasting pan, pour over the wine and poach in the oven for 15 minutes. Slice and serve hot.

Salt Cod & Potato Fritters

These little fritters are extremely easy to make and taste really delicious. Serve them simply with a wedge of fresh lemon and some green salad. Offer guests a bowl of garlic mayonnaise for dipping.

MAKES ABOUT 24

INGREDIENTS
450g/1lb salt cod fillets
500g/1¼lb floury potatoes, unpeeled
plain (all-purpose) flour, for coating
vegetable oil, for deep-frying

1 Put the salt cod in a bowl, pour over cold water and leave to soak for 24 hours, changing the water every 6–8 hours. Drain, rinse and place in a pan of cold water. Slowly bring to the boil and simmer for 5 minutes, then drain and cool. When cooled, remove any bones and skin and mash the fish with a fork.

2 Cook the potatoes in their skins in a pan of salted boiling water for 20–25 minutes, or until just tender. Peel and mash.

3 Add the fish to the potatoes and mix well. Season to taste with salt and pepper. Break off walnut-sized pieces of the mixture and roll into balls. Place on a floured plate, cover and chill for 20–30 minutes. Roll each ball lightly in flour, dusting off any excess.

4 Heat enough oil for deep-frying in a large pan and fry the balls for 5–6 minutes, or until golden. Remove with a slotted spoon and drain on kitchen paper. Serve hot or warm.

Haddock with Fennel Butter & Lemon

Fresh fish tastes fabulous cooked in a simple herb butter. Here the liquorice flavour of fennel complements the haddock beautifully to make a simple dish ideal for a dinner party. Fold small fillets in half before baking.

SERVES 4

INGREDIENTS
675g/1½lb haddock fillet, skinned and cut into 4 portions
50g/2oz/¼cup butter
1 lemon
45ml/3 tbsp coarsely chopped fennel

1 Preheat the oven to 220°C/425°F/Gas 7. Season the fish on both sides with salt and pepper. Melt one-quarter of the butter in a frying pan, preferably non-stick, and cook the fish over a medium heat briefly on both sides.

2 Transfer the fish to a shallow ovenproof dish. Cut four wafer-thin slices from the lemon and squeeze the juice from the remainder over the fish. Place the lemon slices on top and then bake for 15–20 minutes, or until the fish is cooked.

3 Meanwhile, melt the remaining butter in the frying pan and add the fennel and a little seasoning.

4 Transfer the cooked fish to plates and pour the cooking juices into the herb butter. Heat gently for a few seconds, then pour the herb butter over the fish. Serve immediately.

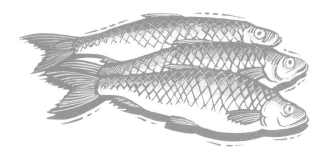

Smoked Haddock Fillets with Quick Parsley Sauce

Make any herb sauce with this method, making sure it is thickened and seasoned well to complement the smoky flavour of the fish. Serve tiny new potatoes and a herb salad with the fish to make a light, summery main course.

SERVES 4

INGREDIENTS
4 × 225g/8oz smoked haddock fillets
75g/3oz/6 tbsp butter, softened
300ml/½ pint/1¼ cups milk
60ml/4 tbsp chopped fresh parsley

1 Smear the fish fillets on both sides with 50g/2oz/4 tbsp butter and pre-heat the grill (broiler).

2 Beat the remaining butter with a little flour to make a thick paste.

3 Grill (broil) the fish for 10–15 minutes, turning when necessary. Meanwhile, heat the milk until just below boiling point. Add the butter and flour mixture in small knobs whilst whisking constantly over the heat. Continue whisking until the sauce is smooth and thick.

4 Stir in the parsley, season the sauce with salt and pepper and serve poured over the fillets.

VARIATION
Try this recipe using unsmoked haddock or other types of white fish. A sauce flavoured with fresh dill, basil or fennel is all excellent with fish.

MACKEREL IN CHERMOULA PASTE

Chermoula is a spice mix used widely in Moroccan and North African cooking. It is now readily available in most large supermarkets. The roast mackerel are best served in their paper parcels, to be unwrapped at the table.

SERVES 4

INGREDIENTS
4 whole mackerel, cleaned and gutted
2–3 tbsp chermoula, to taste
75ml/5 tbsp olive oil
2 red onions, sliced

1 Preheat the oven to 190°C/375°F/Gas 5. Place each mackerel on a large sheet of baking parchment. Using a sharp knife, slash each fish several times.

2 In a small bowl, mix the chermoula with the olive oil, and spread over the mackerel, rubbing the mixture into the cuts.

3 Spread the red onion slices over the mackerel, and season with salt and pepper. Wrap the fish in the parchment, twisting or folding the ends to seal the parcels and place on a baking tray. Bake for 20 minutes, until the mackerel is cooked through. Serve immediately.

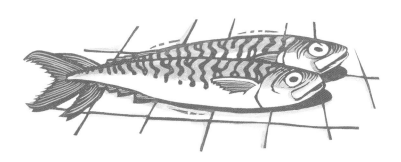

TONNO CON PISELLI

This Jewish Italian dish of fresh tuna and peas is traditional at Passover, which falls in spring. Little peas were eaten only at this time of year when they were in season. At other times of the year chickpeas were used instead – they give a heartier result.

SERVES 4

INGREDIENTS
350g/12oz tuna steaks
600ml/1 pint/2½ cups fresh tomato sauce
350g/12oz/3 cups fresh shelled or frozen peas
45ml/3 tbsp chopped fresh flat leaf parsley

1 Preheat the oven to 190°C/375°F/Gas 5. Sprinkle the tuna steaks on each side with salt and plenty of freshly ground black pepper and place in a shallow ovenproof dish, in a single layer.

2 Bring the tomato sauce to the boil, then add the fresh shelled or frozen peas and chopped fresh flat leaf parsley. Pour the sauce and peas evenly over the fish steaks in the ovenproof dish and bake in the preheated oven, uncovered, for about 20 minutes, or until the fish is tender. Serve the fish, sauce and peas immediately, straight from the dish.

VARIATION
This recipe works well with other types and cuts of fish. Use tuna fillets in place of the steaks or try different fish steaks, such as salmon or swordfish.

Seared marinated Tuna steaks

These steaks are delicious with a green salad or steamed vegetable and new potaotes. Alternatively, serve them cold, along with cooked and cooled green beans, potatoes and olives, for a traditional salade Niçoise

SERVES 4

INGREDIENTS
4 tuna steaks, about 150g/5oz each
45ml/3 tbsp garlic-infused olive oil
30ml/2 tbsp sherry vinegar
2 eggs

1 Put the tuna steaks in a shallow non-metallic dish. Mix the oil and vinegar together and season with salt and pepper.

2 Pour the mixture over the tuna steaks and turn them to coat in the marinade. Cover and chill for up to 1 hour.

3 Heat a griddle pan until smoking hot. Remove the tuna steaks from the marinade and lay them on the griddle pan. Cook for 2–3 minutes on each side, so that they are still pink in the centre. Remove from the pan and set aside.

4 Meanwhile, cook the eggs in a pan of boiling water for 6 minutes, then cool under cold running water. Shell the eggs and cut in half lengthways.

5 Pour the marinade on to the griddle pan and cook until it starts to bubble. Divide the tuna steaks among four serving plates and top each with half an egg. Drizzle the marinade over the top and serve immediately.

SEA BASS IN A SALT CRUST

Baking fish in a crust of sea salt seals in and enhances its flavour. Any firm fish can be cooked in this way. Decorate with a garnish of seaweed or blanched samphire and lemon slices, and break open the crust at the table to release the glorious aroma.

SERVES 4

INGREDIENTS
1 sea bass, about 1kg/2¼lb, cleaned and scaled
1 sprig each of fresh fennel, rosemary and thyme
mixed peppercorns
2kg/4½lb coarse sea salt

1 Preheat the oven to 240°C/475°F/Gas 9. Fill the cavity of the fish with the fresh fennel, rosemary and thyme, and grind over some of the mixed peppercorns.

2 Spread half the salt in an ovenproof dish (ideally oval) and lay the sea bass on it. Cover the fish all over with a 1cm/½in layer of salt, pressing it down firmly. Moisten the salt lightly by spraying with water from an atomizer. Bake the fish for 30–40 minutes, until the salt crust is just beginning to colour.

3 Bring the sea bass to the table in its salt crust. Use a sharp knife to break open the crust and cut into four portions.

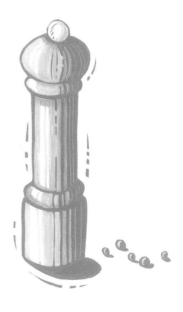

SEA BASS WITH PARSLEY & LIME BUTTER

The delicate but firm, sweet flesh of sea bass goes beautifully with citrus flavours, and in this recipe it is cooked with lime. Roast fennel and sautéed diced potatoes would be excellent accompaniments to this dish.

SERVES 6

INGREDIENTS
50g/2oz/¼ cup butter
6 sea bass fillets, about 150g/5oz each
grated rind and juice of 1 large lime
30ml/2 tbsp chopped fresh parsley

1 Heat the butter in a large frying pan and add three of the sea bass fillets, skin side down. Cook for 3–4 minutes, or until the skin is crisp and golden. Flip the fish over and cook for a further 2–3 minutes, or until cooked through.

2 Remove the fillets from the pan with a metal spatula. Place each on a serving plate and keep them warm. Cook the remaining fish in the same way and transfer to serving plates.

3 Add the lime rind and juice to the pan with the parsley, and season with salt and black pepper. Allow to bubble for 1–2 minutes, then pour a little over each fish portion and serve immediately.

GRILLED HAKE WITH LEMON & CHILLI

Choose firm hake fillets, as thick as possible. This is an ideal recipe if you are counting the calories, because it is low in fat. Serve with baby new potatoes and steamed fine green beans or broccoli.

SERVES 4

INGREDIENTS
4 hake fillets, each 150g/5oz
olive oil, for brushing
finely grated rind and juice of 1 unwaxed lemon
15ml/1 tbsp crushed chilli flakes

1 Preheat the grill (broiler) to high. Brush the hake fillets all over with the olive oil and place them skin side up on a baking sheet.

2 Grill (broil) the fish for 4–5 minutes, until the skin is crispy, then carefully turn them over using a metal spatula.

3 Sprinkle the fillets with the lemon rind and chilli flakes and season with salt and ground black pepper.

4 Grill the fillets for a further 2–3 minutes, or until the hake is cooked through. (Test using the point of a sharp knife; the flesh should flake.) Squeeze over the lemon juice just before serving.

Teriyaki Salmon

Bottles of teriyaki sauce – a lovely rich Japanese glaze with a sweet, salty flavour – are available in most large supermarkets and Asian stores. This salmon dish is good served with sticky rice or soba noodles.

SERVES 4

INGREDIENTS
4 salmon fillets, 150g/5oz each
75ml/5 tbsp teriyaki sauce
15ml/¼ pint/⅔ cup sunflower oil
5cm/2in piece of fresh root ginger, peeled and cut into matchsticks

1 Put the salmon in a shallow, non-metallic dish and pour over the teriyaki sauce. Cover and chill for 2 hours.

2 Meanwhile, heat the sunflower oil in a small pan and add the ginger. Fry for 1–2 minutes, or until golden and crisp. Remove with a slotted spoon and drain on kitchen paper.

3 Heat a griddle pan until smoking hot. Remove the salmon from the marinade and add, skin side down, to the pan. Cook for 2–3 minutes, turn over and cook for a further 1–2 minutes, or until cooked through. Remove from the pan and divide among four serving plates. Top the salmon fillets with the crispy fried ginger.

4 Pour the marinade into the pan and cook for 1–2 minutes. Pour over the salmon and serve.

COOK'S TIP
When buying salmon, check that the flesh is firm. It should be dark pink – not pale or greyish – with creamy marbling and not too much fat.

Salmon with Green Sauce

Baking a salmon in foil produces a moist result, and is one of the easiest ways of cooking it. Garnish the fish with thin slices of cucumber and dill to conceal any flesh that may look ragged after skinning, and serve with lemon wedges.

SERVES 6–8

INGREDIENTS
2–3kg/4½–6¾lb salmon, cleaned with head and tail left on
3–5 spring onions (scallions), thinly sliced
1 lemon, thinly sliced
600ml/1 pint/2½ cups watercress sauce or herb mayonnaise

1 Preheat the oven to 180°C/350°F/Gas 4. Rinse the salmon and lay it on a large piece of foil. Stuff the fish with the sliced spring onions and layer the lemon slices inside and around the fish. Sprinkle with salt and ground black pepper.

2 Loosely fold the foil around the fish and fold the edges over to seal. Bake for about 1 hour.

3 Remove the fish from the oven and leave to stand, still wrapped in the foil, for about 15 minutes, then unwrap the parcel and leave the fish to cool.

4 When the fish is cool, carefully lift it on to a large plate, retaining the lemon slices. Cover the fish tightly with clear film (plastic wrap) and chill for several hours in the refrigerator.

5 Before serving, discard the lemon slices from around the fish. Using a blunt knife to lift up the edge of the skin, carefully peel the skin away from the flesh, avoiding tearing the flesh, and pull out any fins at the same time.

6 Chill the watercress sauce or herb mayonnaise before serving. Transfer the fish to a serving platter and serve the sauce separately.

Marinated Smoked Salmon with Lime & Coriander

If you want an elegant appetizer that is quick to put together, then this is the one for you. The tangy lime juice and aromatic coriander leaves contrast perfectly with the smoky flavour of the salmon. Serve with thinly sliced brown bread and butter.

SERVES 6

INGREDIENTS
200g/7oz smoked salmon
a handful of fresh coriander (cilantro) leaves
grated rind and juice of 1 lime
15ml/1 tbsp extra virgin olive oil

1 Using a sharp knife or pair of kitchen scissors, cut the salmon into strips and arrange on a serving platter.

2 Sprinkle the coriander leaves and lime rind over the salmon and squeeze over the lime juice. Drizzle with the olive oil and season with black pepper. Cover with clear film (plastic wrap) and chill for 1 hour before serving.

COOK'S TIP
Making this dish an hour in advance allows the flavours to mingle. You should not leave it for longer than this because the lime juice will discolour the salmon and spoil the look of the dish.

PAN-FRIED SKATE WINGS WITH CAPERS

This sophisticated way of serving skate wings is perfect for a special dinner party. The lime juice and capers add an interesting piquant flavour. Serve the fish with a mixed green salad and baby new potatoes.

SERVES 6

INGREDIENTS
50g/2oz/¼ cup butter
6 small skate wings
grated rind and juice of 2 limes
30ml/2 tbsp salted capers, rinsed and drained

1 Heat the butter in a large frying pan and add one of the skate wings. Fry for 4–5 minutes on each side, until golden and cooked through.

2 Using a fish slice or metal spatula carefully transfer the cooked skate wing to a warmed serving plate and keep warm while you cook each of the remaining skate wings in the same way.

3 Return the pan to the heat and add the lime rind and juice, and the drained capers. Season with salt and freshly ground black pepper and allow to bubble for 1–2 minutes.

4 Spoon a little of the pan juices and the capers over each skate wing and serve the fish immediately.

PRAWN & NEW POTATO STEW

This spicy shellfish stew is just the thing for a really easy-to-prepare supper dish. Do not overheat the prawns or they will shrivel and become tough and tasteless. Serve with warm, crusty bread to mop up the delicious sauce, and a mixed green salad.

SERVES 4

INGREDIENTS
675g/1½lb small new potatoes, scrubbed
15g/½oz fresh coriander (cilantro)
350g/12oz jar tomato and chilli sauce
300g/11oz cooked peeled prawns (shrimp), thawed and drained if frozen

1 Cook the potatoes in lightly salted, boiling water for 15 minutes, until tender. Drain and return to the pan.

2 Finely chop half the coriander and add to the pan with the tomato and chilli sauce and 90ml/6 tbsp water. Bring to the boil, reduce the heat, cover and simmer gently for 5 minutes.

3 Stir in the prawns and heat briefly until they are warmed through, but do not overheat. Spoon the stew into shallow bowls and serve sprinkled with the remaining coriander, torn into pieces.

COOK'S TIPS
Choose new potatoes that have plenty of flavour, such as Jersey Royals, Maris Piper or Nicola, for this stew. Use a good-quality tomato and chilli sauce; there are now several different varieties available in the supermarkets.

CRAB & CUCUMBER WRAPS

This dish is a modern twist on the ever-popular Chinese classic, crispy Peking duck with pancakes. In this quick and easy version, crisp, refreshing cucumber and full-flavoured dressed crab are teamed with spicy-sweet hoisin sauce in tortilla wraps.

SERVES 2

INGREDIENTS
½ cucumber
1 medium dressed crab
4 small wheat tortillas
120ml/8 tbsp hoisin sauce

1 Cut the cucumber into small even-sized batons. Scoop the dressed crab into a small mixing bowl, add a little freshly ground black pepper and mix lightly.

2 Heat the tortillas gently, one at a time, in a heavy frying pan until they begin to colour on each side.

3 Spread a tortilla with 30ml/2 tbsp hoisin sauce, then sprinkle with one-quarter of the cucumber. Arrange one-quarter of the crab meat down the centre of each tortilla and roll up. Repeat with the remaining ingredients. Serve immediately.

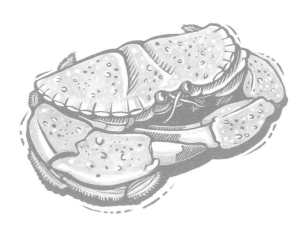

ASIAN-STYLE CRAB CAKES

You could serve these patties as a simple supper for four, or an appetizer for eight people. Use a mixture of white and brown crab meat, as the dark adds a depth of flavour and texture. Serve with a small bowl of sweet chilli sauce.

MAKES 16

INGREDIENTS
450g/1lb/2⅔ cups fresh crab meat, white and brown
15ml/1 tbsp grated fresh root ginger
15–30ml/1–2 tbsp plain (all-purpose) flour
60ml/4 tbsp sunflower oil

1 Put the crab meat in a bowl and add the ginger, some salt and ground black pepper and enough flour to produce a stiff or workable texture. Stir well until thoroughly mixed.

2 Using floured hands, divide the crab mixture into 16 equal-sized pieces and shape roughly into patties.

3 Heat the sunflower oil in a frying pan and add the patties, four at a time. Cook for 2–3 minutes on each side, until golden. Remove with a metal spatula and leave to drain on kitchen paper for a few minutes.

4 Keep the cooked crab cakes warm while you cook the remaining patties in the same way. Serve immediately.

COOK'S TIP
Always buy live crab whenever possible, so that you can be sure of its freshness. A crab was traditionally cooked by dropping it into boiling water. A more humane alternative is to put the live crab in cold water and slowly bring the water to boiling point.

MUSSELS IN WHITE WINE

This simple yet delicious dish is perfect for informal entertaining. Serve the mussels with plenty of warm bread to mop up the juices. To make a variation, cook the mussels in beer instead of wine – they taste fantastic.

SERVES 2

INGREDIENTS
25g/1oz/2 tbsp butter
300ml/½ pint/1¼ cups dry white wine
1kg/2¼lb mussels, cleaned
45ml/3 tbsp chopped fresh parsley

1 Heat the butter in a large pan until foaming, then pour in the wine. Bring to the boil. Discard any open mussels that do not close when sharply tapped, and add the remaining ones to the pan. Cover with a tight-fitting lid and cook over a medium heat for 4–5 minutes, shaking the pan every now and then. By this time, all the mussels should have opened. Discard any that are still closed.

2 Line a large strainer with kitchen paper and strain the mussels and their liquid through it. Transfer the mussels to warmed serving bowls. Pour the liquid into a small pan and bring to the boil. Season with salt and pepper and stir in the parsley. Pour over the mussels and serve immediately.

MEAT & POULTRY

With the simple addition of a few well-chosen ingredients, meat and poultry can be transformed into exciting, innovative dishes. For a quick and easy family supper, try Pork Kebabs or Honey Mustard Chicken, perhaps with a simple salad and rice or bread. With a little more advance preparation, but minimal effort, you can make Beef Cooked in Red Wine, Marinated Lamb with Oregano and Basil, or Soy-marinated Chicken with Asparagus. Or try Chicken Escalopes with Lemon and Serrano Ham for a really unusual, sophisticated dinner party dish.

Sicilian Meatballs in Tomato Sauce

Cooking the meatballs in their sauce keeps them moist, and there's no need to fry them first. Serve the meatballs in the traditional way with spaghetti and shavings of Parmesan cheese, accompanied by a green salad.

SERVES 4

INGREDIENTS
225g/8oz/1 cup minced (ground) beef
4 Sicilian-style sausages
2 × 400g/14oz cans pomodorino tomatoes

1 Put the minced beef in a bowl and season with salt and pepper. Remove the sausages from their skins and mix thoroughly into the beef.

2 Shape the mixture into balls about the size of large walnuts and arrange in a single layer in a shallow baking dish. Cover and chill for 30 minutes.

3 Preheat the oven to 180°C/350°F/Gas 4. Process the tomatoes in a food processor until just smooth, and season to taste. Pour over the meatballs, making sure they are all covered.

4 Bake the meatballs for 40 minutes, stirring once or twice, until they are cooked through. Serve immediately.

Beef Patties with Onions & Peppers

This family favourite is easy to make and can be varied by adding other vegetables,
such as broccoli or mushrooms. The patties can be served in burger buns with
salad and relish, with crusty bread, or with rice and a ready-made tomato sauce.

SERVES 4

INGREDIENTS
500g/1¼lb lean minced (ground) beef
4 onions, 1 finely chopped and 3 sliced
30ml/2 tbsp garlic-flavoured or plain olive oil
3 green (bell) peppers, seeded and sliced lengthways into strips

1 Place the minced beef, chopped onion and 15ml/1 tbsp of the oil in a bowl and season with salt and freshly ground black pepper. Stir well until thoroughly mixed. Form into four large or eight small patties.

2 Heat the remaining oil in a large, deep non-stick frying pan, then add the beef patties and cook on both sides until browned. Sprinkle over 15ml/1 tbsp water and add a little seasoning.

3 Cover the patties with the sliced onions and peppers. Sprinkle in another 15ml/1 tbsp water and a little seasoning, then cover the pan. Reduce the heat to very low and braise for 20–30 minutes, depending on the size of the patties and how well done you like them.

4 When the onions are turning golden brown, remove the pan from the heat. Serve the patties with the onions and peppers.

Beef Cooked in Red Wine

Shin of beef is a tough cut of meat, but marinating it overnight in red wine will ensure a tender result. Although this dish takes a long time to cook, it is very easy to prepare – once it is in the oven you can sit down and relax with a glass of wine. Sprinkle the stew with rosemary and serve with mashed potatoes.

Serves 4–6

INGREDIENTS
675g/1½lb boned and cubed shin of beef
3 large garlic cloves, finely chopped
1 bottle fruity red wine

1 Put the beef in a casserole dish with the garlic and some black pepper, and pour over the red wine. Stir to combine, then cover and chill for at least 12 hours.

2 Preheat the oven to 160°C/325°F/Gas 3. Cover the casserole with a tight-fitting lid and transfer to the oven. Cook for 2 hours, or until the beef is very tender. Season with salt and pepper to taste, and serve piping hot.

VARIATION
Marinate the beef in a mixture of half port and half beef stock instead of the red wine. Port cooks down to produce a lovely rich sauce, but be sure to dilute it with stock because it can be quite overpowering on its own. A half-and-half mixture will give the perfect balance of taste.

STEAK WITH TOMATO SALSA

A refreshing, tangy salsa of tomatoes, spring onions and balsamic vinegar makes a colourful topping for chunky, pan-fried steaks. Choose rump, sirloin or fillet, and if you do not have a non-stick pan, grill (broil) the steak instead for the same length of time. Serve with potato wedges and a mixed leaf salad with a mustard dressing.

SERVES 2

INGREDIENTS
2 steaks, about 2cm/³⁄₄in thick
4 large plum tomatoes
2 spring onions (scallions)
30ml/2 tbsp balsamic vinegar

1 Trim any excess fat from the steaks, then season on both sides with salt and freshly ground black pepper. Heat a non-stick frying pan and cook the steaks for about 3 minutes on each side if you like them medium rare. Cook for a little longer if you prefer your steak well cooked.

2 Meanwhile, put the tomatoes in a heatproof bowl, cover with boiling water and leave for 1–2 minutes, until the skins start to split. Drain the tomatoes, and when they are cool enough to handle, halve them and scoop out the seeds. Dice the tomato flesh. Thinly slice the spring onions.

3 Transfer the steaks to warmed plates and keep warm. Add the vegetables, balsamic vinegar, 30ml/2 tbsp water and a little seasoning to the cooking juices in the pan and stir briefly until warm, scraping up any meat residue. Spoon the salsa over the steaks and serve immediately.

MARINATED LAMB WITH OREGANO & BASIL

Lamb leg steaks are a tender, chunky cut of meat with a small round of bone in the middle, ideal for pan frying. The sweet flavour of lamb goes well with oregano and basil. However, you could use finely chopped rosemary or thyme instead. Serve the lamb steaks with couscous and steamed fresh vegetables such as broccoli, cauliflower or fine green beans.

SERVES 4

INGREDIENTS
4 large or 8 small lamb leg steaks
60ml/4 tbsp garlic-infused olive oil
1 small bunch of fresh oregano, roughly chopped
1 small bunch of fresh basil, torn

1 Put the lamb steaks in a shallow, non-metallic dish. Mix 45ml/3 tbsp of the garlic-infused oil with the oregano, basil and some salt and pepper, reserving some of the herbs for garnishing. Pour over the lamb and turn to coat in the marinade. Cover and chill for up to 8 hours.

2 Heat the remaining oil in a large frying pan. Remove the lamb from the marinade and fry for 5–6 minutes on each side, until slightly pink in the centre. Add the marinade and cook for 1–2 minutes until warmed through. Place on a serving dish, pour over the sauce, garnish with the reserved herbs and serve.

North African Lamb with Prunes

This dish is full of contrasting flavours that create a rich, spicy main course. Use lamb that still retains some fat, as this will help keep the meat moist and succulent. Serve with salad and couscous or mixed white and wild rice, sprinkled with chopped fresh herbs. You can also roast a selection of vegetables, cut into chunks, along with the lamb and onions.

SERVES 4

INGREDIENTS
675g/1½lb lamb fillet or shoulder steaks, cut into chunky pieces
5 small onions
7.5ml/1½ tsp harissa
115g/4oz ready-to-eat pitted prunes, halved

1 Preheat the oven to 200°C/400°F/Gas 6. Season the lamb with salt and pepper. Heat a frying pan, preferably non-stick, and cook the lamb on all sides until beginning to brown. Transfer to a roasting pan, reserving any fat in the frying pan.

2 Peel the onions and cut each into six wedges. Toss with the lamb and roast for about 30–40 minutes, until the lamb is cooked through and the onions are deep golden brown in colour.

3 Put the lamb and onions back into the frying pan. Mix the harissa with 250ml/8fl oz/1 cup boiling water and add to the roasting pan. Scrape up any residue in the pan and pour the mixture over the lamb and onions. Stir in the prunes and heat until just simmering. Cover and simmer for 5 minutes, then serve.

Lamb Steaks with Redcurrant Glaze

This classic, simple dish is delicious and is an excellent, quick recipe for cooking on the barbecue. The tangy flavour of redcurrants is a traditional accompaniment to lamb. It is good served with new potatoes and fresh garden peas tossed in butter.

SERVES 4

INGREDIENTS
4 large fresh rosemary sprigs
4 lamb leg steaks
75ml/5 tbsp redcurrant jelly
30ml/2 tbsp raspberry or red wine vinegar

1 Reserve the tips of the rosemary and finely chop the remaining leaves. Rub the chopped rosemary, salt and pepper all over the lamb.

2 Preheat the grill (broiler) to medium, or prepare a barbecue. Heat the redcurrant jelly gently in a small pan with 30ml/2 tbsp water and a little seasoning. Stir in the vinegar.

3 Place the lamb steaks on a foil-lined grill rack and brush with a little of the redcurrant glaze. Cook under the grill or on the barbecue for about 5 minutes on each side, until deep golden, brushing frequently with more redcurrant glaze.

4 Transfer the lamb to warmed plates. Pour any juices from the foil into the remaining glaze and heat through gently. Pour the glaze over the lamb and serve, garnished with the reserved rosemary sprigs.

COOK'S TIP
To make raspberry vinegar, macerate 450g/1lb fresh raspberries in 1.2 litres/2 pints/5 cups good-quality wine vinegar for 2–3 weeks. Strain before use.

ROAST SHOULDER OF LAMB WITH WHOLE GARLIC CLOVES

The potatoes catch the lamb fat as it cooks, giving garlicky, juicy results. Return the potatoes to the oven to keep them warm while you leave the lamb to rest before carving. Serve with fresh seasonal vegetables.

SERVES 4–6

INGREDIENTS
675g/1½lb waxy potatoes, peeled and cut into large dice
12 garlic cloves, unpeeled
45ml/3 tbsp olive oil
1 whole shoulder of lamb

1 Preheat the oven to 180°C/350°F/Gas 4. Put the potatoes and garlic cloves into a large roasting pan and season with salt and pepper. Pour over 30ml/2 tbsp of the oil and toss the potatoes and garlic to coat.

2 Place a rack over the roasting pan, so that it is not touching the potatoes. Place the lamb on the rack and drizzle over the remaining oil. Season with salt and freshly ground black pepper.

3 Roast the lamb and potatoes for 2–2½ hours, or until the lamb is cooked through. Halfway through the cooking time, carefully take the lamb and the rack off the roasting pan and turn the potatoes to ensure even cooking.

STICKY GLAZED PORK RIBS

These spare ribs have a lovely sweet-and-sour flavour and are popular with children as well as adults, making them the perfect choice for a family meal. They're also great for cooking over a barbecue; for the best flavour, marinate them first for at least 3 minutes in the honey and soy sauce, and brush frequently with the mixture during cooking To enjoy the ribs at their best, get stuck in and eat them with your fingers.

SERVES 4

INGREDIENTS
900g/2lb pork spare ribs
75ml/5 tbsp clear honey
75ml/5 tbsp light soy sauce

1 Preheat the oven to 190°C/375°F/Gas 5. Put the spare ribs in a roasting pan and season well with plenty of salt and ground black pepper.

2 In a small bowl, mix together the honey and soy sauce and pour over the ribs. Turn the ribs several times, spooning over the mixture until thoroughly coated.

3 Bake the spare ribs for 30 minutes, then increase the oven temperature to 220°C/425°F/Gas 7 and cook for a further 10 minutes, or until the honey and soy sauce mixture turns into a thick, sticky glaze.

CHINESE SPICED PORK CHOPS

Five-spice powder is a useful ingredient for perking up dishes and adding a good depth of flavour. The five different spices – Szechuan pepper, cinnamon, cloves, fennel seeds and star anise – are perfectly balanced, with the aniseed flavour of star anise predominating. Serve the spiced pork chops with lightly steamed green vegetables and plain boiled rice.

SERVES 4

INGREDIENTS
4 large pork chops, about 200g/7oz each
15ml/1 tbsp Chinese five-spice powder
30ml/2 tbsp soy sauce
30ml/2 tbsp garlic-infused olive oil

1 Arrange the pork chops in a non-metallic baking dish. Sprinkle the five-spice powder over the chops, then drizzle over the soy sauce and garlic-infused olive oil. (Alternatively, mix together the oil and five-spice powder, and pour over the chops.)

2 Using your hands, rub the mixture into the meat. Cover the dish with clear film (plastic wrap) and chill for 2 hours.

3 Preheat the oven to 160°/325°F/Gas 3. Uncover the dish and bake for 30–40 minutes, or until the pork is cooked through and tender. Serve immediately.

COOK'S TIP
To make garlic-infused olive oil, peel and halve a large garlic clove and place in a clean bottle with 600ml/1 pint/2½ cups extra virgin olive oil. Cover tightly and leave to stand in a cool place for 2 weeks.

PORK WITH JUNIPER BERRIES

Juniper berries have a strong, pungent taste and are an ideal flavouring for rich, fatty meats such as pork, while bay leaves add a lovely aroma. Serve the roast pork with roast potatoes and some lightly cooked leafy green vegetables.

SERVES 4–6

INGREDIENTS
1kg/2¼lb boned leg of pork
5 fresh bay leaves
6 juniper berries
15ml/1 tbsp olive oil

1 Preheat the oven to 180°/350°F/Gas 4. Open out the pork and season with plenty of salt and freshly ground black pepper.

2 Lay the bay leaves on the pork, evenly spaced, and sprinkle over the juniper berries. Carefully roll up the pork to enclose the bay leaves and juniper berries and tie with string to secure.

3 Rub the skin with the oil and then rub in plenty of salt. Roast the pork for 1–1¼ hours, until cooked through.

4 Remove the pork from the oven and leave to rest for about 10 minutes before carving, then serve immediately.

COOK'S TIP
If you want to cook a larger or smaller leg of pork in this way, roast it for about 20 minutes per 450g/1lb, plus an extra 20 minutes.

Paprika Pork

This chunky, goulash-style dish is rich with peppers and paprika. Grilling the peppers before adding them to the meat really brings out their sweet, vibrant flavour. Rice or buttered boiled potatoes go particularly well with the rich pork.

SERVES 4

INGREDIENTS
2 red, 1 yellow and 1 green (bell) pepper, seeded
500g/1¼lb lean pork fillet (tenderloin)
45ml/3 tbsp paprika
300g/11oz jar or tub of tomato sauce with herbs or garlic

1 Preheat the grill (broiler). Cut the peppers into thick strips and sprinkle in a single layer on a foil-lined grill rack. Cook under the grill for 20–25 minutes, until the edges of the strips are lightly charred.

2 Meanwhile, cut the pork into chunks. Season with salt and pepper and cook in a non-stick frying pan for about 5 minutes, until beginning to brown.

3 Transfer the meat to a heavy pan and add the paprika, tomato sauce 300ml/ ½ pint/1¼ cups water. Bring to the boil, reduce the heat, cover and simmer gently for 30 minutes.

4 Add the peppers and cook for a further 10–15 minutes, until the meat is tender. Taste for seasoning and serve immediately.

Pork Kebabs

The word kebab comes from Arabic and means "on a skewer". Use pork fillet because it is lean and tender, and cooks quickly. Kebabs are good served with rice, or stuffed into warmed pitta bread with shredded lettuce leaves.

SERVES 4

INGREDIENTS
500g/1¼lb lean pork fillet (tenderloin)
8 large, thick spring onions (scallions), trimmed
120ml/4fl oz/½ cup barbecue sauce
1 lemon

1 Cut the fillet of pork into 2.5cm/1in cubes. Chop the spring onions into 2.5cm/1in long sticks.

2 Preheat the grill (broiler) to high. Oil the wire rack and spread out the pork cubes on it. Grill the pork until the juices drip, then dip the pieces in the barbecue sauce and put back on the grill. Grill for 30 seconds on each side, then repeat the dipping and cooking process twice more. Set aside and keep warm.

3 Gently grill the spring onions until soft and slightly brown outside. Do not dip in the barbecue sauce. Thread about four pieces of pork and three spring onion pieces on to each of eight bamboo skewers.

4 Arrange the skewers on a platter. Cut the lemon into wedges and squeeze a little lemon juice over each skewer. Serve immediately, offering the remaining lemon wedges separately.

COOK'S TIP
If you are cooking the pork on a barbecue, soak the skewers for 30 mintues in water to prevent burning, and thread the meat and spring onions on them before cooking.

ONION & SAUSAGE TARTE TATIN

The traditional French tarte Tatin is sweet, and is made with apples, but this is a savoury version. Toulouse sausages have a meaty texture and a garlicky flavour that is delicious with caramelized onions. Serve the tart with a green salad of bitter leaves.

SERVES 4

INGREDIENTS
45ml/3 tbsp sunflower oil
450g/1lb Toulouse sausages
2 large onions, sliced
250g/9oz ready-made puff pastry, thawed if frozen

1 Heat the oil in a 23cm/9in non-stick frying pan with an ovenproof handle, and add the sausages. Cook over a gentle heat, turning occasionally, for 7–10 minutes, or until golden and cooked through. Remove from the pan and set aside.

2 Preheat the oven to 190°C/375°F/Gas 5. Pour the oil (left behind after cooking the sausages) into the frying pan and add the onions. Season with salt and pepper and cook over a gentle heat for 10 minutes, stirring occasionally, until caramelized and tender.

3 Slice each sausage into four or five chunks and stir into the onions. Remove from the heat and set aside.

4 Roll out the puff pastry and cut out a circle slightly larger than the frying pan. Lay the pastry over the sausages and onions, tucking the edges in all the way around. Bake for 20 minutes, or until the pastry is risen and golden. Turn out on to a board, pastry side down, cut into wedges and serve.

Spicy Chorizo Sausage & Spring Onion Hash

You can use up leftover boiled potatoes for this recipe. If you have to cook them first, do this while you are frying the sausages. Fresh chorizo sausages – some of which are very hot and spicy – are available from good butchers and Spanish delicatessens.

SERVES 4

INGREDIENTS
15ml/1 tbsp olive oil
450g/1lb fresh chorizo sausages
450g/1lb cooked potatoes, diced
1 bunch of spring onions (scallions), sliced

1 Heat a large frying pan over a medium heat and add the sausages. Cook for 8–10 minutes, turning occasionally, until cooked through. Remove from the pan and set aside.

2 Add the olive oil to the sausage fat in the pan and then add the potatoes. Cook over a low heat for 5–8 minutes, turning occasionally, until golden. Meanwhile, cut the sausages into bite size chunks and add to the pan.

3 Add the spring onions to the pan and cook for a couple more minutes, until they are piping hot. Season with salt and pepper, and serve immediately.

Fragrant Lemon Grass & Ginger Pork Patties

Lemon grass lends a fragrant citrus flavour to pork, enhanced by the fresh zing of ginger. Serve the patties in burger buns with thick slices of juicy tomato, crisp, refreshing lettuce and a splash of chilli sauce.

SERVES 4

INGREDIENTS
450g/1lb/2 cups minced (ground) pork
15ml/1 tbsp fresh root ginger, grated
1 lemon grass stalk
30ml/2 tbsp sunflower oil

1 Put the pork in a bowl and stir in the ginger. Season with salt and freshly ground black pepper. Remove the tough outer layers from the lemon grass stalk and discard. Chop the centre part as finely as possible and mix into the pork. Shape into four patties and chill for about 20 minutes.

2 Heat the oil in a large, non-stick frying pan and add the patties. Fry for 3–4 minutes on each side over a gentle heat, until cooked through. Remove from the pan with a metal spatula and drain on kitchen paper, then serve.

PAN-FRIED GAMMON WITH CIDER

Gammon and cider make a delicious combination with the sweet, tangy flavour of cider complementing the gammon perfectly. Serve this dish with mustard mashed potatoes and a selection of fresh seasonal vegetables.

SERVES 4

INGREDIENTS
30ml/2 tbsp sunflower oil
4 gammon steaks (smoked or cured ham), 225g/8oz each
150ml/¼ pint/⅔ cup dry (hard) cider
45ml/3 tbsp double (heavy) cream

1 Heat the oil in a large frying pan until hot. Make a few cuts in the rind on the gammon steaks to stop them curling up and add them to the pan.

2 Cook the steaks for 3–4 minutes on each side, then pour in the cider. Allow to boil for a couple of minutes, then stir in the cream and cook for 1–2 minutes, or until thickened. Season with salt and black pepper, and serve immediately.

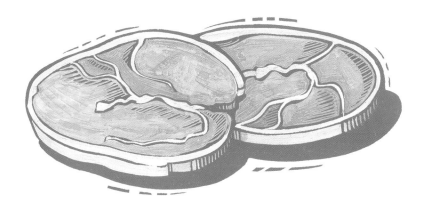

HONEY MUSTARD CHICKEN

Chicken thighs have a rich flavour, but if you want to cut down on the fat content, use four chicken breast portions instead and cook for only 20–25 minutes. Serve the chicken with a chunky tomato and red onion salad.

SERVES 4

INGREDIENTS
8 chicken thighs
60ml/4 tbsp wholegrain mustard
60ml/4 tbsp clear honey

1 Preheat the oven to 190°/375°/Gas 5. Put the chicken thighs in a single layer in a roasting pan.

2 Mix together the mustard and honey, season with salt and ground black pepper to taste and brush the mixture all over the chicken thighs.

3 Cook for 25–30 minutes, brushing the chicken with the pan juices occasionally, until cooked through. (To check the chicken is cooked through, pierce the thickest part with a sharp knife; the juices should run clear.)

VARIATION
Instead of honey and mustard, try coating the chicken with crushed garlic, mixed with grated lemon rind or finely chopped fresh herbs.

Stir-fried Chicken with Thai Basil

Thai basil, sometimes called holy basil, has purple-tinged leaves and a more pronounced, slightly aniseedy flavour than the usual varieties. Serve this fragrant stir-fry with plain steamed rice or boiled noodles and soy sauce on the side.

Serves 4

Ingredients
4 skinless chicken breast fillets, cut into strips
2 red (bell) peppers
30ml/2 tbsp garlic-infused olive oil
1 small bunch of fresh Thai basil

1 Slice the chicken breast portions into strips, using a sharp knife. Halve the peppers, remove the seeds, then cut each piece of pepper into strips.

2 Heat the oil in a wok or large frying pan. Add the chicken and red peppers and stir-fry over a high heat for about 3 minutes, until the chicken is golden and cooked through. Season with salt and freshly ground black pepper.

3 Roughly tear up the basil leaves, add to the chicken and peppers and toss briefly to combine. Serve immediately.

Cook's Tip
Thai basil is usually available in most Asian food stores, but if you can't find any, substitute a handful of ordinary basil instead.

QUICK-AND-EASY TANDOORI CHICKEN

This is a really easy version of the very popular Indian/Pakistani dish. If you have time, prepare the chicken when you get up in the morning, so that it's ready to cook for supper. Serve with a red onion and cucumber salad and warmed naan bread.

SERVES 4

INGREDIENTS
4 skinless chicken breast fillets and 4 skinless chicken thigh fillets
200ml/7fl oz/scant 1 cup Greek (US strained plain) yogurt
45ml/3 tbsp tandoori curry paste

1 Using a sharp knife, slash the chicken breasts and thighs and place in a shallow, non-metallic ovenproof dish.

2 Put the curry paste and yogurt in a bowl and mix together. Season with salt and pepper, then pour over the chicken and toss to coat well. Cover the dish with clear film (plastic wrap) and chill for at least 8 hours.

3 Preheat the oven to 190°C/375°F/Gas 5. Remove the clear film from the chicken and transfer the dish to the oven. Bake for 20–30 minutes, or until the chicken is cooked through. Serve immediately.

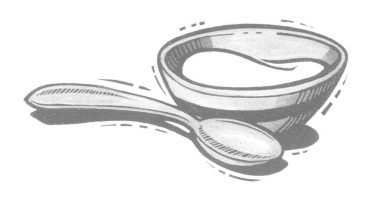

Roast Chicken with Black Pudding & Sage

The combination of juicy roast chicken and black pudding, complemented with fresh sage leaves, is wonderful. Choose an organic chicken if you want the best flavour. Serve as a Sunday roast with roast vegetables, or simply with a salad.

SERVES 4

INGREDIENTS
1 medium oven-ready chicken
115g/4oz black pudding (blood sausage), skinned
30ml/2 tbsp fresh sage leaves
25g/1oz/2 tbsp softened butter

1 Preheat the oven to 190°C/375°F/Gas 5. Carefully push your fingers between the skin and the flesh at the neck end of the bird to loosen it, making sure you don't tear the skin in the process.

2 Shape the black pudding into a flat, roundish shape, to fit the space between the skin and the breast meat. Push it under the skin with half the sage leaves.

3 Truss the chicken and place in a roasting pan. Spread the butter over the breast and thighs, and season with salt and ground black pepper. Sprinkle over the remaining sage leaves and roast for 1½ hours, or until the chicken is cooked through. Leave to rest for 10 minutes before carving.

COOK'S TIP
To truss a chicken, lay it down breast uppermost and away from you. Tuck the wing tips and neck flap underneath. Tie a piece of string around the legs and under the flap of skin. Bring the string back towards the neck end, passing it between the legs. Turn the bird over and wrap the string around the wings to keep them flat. Finally, pull the string tight to bring the wings together and tie neatly.

Soy-marinated Chicken with Asparagus

Two simple flavours, soy sauce and orange, combine in this mouthwatering dish. Serving the chicken on a bed of asparagus turns it into a special treat. Wilted spinach or shredded greens work well as an everyday alternative.

SERVES 4

INGREDIENTS
4 skinless chicken breast fillets
1 large orange
30ml/2 tbsp dark soy sauce
400g/14oz medium asparagus spears

1 Slash each chicken portion diagonally and place them in a single layer in a shallow, ovenproof dish. Halve the orange, squeeze the juice from one half and mix it with the soy sauce. Pour this over the chicken. Cut the remaining orange into wedges and place these on the chicken. Cover and marinate for several hours.

2 Preheat the oven to 180°C/350°F/Gas 4. Turn the chicken over and bake, uncovered, for 20 minutes. Turn the chicken over again and bake for a further 15 minutes, or until cooked through.

3 Meanwhile, cut off any tough ends from the asparagus and place in a frying pan. Pour in enough boiling water just to cover and cook gently for 3–4 minutes, until just tender. Drain and arrange on warmed plates, then top with the chicken and orange wedges. Spoon over the cooking juices and season with freshly ground black pepper. Serve immediately.

Chicken Escalopes with Lemon & Serrano Ham

Chicken escalopes are flattened chicken breast fillets – they cook quicker than normal breast portions and absorb flavours more readily. In this light summery dish, the chicken is flavoured with ham and lemon. It can be assembled in advance, so is good for entertaining. Serve with new potatoes and freshly cooked vegetables.

Serves 4

Ingredients
40g/1½oz/3 tbsp butter, softened
4 skinless chicken breast fillets
4 slices Serrano ham
1 lemon

1 Preheat the oven to 180°C/350°F/Gas 4. Beat the butter with plenty of freshly ground black pepper and set aside. Place the chicken portions on a large sheet of clear film (plastic wrap), spacing them well apart. Cover with a second sheet, then beat with a rolling pin until the portions are half their original thickness.

2 Transfer the chicken to a large, shallow ovenproof dish and crumple a slice of ham on top of each portion. Cut eight thin slices from the lemon and place two on each slice of ham.

3 Dot with the pepper butter and bake for about 30 minutes, until the chicken is cooked. Transfer to serving plates and spoon over any juices from the dish.

Thyme and Lime-flavoured Turkey Patties

So much better than store-bought burgers, these light patties are delicious served hamburger-style in split and toasted buns with relish, salad leaves and chunky fries. If you are making them for children, shape the mixture into 12 equal-sized rounds and serve in mini-rolls or in rounds stamped out from sliced bread.

SERVES 6

INGREDIENTS
675g/1½lb minced (ground) turkey
1 small red onion, finely chopped
small handful of fresh thyme leaves
30ml/2 tbsp lime-flavoured olive oil

1 Mix together the turkey, onion, thyme, 15ml/1 tbsp of the oil and seasoning. Cover and chill for up to 4 hours to let the flavours develop, then divide the mixture into six equal portions and shape into round patties.

2 Preheat a griddle pan. Brush the patties with half of the remaining lime-flavoured olive oil, then place them on the pan and cook for 10–12 minutes. Turn the patties over, brush with more oil, and cook for 10–12 minutes on the second side, or until cooked right through. Serve the patties immediately.

VARIATIONS
These patties can also be made using minced chicken, lamb, pork or beef. And you could try chopped oregano or parsley in place of the thyme, and lemon-flavoured oil instead of lime.

PHEASANT COOKED IN PORT

This warming dish is delicious served with mashed root vegetables and shredded cabbage or leeks. Marinating the pheasant in port helps to moisten and tenderize the meat, which can often be slightly dry. If you prefer, marinate the pheasant in a full-bodied red wine, and add a chopped red onion with the mushrooms

SERVES 4

INGREDIENTS
2 pheasants, cut into portions
300ml/½ pint/1¼ cups port
50g/2oz/¼ cup butter
300g/11oz chestnut mushrooms, halved if large

1 Place the pheasant portions in a bowl and pour over the port. Cover and marinate for 3–4 hours or overnight, turning the portions occasionally.

2 Drain the meat thoroughly, reserving the marinade. Pat the portions dry on kitchen paper and season lightly with salt and pepper. Melt three-quarters of the butter in a frying pan and cook the pheasant portions on all sides for about 5 minutes, until deep golden. Drain well, transfer to a plate, then cook the mushrooms in the fat remaining in the pan for 3 minutes.

3 Return the pheasant to the pan and pour in the reserved marinade with 200ml/7fl oz/scant 1 cup water. Bring to the boil, reduce the heat and cover, then simmer gently for about 45 minutes, until the pheasant is tender.

4 Using a slotted spoon, carefully remove the pheasant portions and mushrooms from the frying pan and keep warm. Bring the cooking juices to the boil and boil vigorously for 3–5 minutes, until they are reduced and slightly thickened. Strain the juices through a fine strainer and return them to the pan. Whisk in the remaining butter over a gentle heat until it has melted, season to taste, then pour the juices over the pheasant and mushrooms and serve.

DUCK WITH PLUM SAUCE

Sharp plums cut the rich flavour of duck wonderfully well in this updated version of an old English dish. Duck is often considered to be a fatty meat but modern breeding methods have made leaner ducks widely available. For an easy dinner party main course, serve the duck with creamy mashed potatoes, celeriac and steamed broccoli.

SERVES 4

INGREDIENTS
4 duck quarters
1 large red onion, finely chopped
500g/1¼lb ripe plums, stoned (pitted) and quartered
30ml/2 tbsp redcurrant jelly

1 Prick the duck skin all over with a fork to release the fat during cooking and help give a crisp result. Place the portions in a heavy frying pan, skin side down.

2 Cook the duck pieces for 10 minutes on each side, or until golden brown and cooked right through. Remove the duck from the frying pan using a slotted spoon and keep warm.

3 Pour away all but 30ml/2 tbsp of the duck fat, then stir-fry the onion for 5 minutes, or until golden. Add the plums and cook for 5 minutes, stirring frequently. Add the jelly and mix well.

4 Replace the duck portions and cook for a further 5 minutes, or until thoroughly reheated. Season to taste before serving.

COOK'S TIP
It is important that the plums used in this dish are very ripe, otherwise the mixture will be too dry and the sauce will be extremely sharp.

VEGETARIAN

Fresh vegetables, mild eggs, rich and creamy cheeses and aromatic herbs and spices are great partners and can be combined to make a delicious array of vegetarian meals. Enjoy wonderful dishes such as Baked Sweet Potatoes with Leeks & Gorgonzola, richly flavoured Tomato & Tapenade Tarts with Mascarpone Topping, and light-as-air Cheese & Tomato Soufflés, as well as classic vegetarian favourites, such as Margherita Pizza and Mushroom Stroganoff.

AUBERGINES WITH CHEESE SAUCE

This wonderfully simple dish can easily be assembled in advance, ready to go in the oven, so it's perfect for entertaining. Kashkaval cheese is particularly good in this recipe – it is a hard yellow cheese made from sheep's milk and is originally from the Balkans. Serve with mixed salad and lots of crusty bread to mop up the delicious cheese sauce.

SERVES 4–6

INGREDIENTS
2 large aubergines (eggplants), cut into 5mm/¼in thick slices
about 60ml/4 tbsp olive oil
*400g/14oz/3½ cups grated cheese, such as kashkaval, Gruyère, or a mixture of
   Parmesan and Cheddar*
600ml/1 pint/2½ cups savoury white sauce or béchamel sauce

1 Layer the aubergine slices in a colander, sprinkling each layer with salt, and leave to drain for at least 30 minutes. Rinse, then pat dry with kitchen paper.

2 Heat the oil in a frying pan, then cook the aubergine slices until golden brown on both sides. Remove from the pan and set aside.

3 Preheat the oven to 180°C/350°F/Gas 4. Mix most of the grated cheese into the savoury white or béchamel sauce, reserving a little to sprinkle over the top of the finished dish.

4 Arrange a layer of the aubergines in an ovenproof dish, then pour over some sauce. Repeat with the remaining ingredients, ending with sauce. Sprinkle with the reserved cheese. Bake for 35–40 minutes, until golden.

CHEESE & TOMATO SOUFFLÉS

Using a ready-made cheese sauce takes the hard work out of soufflé making. The key to success when making soufflés is to whisk the egg whites thoroughly to incorporate as much air as possible. During the cooking time don't open the oven door – the cold draught could cause the delicate mixture to collapse. For the same reason, serve the soufflés as soon as you remove them from the oven.

SERVES 6

INGREDIENTS
350g/12oz tub fresh cheese sauce
50g/2oz sun-dried tomatoes in olive oil, drained, plus 10ml/2 tsp of the oil
130g/4½oz/1⅓ cups grated Parmesan cheese
4 large (US extra large) eggs, separated

1 Preheat the oven to 200°C/400°F/Gas 6. Turn the cheese sauce into a bowl. Thinly slice the sun-dried tomatoes and add to the bowl with 90g/3½oz/ generous 1 cup of the Parmesan, the egg yolks and seasoning. Stir to combine.

2 Brush the base and sides of six 200ml/7fl oz/scant 1 cup ramekins with the oil and then coat the insides of the dishes with half the remaining cheese, tilting them until evenly covered.

3 Whisk the egg whites in a clean bowl until they are stiff. Use a large metal spoon to stir one-quarter of the egg whites into the sauce, then fold in the remainder. Spoon the mixture into the prepared dishes and sprinkle the remaining Parmesan cheese on top. Place on a baking sheet and bake for 15–18 minutes, until well risen and golden. Serve immediately.

CLASSIC MARGHERITA PIZZA

Bought pizza base mixes are a useful storecupboard stand-by. A Margherita Pizza makes a lovely simple supper, but of course you can add any extra toppings you like. Mushrooms and olives make a great addition – just add them to the pizza before cooking. The pizza is good just on its own, or served with a green salad.

SERVES 2

INGREDIENTS
half a 300g/11oz packet pizza base mix
15ml/1 tbsp herb-infused olive oil
45ml/3 tbsp ready-made tomato and basil sauce
150g/5oz mozzarella cheese, sliced

1 Make the pizza base mix according to the instructions on the packet. Brush the base with a little of the olive oil and spread over the tomato and basil sauce, making sure that it doesn't quite reach the edges.

2 Arrange the slices of mozzarella on top of the pizza and bake for 25–30 minutes, or until golden and the cheese is melted and bubbling.

3 Drizzle the remaining oil on top of the pizza, season with salt and black pepper and serve immediately.

GOAT'S CHEESE PASTRIES

These attractive little tartlets couldn't be easier to make. Garnish them with fresh thyme sprigs and serve with a selection of salad leaves and a tomato and basil salad for a light lunch or quick supper. Several types of goat's cheeses are available – the creamy log-shaped types without a rind are most suitable for these pastries.

SERVES 4

INGREDIENTS
15ml/1 tbsp olive oil
450g/1lb red onions, sliced
425g/15oz packet ready-rolled puff pastry
115g/4oz/1 cup goat's cheese, cubed

1 Heat the oil in a large, heavy frying pan, add the onions and cook over a gentle heat for 10 minutes, or until softened, stirring occasionally to prevent them from browning. Add seasoning to taste and cook for a further 2 minutes. Remove the pan from the heat and leave to cool.

2 Preheat the oven to 220°C/425°F/Gas 7. Unroll the puff pastry and using a 15cm/6in plate as a guide, cut out four rounds. Place the pastry rounds on a dampened baking sheet and, using the point of a sharp knife, score a border, 2cm/¾in inside the edge of each pastry round.

3 Divide the onions among the pastry rounds and top with the goat's cheese. Bake for 25–30 minutes, until golden brown.

VARIATION
To make richer-flavoured pastries ring the changes by spreading the pastry base with red or green pesto or tapenade before you top with the cooked onions and the goats cheese. Ordinary onions can be used instead of red, if you prefer.

Toasted Sourdough with Goat's Cheese

This is a cheese on toast recipe with a touch of the exotic – but it is quick and easy to make and ideal as a quick tasty snack at any time of day. Choose a good quality, firm goat's cheese because it needs to keep its shape during cooking. Serve with a green salad – baby spinach leaves are a good choice.

SERVES 2

INGREDIENTS
2 thick sourdough bread slices
30ml/2 tbsp garlic-infused olive oil
30ml/2 tbsp chilli jam
2 firm goat's cheese slices, about 90g/3½oz each

1 Preheat the grill (broiler) to high. Brush the slices of sourdough bread on both sides with the oil, and grill (broil) one side until golden. Spread the untoasted side of each slice with the chilli jam and top with the goat's cheese.

2 Return the bread to the grill and cook for 3–4 minutes, or until the cheese is beginning to melt and turn golden and bubbling. Season with ground black pepper and serve immediately.

COOKS TIP
Sourdough bread is not as readily available in Britain as it is in the United States and other European countries. Other types of bread could be substituted.

Tomato & Tapenade Tarts with Mascarpone Topping

These delicious individual tarts look and taste fantastic, despite the fact that they demand very little time or effort. The mascarpone cheese topping melts as it cooks to make a smooth, creamy sauce. Cherry tomatoes have a delicious sweet flavour with a low acidity, but plum tomatoes or vine-ripened tomatoes can also be used.

SERVES 4

INGREDIENTS
500g/1¼lb puff pastry, thawed if frozen
60ml/4 tbsp black or green olive tapenade
500g/1¼lb cherry tomatoes
90g/3½oz/scant ½ cup mascarpone cheese

1 Preheat the oven to 220°C/425°F/Gas 7. Lightly grease a large baking sheet with oil and sprinkle it with water. Roll out the pastry on a lightly floured surface and cut out four 16cm/6½in rounds, using a bowl or small plate as a guide.

2 Transfer the pastry rounds to the prepared baking sheet. Using the tip of a sharp knife, carefully mark a shallow cut 1cm/½in in from the edge of each round to form a rim.

3 Reserve half the tapenade and spread the rest over the pastry rounds, keeping the paste inside the marked rim. Cut half the tomatoes in half. Pile all the tomatoes, whole and halved, on the pastry, again keeping them inside the rim. Season lightly with salt and freshly ground black pepper.

4 Bake for 20 minutes, until the pastry is well risen and golden. Dot with the remaining tapenade. Spoon the mascarpone on the centre of the tomatoes and season with black pepper. Bake for a further 10 minutes, until the mascarpone has melted to make a sauce. Serve the tarts warm.

Mushroom Polenta

This simple recipe uses freshly made polenta, but for an even easier version you can substitute ready-made polenta and slice it straight into the dish, ready for baking. The cheesy mushroom topping is also delicious on toasted herb or sun-dried tomato bread as a light lunch or supper. To add variety, you can replace some of the mushrooms with a mixture of different wild ones.

SERVES 4

INGREDIENTS
250g/9oz/1½ cups quick-cook polenta
50g/2oz/¼ cup butter
400g/14oz chestnut mushrooms, sliced
175g/6oz/1½ cups grated Gruyère cheese

1 Line a 28 × 18cm/11 × 7in shallow baking tin (pan) with baking parchment. Bring 1 litre/1¾pints/4 cups water with 5ml/1 tsp salt to the boil in a large pan. Add the polenta in a steady stream, stirring constantly. Bring back to the boil, stirring, and cook for 5 minutes, until thick and smooth. Turn the polenta into the prepared tin and spread it out into an even layer. Leave to cool.

2 Preheat the oven to 200°C/400°F/Gas 6. Melt the butter in a frying pan and cook the mushrooms for 3–5 minutes, until golden. Season with salt and lots of freshly ground black pepper.

3 Turn out the polenta on to a chopping board. Peel away the parchment and cut the polenta into large squares. Pile the squares into a shallow, ovenproof dish. Sprinkle with half the cheese, then pile the mushrooms on top and pour over their buttery juices. Sprinkle with the remaining cheese and bake for about 20 minutes, until the cheese is melting and pale golden.

Mushroom Stroganoff

This creamy mixed mushroom sauce is ideal for a dinner party. Serve it with toasted buckwheat, brown rice or a mixture of wild rices and garnish with chopped chives. For best results, choose a variety of different mushrooms – wild mushrooms such as chanterelles, ceps and morels add a delicious flavour and texture to the stroganoff, as well as adding colour and producing a decorative appearance.

Serves 4

INGREDIENTS
25g/1oz/2 tbsp butter
900g/2lb mixed mushrooms, cut into bitesize pieces, including ⅔ button (white)
   mushrooms and ⅓ assorted wild or unusual mushrooms
350ml/12fl oz/1½ cups white wine sauce
250ml/8fl oz/1 cup sour cream

1 Melt the butter in a large frying pan and quickly cook the mushrooms, in batches, over a high heat, until brown. Transfer the cooked mushrooms to a bowl.

2 Add the sauce to the juices remaining in the pan and bring to the boil, stirring. Reduce the heat and replace the mushrooms with any juices from the bowl. Stir well and heat for a few seconds, then remove from the heat.

3 Stir the sour cream into the cooked mushroom mixture and season to taste with salt and lots of freshly ground black pepper. Heat through gently for a few seconds, then transfer to warm plates and serve immediately.

Spicy Chickpea Samosas

A blend of crushed chickpeas and spices makes an interesting alternative to the more familiar meat or vegetable fillings in these little pastries. These samosas look pretty garnished with fresh coriander leaves and finely sliced onion and are delicious served with a simple dip made from yogurt and chopped fresh mint leaves. They make a tasty addition to a vegetarian buffet.

MAKES 18

INGREDIENTS
2 × 400g/14oz cans chickpeas, drained and rinsed
120ml/4fl oz/½ cup hara masala or curry paste
275g/10oz filo pastry
60ml/4 tbsp chilli and garlic oil

1 Preheat the oven to 220°C/425°F/Gas 7. Process half the chickpeas to a paste in a food processor. Spoon the paste into a bowl and add the whole chickpeas, the hara masala or coriander sauce. Mix until well combined.

2 Lay a sheet of filo pastry on a work surface and cut into three strips. Brush the strips with a little of the oil. Place a dessertspoon of the filling at one end of a strip. Turn one corner diagonally over the filling to meet the long edge. Continue folding the filling and the pastry along the length of the strip, keeping the triangular shape. Transfer to a baking sheet and repeat with the remaining filling and pastry.

3 Brush the pastries with any remaining oil and bake for 15 minutes, until the pastry is golden. Cool slightly before serving.

COOK'S TIP
Hara masala is available bottled in Asian stores. You can make your own by pounding together fresh coriander (cilantro) and mint leaves, garlic, chillies, fresh root ginger, garam masala and a little yogurt to form a paste. Adjust the quantities to taste.

Tofu & Pepper Kebabs

A simple coating of ground, dry-roasted peanuts pressed on to cubed tofu provides plenty of additional flavour along with the peppers. Use metal or bamboo skewers for the kebabs – if you use bamboo, then soak them in cold water for 30 minutes before using to prevent them from scorching during cooking. The kebabs can also be cooked on a barbecue, if you prefer.

SERVES 4

INGREDIENTS
250g/9oz firm tofu
50g/2oz/½ cup dry-roasted peanuts
2 red and 2 green (bell) peppers
60ml/4 tbsp sweet chilli dipping sauce

1 Pat the tofu dry on kitchen paper and then cut it into small cubes. Grind the peanuts in a blender or food processor and transfer to a plate. Turn the tofu cubes in the ground nuts to coat.

2 Preheat the grill (broiler) to medium. Halve and seed the peppers, and cut them into large chunks. Thread the chunks of pepper on to four large skewers with the tofu cubes and place on a foil-lined grill rack.

3 Grill (broil) the kebabs, turning frequently, for 10–12 minutes, or until the peppers and peanuts are beginning to brown. Transfer the kebabs to plates and serve with the dipping sauce.

Mixed Bean & Tomato Chilli

Here, mixed beans, fiery red chilli and plenty of freshly chopped coriander are simmered in a tomato sauce to make a delicious vegetarian chilli. Always a popular dish, chilli can be served with a variety of accompaniments – choose from baked potatoes, boiled rice, crusty bread or tortillas. Garnish with slices of tomato, chopped celery or red onion and top with yogurt.

Serves 4

Ingredients
400g/14oz jar tomato and herb sauce
2 × 400g/14oz cans mixed beans, drained and rinsed
1 fresh red chilli
large handful of fresh coriander (cilantro)

1 Pour the tomato sauce and mixed beans into a pan. Seed and thinly slice the chilli, then add it to the pan. Reserve a little of the coriander, chop the remainder and add it to the pan.

2 Bring the mixture to the boil, reduce the heat, cover and simmer gently for 10 minutes. Stir the mixture occasionally and add a dash of water if the sauce starts to dry out.

3 Ladle the chilli into warmed individual serving bowls and top with the reserved coriander. Serve immediately.

LENTILS WITH FETA CHEESE

The combination of lentils, tomatoes and cheese is widely used in Mediterranean cooking. The tang of feta cheese complements the slightly earthy flavour of the attractive dark lentils. True Puy lentils come from the region of France, Le Puy, which has a unique climate and volcanic soil in which they thrive. They are considered to be far superior in taste and texture to other varieties of lentils.

SERVES 4

INGREDIENTS
250g/9oz/1½ cups Puy lentils
200g/7oz feta cheese
75ml/5 tbsp sun-dried tomato purée (paste)
small handful of fresh chervil or flat leaf parsley, chopped, plus extra to garnish

1 Place the lentils in a heavy pan with 600ml/1 pint/2½ cups water. Bring to the boil, reduce the heat and cover the pan. Simmer gently for about 20 minutes, until the lentils are just tender and most of the water has been absorbed.

2 Crumble half the feta cheese into the pan. Add the sun-dried tomato purée, chopped chervil or flat leaf parsley and a little salt and freshly ground black pepper. Heat through for 1 minute.

3 Transfer the lentil mixture and juices to warmed plates or bowls. Crumble the remaining feta cheese on top and sprinkle with the fresh herbs to garnish. Serve the lentils immediately.

Roasted Pepper & Hummus Wrap

At lunchtime stuffed wraps make a tasty change from sandwiches. They also have the bonus that they can be made a few hours in advance without going soggy in the way that bread sandwiches often can. You can introduce all kinds of variation to this basic combination. Try using chopped red onion, raw or fried, in place of the red pepper, or guacamole in place of the hummus.

Serves 2

Ingredients
1 large red (bell) pepper, halved and seeded
15ml/1 tbsp olive oil
4 tbsp hummus
2 soft flour tortillas

1 Preheat the grill (broiler) to high. Brush the pepper halves with the oil and place cut side down on a baking sheet. Grill for 5 minutes, until charred. Put the pepper halves in a sealed plastic bag and leave to cool.

2 When cooled, remove the peppers from the bag. Carefully peel away and discard the charred skin. Thinly slice the flesh using a sharp knife.

3 Spread the hummus over the tortillas in a thin, even layer and top with the roasted pepper slices. Season with salt, if necessary and plenty of ground black pepper, then roll them up and cut in half to serve.

Variation
As well as plain flour tortillas, some large supermarkets also sell flavoured tortillas.

Baked Sweet Potatoes with Leeks & Gorgonzola

Sweet potatoes have a distinctive sugary and spicy flavour, which makes them an excellent addition to vegetarian recipes. This dish tastes wonderful and looks stunning if you buy the beautiful orange-fleshed sweet potatoes, which have a higher nutritional content because they are richer in the anti oxidant betacarotene. The Gorgonzola cheese topping adds a sharp, distinctive flavour.

SERVES 4

INGREDIENTS
4 large sweet potatoes, scrubbed
30ml/2 tbsp olive oil
2 large leeks, washed and sliced
115g/4oz Gorgonzola cheese, sliced

1 Preheat the oven to 190°C/375°F/Gas 5. Dry the sweet potatoes with kitchen paper and rub them all over with 15ml/1 tbsp of the oil. Place them on a baking sheet and sprinkle with salt. Bake for 1 hour, or until tender.

2 Meanwhile, heat the remaining oil in a frying pan and add the sliced leeks. Cook for 3–4 minutes, or until softened and just beginning to turn golden.

3 Cut the sweet potatoes in half lengthways and place them cut side up on the baking sheet. Top with the cooked leeks and season.

4 Lay the cheese slices on top and grill (broil) under a high heat for 2–3 minutes, until the cheese is bubbling. Serve immediately.

POTATO & ONION TORTILLA

This deep-set omelette with sliced potatoes and onions is the best-known Spanish tortilla and makes a deliciously simple lunch or supper dish when served with a leafy green salad and crusty bread. Tortillas are often made with a variety of ingredients – olives, chopped tomatoes, cooked peas, corn kernels, or grated Cheddar or Gruyère cheese can all be added to the mixture in step 2, if you like.

SERVES 4–6

INGREDIENTS
800g/1¾lb medium potatoes
100ml/3½fl oz/scant ½ cup extra virgin olive oil
2 onions, thinly sliced
6 eggs

1 Thinly slice the potatoes. Heat 75ml/5 tbsp of the oil in a frying pan and cook the potatoes, turning frequently, for 10 minutes. Add the onions and seasoning, and continue to cook gently for a further 10 minutes, until the vegetables are tender.

2 Meanwhile, break the eggs into a large bowl, add a little salt and ground black pepper, and beat well. Add the potatoes and onions to the beaten eggs and mix gently. Leave to stand for 10 minutes.

3 Wipe out the pan with kitchen paper and heat the remaining oil in it. Pour the egg mixture into the pan and spread it out in an even layer. Cover and cook over a gentle heat for 20 minutes, until the eggs are just set. Serve cut into wedges.

BAKED LEEK & POTATO GRATIN

Potatoes baked in a delicious creamy cheese sauce make the ultimate comfort dish, whether they are served as an accompaniment to pork or fish dishes or, as in this recipe, with plenty of leeks and melted cheese as a main course. When preparing leeks, separate the leaves and rinse them thoroughly under cold running water, as soil and grit often get caught between the layers.

SERVES 4–6

INGREDIENTS
900g/2lb medium potatoes, thinly sliced
2 large leeks, trimmed
200g/7oz ripe Brie or Camembert cheese, sliced
450ml/³⁄₄ pint/scant 2 cups single (light) cream

1 Preheat the oven to 180°C/350°F/Gas 4. Cook the potatoes in plenty of lightly salted, boiling water for 3 minutes, until slightly softened, then drain. Cut the leeks into 1cm/½in lengths and blanch them in boiling water for 1 minute, until softened, then drain.

2 Turn half the potatoes into a shallow, ovenproof dish and spread them out to the edge. Cover with two-thirds of the leeks, then add the remaining potatoes. Tuck the slices of cheese and the remaining leeks in among the top layer of potato slices. Season with salt and pepper and pour the cream over.

3 Bake for 1 hour, until tender and golden. Cover with foil if the top starts to overbrown before the potatoes are tender.

PASTA & RICE

Pasta and rice are the perfect staples on which to base simple, tasty meals. You need only a few ingredients to rustle up delicious dishes, from a simple midweek supper of Fettucine all'Alfredo or Spaghettini with Roasted Garlic to more elegant dishes for entertaining, such as Pasta with Roast Tomatoes & Goat's Cheese. Whether you choose a substantial bowl of pasta or a fragrant seafood risotto – the recipes in this chapter are sure to delight.

Fettucine all'Alfredo

This simple but delicious recipe was invented by a Roman restaurateur called Alfredo, who became famous for serving it with a gold fork and spoon. Today's busy cooks will find cartons of long-life cream invaluable for this type of recipe. If you can't get fettucine, any long ribbon-like pasta can be used in this dish – try tagliatelle or slightly wider pappardelle instead.

Serves 4

Ingredients
50g/2oz/¼ cup butter
200ml/7fl oz/scant 1 cup double (heavy) cream
50g/2oz/⅔ cup freshly grated Parmesan cheese, plus extra to serve
350g/12oz fresh fettucine

1 Melt the butter in a large pan. Add the cream and bring it to the boil. Simmer for 5 minutes, stirring constantly, then add the Parmesan cheese, with salt and freshly ground black pepper to taste, and remove from the heat.

2 Bring a large pan of salted water to the boil. Add the pasta and quickly bring the water back to the boil, stirring occasionally. Cook the pasta for 2–3 minutes, or according to the instructions on the packet, until al dente. Drain well.

3 Place the pan of cream on a low heat, add the cooked pasta and toss until it is thoroughly coated in the sauce. Taste the sauce for seasoning and add more if necessary. Serve immediately, with extra grated Parmesan handed around separately.

TAGLIATELLE WITH VEGETABLES

Narrow strips of courgette and carrot mingle well with tagliatelle to resemble coloured pasta. Serve as a side dish, or sprinkle with freshly grated Parmesan cheese for a light appetizer or vegetarian main course. You can use a different flavoured oil if you prefer – oils infused with herbs such as rosemary or basil are also widely available and are a quick way of adding flavour to pasta.

SERVES 4

INGREDIENTS
2 large courgettes (zucchini)
2 large carrots
250g/9oz fresh egg tagliatelle
60ml/4 tbsp garlic or chilli-flavoured oil

COOK'S TIP
To make chilli oil, put about 20 seeded and chopped dried chillies in a heatproof container. Heat 250ml/ 8fl oz/1 cup groundnut (peanut) or corn oil in a small pan until the oil just reaches smoking point. Leave the oil to cool for 5 minutes, then pour over the chillies and leave for 1–2 hours. Strain into a clean bottle and store in the refrigerator.

---

1 With a vegetable peeler, cut the courgettes and carrots into long thin ribbons. Bring a pan of salted water to the boil and add the vegetable ribbons. Bring the water back to the boil and boil for 30 seconds. Drain and set aside.

2 Cook the tagliatelle in a large pan of salted water, according to the instructions on the packet. Drain the pasta and return it to the pan. Add the vegetable ribbons, oil and seasoning and toss over a medium to high heat until the pasta and vegetables are glistening with oil. Serve the pasta immediately.

Linguine with Courgettes & Mint

Sweet, mild courgettes and refreshing mint are a great combination and are delicious with pasta. Dried linguine has been used here but you can use any type of pasta you like. Couscous also works well in place of pasta if you prefer.

Serves 4

Ingredients
450g/1lb dried linguine
75ml/5 tbsp garlic-infused olive oil
4 small courgettes (zucchini), sliced
1 small bunch of fresh mint, roughly chopped

1 Cook the linguine in plenty of salted, boiling water according to the instructions on the packet.

2 Meanwhile, heat 45ml/3 tbsp of the oil in a large frying pan and add the courgettes. Fry for 2–3 minutes, stirring occasionally, until tender and golden.

3 Drain the pasta well and toss with the courgettes and chopped mint. Season with salt and pepper, drizzle over the remaining oil and serve immediately.

Pasta with Roast Tomatoes & Goat's Cheese

Roasting tomatoes brings out their flavour and sweetness, which contrasts perfectly with the sharp taste and creamy texture of goat's cheese. This elegant dish is ideal for entertaining. Serve it with a crisp green salad flavoured with herbs.

SERVES 4

INGREDIENTS

8 large ripe tomatoes
60ml/4 tbsp garlic-infused olive oil
450g/1lb any dried pasta shapes
200g/7oz firm goat's cheese, crumbled

COOK'S TIP
Any tomatoes can be roasted, but plum tomatoes have a particularly rich flavour when cooked. Tomatoes sold on the vine also have a good flavour.

1 Preheat the oven to 190°C/375°F/Gas 5. Place the tomatoes in a roasting pan and drizzle over 30ml/2 tbsp of the oil. Season well with salt and pepper and roast for 20–25 minutes, or until soft and slightly charred.

2 Meanwhile, cook the pasta in plenty of salted, boiling water, according to the instructions on the packet. Drain well and return to the pan.

3 Roughly mash the tomatoes with a fork, and stir the contents of the roasting pan into the pasta. Gently stir in the goat's cheese and the remaining oil and serve.

Warm Pasta with Crushed Tomatoes & Basil

It doesn't matter which type of pasta you use for this recipe – any kind you have in the storecupboard will work well. This is an excellent dish to prepare ahead of time – all you have to do before sitting down to eat is cook the pasta.

SERVES 4

INGREDIENTS
6 small ripe tomatoes, halved
45ml/3 tbsp extra virgin olive oil
a small handful of fresh basil leaves
450g/1lb dried pasta shapes

1 Put the halved tomatoes in a bowl and, using your hands, gently squash them until the juices start to run freely. Stir in the olive oil and tear in the basil leaves.

2 Season the tomatoes with salt and ground black pepper and mix well to combine. Cover the bowl with clear film (plastic wrap) and chill for 2–3 hours, to allow the flavours to develop.

3 Remove the tomato and basil mixture from the refrigerator and allow it to return to room temperature.

4 Meanwhile, cook the pasta according to the instructions on the packet. Drain well, toss with the crushed tomato and basil mixture and serve immediately.

COOK'S TIP
Basil leaves bruise easily, so are best torn or used whole, rather than cut with a knife. The herb is usually used raw, as cooking destroys the flavour.

SPAGHETTINI WITH ROASTED GARLIC

If you have never tried roasting garlic, then this is the recipe that will convert you to its delicious mellowed sweetness. Spaghettini is very fine spaghetti, but any long thin pasta can be used in this dish – try spaghetti, linguine, tagliatelle or capellini.

SERVES 4

INGREDIENTS
1 whole head of garlic
120ml/4fl oz/½ cup extra virgin olive oil
400g/14oz fresh or dried spaghettini
coarsely shaved Parmesan cheese

1 Preheat the oven to 180°C/350°F/Gas 4. Place the unpeeled garlic in an oiled roasting pan and roast it for 30 minutes.

2 Leave the garlic to cool, then lay it on its side and slice off the top one-third with a sharp knife.

3 Hold the garlic over a bowl and dig out the flesh from each clove with the point of the knife. When all the flesh has been added to the bowl, pour in the oil and add plenty of black pepper. Mix well.

4 Cook the pasta in a pan of salted boiling water according to the instructions on the packet. Drain the pasta and return it to the clean pan. Pour in the oil and garlic mixture and toss the pasta vigorously over a medium heat until all the strands are thoroughly coated. Serve immediately, with shavings of Parmesan.

Spaghetti with Raw Tomato Sauce & Ricotta

This wonderfully simple uncooked sauce goes well with many different kinds of pasta, both long strands such as spaghetti, tagliatelle or linguini, and short shapes such as macaroni, rigatoni or penne. It is always at its best in summer.

SERVES 4

INGREDIENTS
500g/1¼lb ripe Italian plum tomatoes
75ml/5 tbsp garlic-flavoured olive oil
350g/12oz dried spaghetti or pasta of your choice
115g/4oz ricotta salata cheese, diced

1 Coarsely chop the plum tomatoes, removing the cores and as many of the seeds as you can.

2 Put the tomatoes and oil in a bowl, adding salt and freshly ground black pepper to taste, and stir well. Cover and leave at room temperature for 1–2 hours to allow the flavours to mingle.

3 Cook the spaghetti or your chosen pasta in plenty of salted boiling water according to the packet instructions, then drain well.

4 Taste the sauce to check the seasoning before tossing it with the hot pasta. Sprinkle with the cheese and serve immediately.

Linguine with Rocket and Parmesan

This fashionable first course is very quick and easy to make at home. Rocket has an excellent peppery flavour which combines beautifully with the rich, creamy tang of fresh Parmesan cheese. Fresh Parmesan keeps in the refrigerator for up to a month.

SERVES 4

INGREDIENTS
350g/12oz fresh or dried linguine
120ml/4fl oz/½ cup extra virgin olive oil
1 large bunch rocket (arugula), about 150g/5oz, stalks removed, shredded or torn
75g/3oz/1 cup freshly grated Parmesan cheese

1 Cook the pasta in a large pan of lightly salted boiling water according to the instructions on the packet, then drain thoroughly.

2 Heat about 60ml/4 tbsp of the olive oil in the pasta pan, then add the drained pasta, followed by the rocket. Toss over a medium to high heat for 1–2 minutes, or until the rocket is just wilted, then remove the pan from the heat.

3 Transfer the cooked pasta and rocket to a large, warmed serving bowl. Add half the freshly grated Parmesan and the remaining olive oil. Add a little salt and freshly ground black pepper to taste.

4 Toss the mixture quickly to mix. Serve immediately, sprinkled with the remaining Parmesan cheese.

FARFALLE WITH TUNA

Bought tomato sauce and canned tuna are endlessly versatile for making weekday suppers. You can add some fresh herbs to the sauce if you like – basil, marjoram or oregano all go beautifully with tomatoes. Use fresh herbs rather than dried, as the short cooking time does not allow the flavour of dried herbs to develop fully.

SERVES 4

INGREDIENTS
400g/14oz/3½ cups dried farfalle
600ml/1 pint/2½ cups tomato sauce
8–10 pitted black olives, cut into rings
175g/6oz can tuna in olive oil

1 Cook the pasta in a large pan of lightly salted boiling water according to the instructions on the packet. Meanwhile, heat the tomato sauce in a separate pan and add the olives.

2 Drain the canned tuna and flake it with a fork. Add the tuna to the sauce with about 60ml/4 tbsp of the hot water used for cooking the pasta. Taste and adjust the seasoning if necessary.

3 Drain the pasta thoroughly and place it in a large, warmed serving bowl. Pour the tuna sauce over the top and toss lightly to mix. Serve immediately.

HOME-MADE POTATO GNOCCHI

*These classic Italian potato dumplings are very simple to make – it just requires a
little patience when it comes to shaping them. Serve them as soon as they are cooked,
tossed in melted butter and fresh sage leaves, sprinkled with grated Parmesan cheese
and plenty of black pepper. They make a fabulous alternative to pasta.*

SERVES 2

INGREDIENTS
900g/2lb floury potatoes, cut into large chunks
2 eggs, beaten
150–175g/5–6oz/1¼–1½ cups plain (all-purpose) flour

1 Cook the potatoes in salted, boiling water for 15 minutes, until tender.
Drain well and return to the pan, set it over a low heat and dry the
potatoes for 1–2 minutes, stirring so that they don't burn or stick.

2 Mash the potatoes until smooth, then gradually stir in the eggs and salt.
Work in enough flour to form a soft dough.

3 Break off small pieces of the dough and roll into balls, using floured
hands. Press the back of a fork into each ball to make indentations.
Repeat until all the dough has been used. Leave the gnocchi to rest for
15–20 minutes before cooking.

4 Bring a large pan of water to a gentle boil. Add the gnocchi, about ten at
a time, and cook for 3–4 minutes, or until they float to the surface. Drain
thoroughly and serve as soon as all the gnocchi have been cooked.

Rosemary Risotto with Borlotti Beans

Select a high-quality risotto in a subtle flavour as the base for this recipe. The savoury beans, heady rosemary and creamy mascarpone will transform a simple product into a feast. For an even more authentic risotto flavour, replace half the water with dry white wine. Serve with a simple salad of mixed leaves and Parmesan shavings dressed with balsamic vinegar and plenty of freshly ground black pepper.

Serves 3–4

INGREDIENTS
400g/14oz can borlotti beans
275g/10oz packet vegetable or chicken risotto
60ml/4 tbsp mascarpone cheese
5ml/1 tsp finely chopped fresh rosemary

1 Drain the beans, rinse thoroughly under cold water and drain again. Process about two-thirds of the beans to a fairly coarse purée in a food processor or blender. Set the remaining beans aside.

2 Make up the risotto according to the packet instructions, using the suggested quantity of water.

3 Immediately the rice is cooked, stir in the bean purée. Add the reserved beans, with the mascarpone and rosemary, then season to taste with salt, if necessary, and freshly ground black pepper. Stir thoroughly, then cover and leave to stand for about 5 minutes so that the risotto absorbs the flavours fully.

VARIATION
Fresh thyme or marjoram could be used for this risotto instead of rosemary, if you like. One of the great virtues of risotto is that it lends itself well to many variations. Experiment with plain or saffron risotto and add different herbs to make your own speciality dish.

Pancetta & Broad Bean Risotto

This moist risotto makes a satisfying, balanced meal, especially when served with cooked fresh seasonal vegetables or a mixed green salad. The broad beans add an interesting texture and flavour. Add some chopped fresh herbs and Parmesan shavings as a garnish, if you like. You can also add bay leaves or sprigs of otegano or thyme when cooking the rice – remove and discard them before serving, if you like.

SERVES 4

INGREDIENTS
175g/6oz smoked pancetta or streaky (fatty) bacon, diced
350g/12oz/1¾ cups risotto rice
1.5 litres/2½ pints/6¼ cups simmering vegetable stock
225g/8oz/2 cups frozen baby broad (fava) beans

1 Place the pancetta or bacon in a non-stick or heavy pan and cook gently, stirring occasionally, for about 5 minutes, until the fat runs.

2 Add the risotto rice to the pan and cook for 1 minute, stirring constantly. Add a ladleful of the simmering stock and cook, stirring constantly, until the liquid has been absorbed.

3 Continue adding ladles of the simmering stock until the rice is tender and almost all the liquid has been absorbed. This will take 30–35 minutes.

4 Meanwhile, cook the broad beans in a pan of lightly salted, boiling water for about 3 minutes until tender. Drain well and stir into the risotto. Season to taste with salt and ground black pepper. Spoon into a bowl and serve immediately.

COOK'S TIP
If the broad beans are large, or if you prefer skinned beans, remove the outer skin after cooking them.

MUSSEL RISOTTO

The addition of freshly cooked mussels, aromatic coriander and a little cream to a packet of instant risotto can turn a simple meal into a decadent treat. Serve with a side salad for a splendid supper. Other types of cooked shellfish, such as clams or prawns (shrimp), can be used instead of mussels.

SERVES 3–4

INGREDIENTS
900g/2lb fresh mussels
275g/10oz packet risotto
30ml/2 tbsp chopped fresh coriander (cilantro)
30ml/2 tbsp double (heavy) cream

1 Scrub the mussels, discarding any that do not close when sharply tapped. Place in a large pan. Add 120ml/4fl oz/½ cup water and seasoning, then bring to the boil. Cover the pan and cook the mussels, shaking the pan occasionally, for 4–5 minutes, until they have opened. Drain, reserving the liquid and discarding any that have not opened. Shell most of the mussels, reserving a few in their shells for garnish. Strain the mussel liquid.

2 Make up the packet risotto according to the instructions, using the cooking liquid from the mussels and making it up to the required volume with water.

3 When the risotto is about three-quarters cooked, add the mussels to the pan. Add the coriander and re-cover the pan without stirring in these ingredients.

4 Remove the risotto from the heat, stir in the cream, cover and leave to rest for a few minutes. Spoon into a warmed serving dish, garnish with the reserved mussels in their shells, and serve.

COOK'S TIP
For speed, use cooked mussels in their shells. Reheat them according to the packet instructions and add to the made risotto with the coriander and cream.

CRAB RISOTTO

This simple risotto has a subtle flavour that makes the most of delicate crab. It makes a tempting main course for 3–4 people, or an appetizer for a dinner party. It is important to use a good quality risotto rice, which will give a deliciously creamy result, but the cooked grains are still firm to the bite.

SERVES 3–4

INGREDIENTS
2 large cooked crabs
275g/10oz/1½ cups risotto rice
1.2 litres/2 pints/5 cups simmering fish stock
30ml/2 tbsp mixed finely chopped fresh herbs such as chives, tarragon and parsley

1 One at a time, hold the crabs firmly and hit the underside with the heel of your hand. This should loosen the shell from the body. Using your thumbs, push against the body and pull away from the shell. Remove and discard the intestines and the grey gills.

2 Break off the claws and legs, then use a hammer or crackers to break them open. Using a skewer, pick out the meat and place on a plate.

3 Using a skewer, pick out the white meat from the body cavities and place with the claw and leg meat, reserving a little white meat to garnish. Scoop out the brown meat from the shell and add to the rest of the crab meat.

4 Place the rice in a pan and add one-quarter of the stock. Bring to the boil and cook, stirring, until the liquid has been absorbed. Adding a ladleful of stock at a time, cook, stirring, until about two-thirds of the stock has been absorbed. Stir in the crab meat and herbs, and continue cooking, adding the remaining stock.

5 When the rice is almost cooked but still has some bite, remove it from the heat and adjust the seasoning. Cover and leave to stand for 3 minutes. Serve garnished with the reserved white crab meat.

SALADS

Whether served as a main course or as an accompaniment, salads are always refreshing and welcome. The most successful are composed of only a few ingredients – cooked or raw – whose colours, textures and flavours complement and balance each other perfectly. Try Halloumi & Grape Salad with Fresh Herbs, or Tomato, Bean and Fried Basil Salad, with crusty bread for a light lunch. Potato & Olive Salad or Asparagus, Bacon & Leaf Salad are ideal as an accompaniment to a main course.

Beetroot with Fresh Mint

This simple and decorative beetroot salad flavoured with fresh mint can be served as part of a selection of salads, as an appetizer, or as an accompaniment to grilled or roasted pork or lamb. Balsamic vinegar is a rich, dark vinegar with a mellow, deep flavour. It can be used to dress a variety of salad ingredients and is particularly good drizzled over a tomato and basil salad.

Serves 4

INGREDIENTS
4 cooked beetroot (beet)
15–30ml/1–2 tbsp balsamic vinegar
30ml/2 tbsp olive oil
1 bunch fresh mint, leaves stripped and thinly shredded

1 Slice the beetroot or cut into even-size dice with a sharp knife. Put the beetroot in a bowl. Add the balsamic vinegar, olive oil and a pinch of salt and toss together to combine.

2 Add half the thinly shredded fresh mint to the salad and toss lightly until thoroughly combined. Place the salad in the refrigerator and chill for about 1 hour. Serve garnished with the remaining thinly shredded mint leaves.

SOUR CUCUMBER WITH DILL

This recipe is half pickle, half salad, and totally delicious served with pumpernickel or other coarse, dark, full-flavoured bread, as a light meal or an appetizer. Choose smooth-skinned, smallish cucumbers for this recipe as larger ones tend to be less tender, with tough skins and bitter indigestible seeds. If you can only buy a large cucumber, peel off the skin before slicing it.

SERVES 4

INGREDIENTS
2 small cucumbers, thinly sliced
3 onions, thinly sliced
75–90ml/5–6 tbsp cider vinegar
30–45ml/2–3 tbsp chopped fresh dill

1 In a large mixing bowl, combine together the thinly sliced cucumbers and onions. Season the vegetables with salt and toss together until they are thoroughly combined. Leave the mixture to stand in a cool place for 5–10 minutes.

2 Add the cider vinegar, 30–45ml/2–3 tbsp water and the chopped fresh dill to the cucumber and onion mixture. Toss all the ingredients together until well combined, then chill in the refrigerator for a few hours, or until ready to serve.

VARIATION
If you prefer a sweet and sour mixture, add 45ml/ 3 tbsp caster (superfine) sugar along with the cider vinegar in step 2.

GLOBE ARTICHOKES WITH GREEN BEANS & GARLIC DRESSING

Piquant garlic dressing or creamy aioli go perfectly with these lightly cooked vegetables. Serve lemon wedges with the artichokes so that their juice may be squeezed over to taste. Artichokes should feel heavy for their size – make sure that the inner leaves are wrapped tightly round the choke and the heart inside.

SERVES 6

INGREDIENTS
225g/8oz green beans
3 small globe artichokes
15ml/1 tbsp lemon-flavoured olive oil
250ml/8fl oz/1 cup garlic dressing or aioli

1 Cook the green beans in boiling water for 1–2 minutes, until they are slightly softened. Drain well and set aside.

2 Trim the artichoke stalks close to the base. Bring a large pan of lightly salted water to the boil and cook the artichokes for about 30 minutes, or until you can easily pull away a leaf from the base. Drain well.

3 Using a sharp knife, halve the artichokes lengthways and carefully ease out their chokes using a teaspoon.

4 Arrange the artichokes and beans on serving plates and drizzle with the lemon-flavoured olive oil. Season with coarse salt and a little ground black pepper. Spoon the garlic dressing or aioli into the hearts and serve warm.

5 To eat the artichokes, pull the leaves from the base one at a time and use to scoop a little of the garlic dressing or aioli. It is only the fleshy end of each leaf that is eaten as well as the base, bottom or "fond".

Halloumi & Grape Salad with Fresh Herbs

Firm and salty halloumi cheese is a great standby ingredient for turning a simple salad into a special dish. In this recipe it is tossed with sweet, juicy grapes, which complement its flavour and texture. Fresh young thyme leaves and dill taste especially good mixed with the salad. Serve with a crusty walnut or sun-dried tomato bread.

SERVES 4

INGREDIENTS
150g/5oz mixed salad leaves and tender fresh herb sprigs
175g/6oz mixed seedless green and black grapes
250g/9oz halloumi cheese
75ml/5 tbsp oil and lemon juice or vinegar dressing

1 Toss together the salad leaves and fresh herb sprigs and the green and black grapes, then transfer to a large serving plate.

2 Thinly slice the halloumi cheese. Heat a large non-stick frying pan. Add the sliced halloumi cheese and cook briefly until it just starts to turn golden brown on the underside. Turn the cheese with a fish slice or metal spatula and cook the other side until it is golden brown.

3 Arrange the fried cheese over the salad on the plate. Pour over the oil and lemon juice or vinegar dressing and serve while the cheese is still hot.

Butter Bean, Tomato & Red Onion Salad

Serve this attractive salad with toasted pitta bread for a fresh summer lunch, or as an accompaniment to meat cooked on a barbecue. The red onion and tomatoes make a colourful contrast to the butter beans.

SERVES 4

INGREDIENTS

2 × 400g/14oz cans butter (lima) beans, rinsed and drained
4 plum tomatoes, roughly chopped
1 red onion, finely sliced
45ml/3 tbsp herb-infused olive oil

1 Mix together the beans, tomatoes and onion in a large bowl. Season with salt and freshly ground black pepper, and stir in the herb-infused olive oil.

2 Cover the bowl with clear film (plastic wrap) and chill in the refrigerator for 20 minutes before serving.

VARIATIONS

- *To make a tasty tuna salad, drain a 200g/7oz can tuna, flake the flesh and stir into the bean salad.*
- *For extra flavour and colour, stir in a handful of pitted black olives and a handful of chopped fresh parsley or coriander (cilantro).*
- *To make a wholesome version of the Italian salad Panzanella, tear half a loaf of ciabatta into bite-size pieces and stir into the salad. Leave to stand for 20 minutes before serving.*

Tomato, Bean & Fried Basil Salad

Infusing basil in hot oil brings out its wonderful, aromatic flavour, which works so well in almost any tomato dish. Any canned beans or chickpeas can be used iin this simple dish, as they all taste good and make a wholesome salad for a light lunch.

SERVES 4

INGREDIENTS
15g/½oz/½ cup fresh basil leaves
75ml/5 tbsp extra virgin olive oil
300g/11oz cherry tomatoes, halved
400g/14oz can mixed beans, drained and rinsed

1 Reserve one-third of the basil leaves for garnish, then tear the remainder into pieces. Pour the olive oil into a small pan. Add the torn basil and heat gently for 1 minute, until the basil sizzles and begins to colour.

2 Place the halved cherry tomatoes and beans in a bowl. Pour in the basil oil and add a little salt, if needed, and plenty of freshly ground black pepper. Toss the ingredients together gently, cover and leave to marinate at room temperature for at least 30 minutes. Serve the salad sprinkled with the remaining basil leaves.

Pink Grapefruit & Avocado Salad

Smooth, creamy avocado and zesty citrus fruit are perfect partners in this refreshing salad. Avocados turn brown quickly when exposed to the air: the acidic grapefruit juice will prevent this, so combine the ingredients as quickly as possible.

SERVES 4

INGREDIENTS
2 pink grapefruit
2 ripe avocados
30ml/2 tbsp chilli oil
90g/3½oz rocket (arugula)

1 Slice the top and bottom off a grapefruit, then cut off all the peel and pith from around the side. Working over a small bowl to catch the juices, cut out the segments from between the membranes and place them in a separate bowl. Squeeze any juices remaining in the membranes into the bowl, then discard them. Repeat with the remaining grapefruit.

2 Halve, stone (pit), peel and slice the avocados. Add the flesh to the grapefruit segments. Whisk a little salt and then the chilli oil into the grapefruit juice.

3 Pile the rocket leaves on to four serving plates, top with the grapefruit segments and avocado, and pour over the dressing. Alternatively, toss the rocket with the grapefruit, avocado and dressing, then divide the salad among plates or bowls.

Spicy Moroccan Carrot Salad with Coriander

In this salad from North Africa, the carrots are lightly cooked before being tossed in a cumin and coriander vinaigrette. Cumin has a strong and spicy aroma and a warm pungent flavour that goes particularly well with root vegetables.

Serves 4–6

Ingredients
3–4 carrots, thinly sliced
1.5ml/¼ tsp ground cumin, or to taste
60ml/4 tbsp garlic-flavoured oil and vinegar dressing
30ml/2 tbsp chopped fresh coriander (cilantro) leaves or a mixture of
  coriander and parsley

1 Cook the thinly sliced carrots by either steaming or boiling in lightly salted water until they are just tender but not soft. Drain the carrots, leave for a few minutes to dry and cool, then put into a mixing bowl.

2 Stir in the cumin, garlic dressing and herbs. Season to taste and chill well before serving. Check the seasoning just before serving and add more ground cumin, salt or black pepper, if required.

Raw Turnip Salad in Sour Cream

Usually served cooked, raw young tender turnips have a tangy, slightly peppery flavour. Serve this as an accompaniment for grilled poultry or meat, or as a light appetizer, garnished with parsley and paprika, and served with warmed pitta bread.

SERVES 4

INGREDIENTS
4 young, tender turnips, peeled
½ onion, finely chopped
2–3 drops white wine vinegar, or to taste
90ml/6 tbsp sour cream

1 Thinly slice or coarsely grate the turnips. Alternatively, thinly slice half the turnips and grate the remaining half. Put in a serving bowl.

2 Add the onion and vinegar and season to taste with salt and freshly ground black pepper. Toss together, then stir in the sour cream. Chill before serving.

POTATO, CARAWAY SEED & PARSLEY SALAD

Leaving the potatoes to cool in garlic-infused oil with the caraway seeds helps them to absorb plenty of flavour. This tasty potato salad goes well with meat or poultry, or can be served as part of a mixed salad buffet meal.

SERVES 4–6

INGREDIENTS
675g/1½lb new potatoes, scrubbed
45ml/3 tbsp garlic-infused olive oil
15ml/1 tbsp caraway seeds, lightly crushed
45ml/3 tbsp chopped fresh parsley

1 Cook the potatoes in salted, boiling water for about 10 minutes, or until just tender. Drain thoroughly and transfer to a large bowl.

2 Stir the garlic-infused oil, caraway seeds and some salt and freshly ground black pepper into the hot potatoes, then set aside to cool. When the potatoes are almost cold, stir in the parsley and serve.

VARIATION
This recipe is also delicious made with sweet potatoes instead of ordinary new potatoes. Peel and roughly chop the sweet potatoes, then follow the recipe as instructed above.

POTATO & OLIVE SALAD

This delicious salad is simple and zesty – the perfect choice for lunch, as an accompaniment, or as an appetizer. Similar in appearance to flat leaf parsley, fresh coriander has a distinctive pungent, almost spicy flavour.

SERVES 4

INGREDIENTS
8 large new potatoes
60ml/4 tbsp garlic-flavoured oil and vinegar dressing
90ml/6 tbsp chopped fresh herbs, such as coriander (cilantro) and chives
15 dry-fleshed black Mediterranean olives

1 Cut the new potatoes into smallish chunks. Put them in a pan, pour in water to cover and add a pinch of salt. Bring to the boil, then reduce the heat and cook gently for about 10 minutes, or until the potatoes are just tender. Drain well and leave in a colander to dry thoroughly and cool slightly.

2 Put the potatoes in a serving bowl and drizzle the garlic dressing over them. Toss well and sprinkle with the chopped fresh herbs and black olives. Chill in the refrigerator for at least 1 hour before serving.

VARIATION
Add a pinch of ground cumin or a sprinkling of roasted whole cumin seeds to spice up the salad.

Anchovy & Pepper Salad

Sweet peppers, salty anchovies and garlic make an intensely flavoured salad that is delicious with meat, poultry or cheese. It also makes a tasty snack with olive bread. If the anchovies are too salty for your liking, soak them in milk for 20 minutes.

SERVES 4

INGREDIENTS
2 red, 2 orange and 2 yellow (bell) peppers, halved and seeded
50g/2oz can anchovies in olive oil
2 garlic cloves
45ml/3 tbsp balsamic vinegar

1 Preheat the oven to 200°C/400°F/Gas 6. Place the peppers, cut side down, in a roasting pan. Roast for 30–40 minutes, until the skins are charred. Transfer the peppers to a bowl, cover with clear film (plastic wrap) and leave for 15 minutes.

2 Peel the peppers, then cut them into chunky strips. Drain the canned anchovies, reserving the oil, and halve the fillets lengthways.

3 Slice the garlic as thinly as possible and place it in a large bowl. Stir in the reserved oil, vinegar and a little pepper. Add the peppers and anchovies and use a spoon and fork to mix gently. Cover and chill until ready to serve.

Asparagus, Bacon & Leaf Salad

This excellent salad turns a roast chicken or simple grilled fish into an interesting meal, especially when served with buttered new potatoes. It also makes an appetizing first course or light lunch, on its own or with bread. A wide range of different salad leaves are readily available – frisée has feathery, curly, slightly bitter tasting leaves and is a member of the chicory family. Frisée leaves range in colour from yellow-white to yellow-green.

SERVES 4

INGREDIENTS
500g/1¼lb medium asparagus spears
130g/4½oz thin-cut smoked back (lean) bacon
250g/9oz frisée lettuce leaves or mixed salad leaves
100ml/3½fl oz/scant ½ cup French dressing

1 Trim off any tough stalk ends from the asparagus and cut the spears into three, setting the tender tips aside. Heat 1cm/½in water in a deep frying pan until simmering. Reserve the asparagus tips and cook the remainder of the spears in the water for about 3 minutes, until almost tender. Add the tips and cook for 1 minute more. Drain and refresh under cold, running water.

2 Dry-fry the bacon until golden and crisp and then set it aside to cool slightly. Use kitchen scissors to snip it into bitesize pieces. Place the frisée or mixed leaves in a bowl and add the bacon.

3 Add the asparagus and a little black pepper to the salad. Pour the dressing over and toss the salad lightly, then serve before the leaves begin to wilt.

WARM CHORIZO & SPINACH SALAD

Spanish chorizo sausage contributes an intense spiciness to any ingredient with which it is cooked. In this hearty salad, spinach has sufficient flavour to compete with the chorizo. Watercress or rocket (arugula) could be used instead of the spinach, if you prefer. For an added dimension use a flavoured olive oil – rosemary, garlic or chilli oil would work perfectly. Serve the salad with warm crusty bread to soak up the juices.

SERVES 4

INGREDIENTS
225g/8oz baby spinach leaves
90ml/6 tbsp extra virgin olive oil
150g/5oz chorizo sausage, very thinly sliced
30ml/2 tbsp sherry vinegar

1 Discard any tough stalks from the spinach. Pour the oil into a large frying pan and add the sausage. Cook gently for 3 minutes, until the sausage slices start to shrivel slightly and colour.

2 Add the spinach leaves and remove the pan from the heat. Toss the spinach in the warm oil until it just starts to wilt. Add the sherry vinegar and a little seasoning. Toss the ingredients briefly, then serve immediately, while still warm.

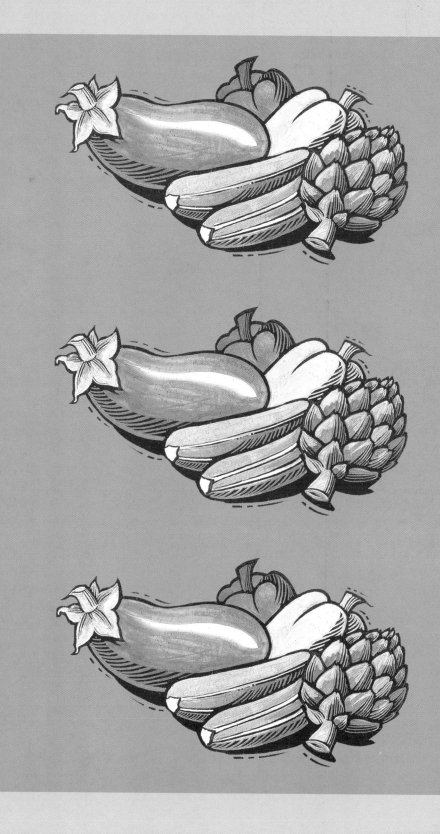

VEGETABLES & SIDE DISHES

A few carefully chosen ingredients can be brought together to create mouthwatering side-dishes and accompaniments that will complement and enhance any main dish. This collection of tasty and colourful combinations of vegetables make healthy eating a tempting treat. Try Cauliflower with Garlic, or stir-fried Broccoli with Soy Sauce & Sesame Seeds, as accompaniments to any main meal. Bubble & Squeak and Cheesy Creamy Leeks are substantial enough to make a meal in themselves.

SPICY POTATO WEDGES

Potato wedges are very popular as a snack food. This recipe is for a spicy version, flavoured with paprika and ground cumin. They are particularly nice with a garlic mayonnaise dip. They could also be served as an appetizer, or as an accompaniment to a main meat or fish course. The wedges need to be served while they are hot and crunchy on the outside – when they are allowed to cool, they become soggy.

SERVES 4

INGREDIENTS
675g/1½lb potatoes
45ml/3 tbsp olive oil
10ml/2 tsp paprika
5ml/1 tsp ground cumin

1 Preheat the oven to 190°C/375°F/Gas 5. Using a sharp knife, cut the potatoes into chunky wedges and place in a roasting pan.

2 In a small bowl, combine the olive oil with the paprika and cumin and season with plenty of salt and freshly ground black pepper. Pour the mixture over the potatoes and toss well to coat thoroughly.

3 Spread the potatoes in a single layer in the roasting pan and bake for 30–40 minutes, or until golden brown and tender. Serve immediately.

COOK'S TIPS
- *To make extra-spicy potato wedges, use chilli powder instead of paprika.*
- *Floury potatoes such as Maris Piper are the best type to use.*

POTATOES ROASTED IN GOOSE FAT

Goose fat gives the best flavour to roast potatoes and is now widely available in cans in supermarkets. However, if you can't find goose fat, or you want to make a vegetarian version of these potatoes, you can use butter or 15ml/1 tbsp olive oil instead. If you like, add a couple of bay leaves to the potatoes before roasting; they impart a lovely flavour. Serve with roast meat or poultry.

SERVES 4

INGREDIENTS
675g/1½lb floury potatoes, such as Maris Piper, peeled
30ml/2 tbsp goose fat
12 garlic cloves, unpeeled

1 Preheat the oven to 190°C/375°F/Gas 5. Cut the potatoes into large chunks and cook in a pan of salted, boiling water for 5 minutes. Drain well and give the colander a good shake to fluff up the edges of the potatoes. Return the potatoes to the pan and place it over a low heat for 1 minute to steam off any excess water.

2 Meanwhile, spoon the goose fat into a roasting pan and place in the oven until hot, about 5 minutes. Add the potatoes to the pan with the garlic and turn to coat in the fat. Season well with salt and ground black pepper and roast for 40–50 minutes, turning occasionally, until the potatoes are golden and tender.

Bubble & Squeak

Whether you have leftovers or cook this old-fashioned classic from fresh, be sure to give it a really good "squeak" in the pan so it turns a rich honey brown. Serve as an accompaniment to grilled pork chops or fried eggs, or simply serve with warm bread for a quick supper. If you prefer, cook the bubble and squeak in individual-sized portions – divide into four and form into patties before cooking.

SERVES 4

INGREDIENTS
60ml/4 tbsp bacon fat or vegetable oil
1 medium onion, finely chopped
450g/1lb floury potatoes, cooked and mashed
225g/8oz cooked cabbage or Brussels sprouts, finely chopped

COOK'S TIP
When made with vegetables from a roast dinner, the mixture can be moistened with leftover gravy, making it bubble as it cooks and giving a really delicious savoury flavour.

1 Heat 30ml/2 tbsp of the bacon fat or vegetable oil in a heavy frying pan. Add the chopped onion and cook over a medium heat, stirring frequently, until softened but not browned.

2 In a large bowl, mix together the potatoes and cooked cabbage or sprouts and season with salt and plenty of freshly ground black pepper to taste.

3 Add the vegetables to the pan with the cooked onions, stir well, then press the vegetable mixture into a large, even cake.

4 Cook over a medium heat for about 15 minutes, until the cake is browned underneath. Remove the pan from the heat.

5 Invert a large plate over the pan, and, holding it tightly against the pan, turn them both over together. Lift off the frying pan, return it to the heat and add the remaining bacon fat or oil. When hot, slide the cake back into the pan, with the browned side uppermost.

6 Cook over a medium heat for 10 minutes, or until the underside is golden brown. Serve hot, cut into wedges.

SAUTÉ POTATOES

These rosemary-scented, crisp golden potatoes are a favourite in French households, transforming any meat, poultry or fish main course into a wonderful treat. If cooked in oil rather than bacon fat, they would be a tasty addition to a vegetarian meal.

SERVES 6

INGREDIENTS
1.3kg/3lb baking potatoes
60–90ml/4–6 tbsp oil, bacon fat or clarified butter
2 or 3 fresh rosemary sprigs, leaves removed and chopped

1 Peel the potatoes and cut into 2.5cm/1in pieces. Place them in a bowl, cover with cold water and leave to soak for 10–15 minutes. Drain, rinse and drain again, then dry thoroughly in a dishtowel.

2 In a large, heavy, non-stick frying pan or wok, heat 60ml/4tbsp of the oil, bacon fat or butter over a medium-high heat, until very hot, but not smoking.

3 Add the potatoes and cook for 2 minutes without stirring so that they seal completely and brown on one side.

4 Shake the pan and toss the potatoes to brown on another side and continue to stir and shake the pan until the potatoes are evenly browned on all sides. Season with salt and and freshly ground black pepper.

5 Add a little more oil, bacon fat or butter and continue cooking the potatoes over a medium to low heat for 20–25 minutes until tender when pierced with a knife, stirring and shaking the pan frequently. About 5 minutes before the end of cooking, sprinkle the potatoes with the chopped rosemary.

Straw Potato Cake

These potatoes are so named in France because of their resemblance to a woven straw doormat. Serve the potato cake as soon as it is cooked, while it is still nice and crisp on the outside. This makes an excellent accompaniment to any main course.

SERVES 4

INGREDIENTS
450g/1lb baking potatoes
25ml/1½ tbsp melted butter
15ml/1 tbsp vegetable oil, plus more if needed

1 Peel the potatoes and grate them coarsely, then immediately toss them with melted butter and season with salt and freshly ground black pepper.

2 Heat the oil in a large frying pan. Add the potato mixture and press down to form an even layer that covers the pan. Cook over a medium heat for 7–10 minutes until the base is well browned.

3 Loosen the potato cake by shaking the pan or running a thin metal spatula under it. To turn it over, invert a large baking tray over the frying pan and holding it tightly against the pan, turn them both over together.

4 Lift off the frying pan, return it to the heat and add a little oil if it looks dry. Slide the potato cake into the frying pan and continue cooking until crisp and browned on both sides. Serve hot, cut into wedges.

COOK'S TIP
You could make several small cakes instead of a large one – just adjust the cooking time accordingly.

CHAMP

This traditional Irish dish of potatoes and spring onions is enriched with a wickedly indulgent amount of butter – for complete indulgence, replace 60ml/4 tbsp of the milk with crème fraîche or buttermilk. Serve the champ as an accompaniment to beef or lamb stew for a warming and hearty winter meal.

SERVES 4

INGREDIENTS
1kg/2¼lb potatoes, cut into chunks
300ml/½ pint/1¼ cups milk
1 bunch spring onions (scallions), thinly sliced, plus extra to garnish
115g/4oz/½ cup slightly salted butter

1 Boil the potatoes in lightly salted water for 20–25 minutes, or until they are tender. Drain and mash the potatoes with a fork or masher until smooth.

2 Place the milk, spring onions and half the butter in a small pan and set over a low heat until just simmering. Cook for 2–3 minutes, until the butter has melted and the spring onions have softened.

3 Beat the milk mixture into the mashed potato using a wooden spoon until the mixture is light and fluffy. Reheat gently, adding seasoning to taste.

4 Turn the potato into a warmed serving dish and make a well in the centre with a spoon. Place the remaining butter in the well and let it melt. Serve immediately, sprinkled with extra spring onion.

VARIATION
To make colcannon, another Irish speciality, follow the main recipe, using half the butter. Cook about 500g/1¼lb finely shredded green cabbage or kale in a little water until just tender, drain thoroughly and then beat into the creamed potato. This is delicious served with sausages and grilled (broiled) ham or bacon. The colcannon may also be fried in butter and then browned under the grill (broiler).

CHEESY CREAMY LEEKS

This is quite a rich accompaniment that could easily be served as a meal in itself with brown rice or couscous. Cheddar and Monterey Jack cheese have a strong flavour, but you could use a milder Swiss cheese, such as Gruyère, if you like. Make sure you wash the leeks really thoroughly to remove any dirt or grit.

SERVES 4

INGREDIENTS

4 large leeks or 12 baby leeks, trimmed and washed
15ml/1 tbsp olive oil
150ml/¼ pint/⅔ cup double (heavy) cream
75g/3oz mature (sharp) Cheddar or Monterey Jack cheese, grated

1 If using large leeks, slice them lengthways. Heat the oil in a large frying pan and add the leeks. Season with salt and pepper and cook for about 4 minutes, stirring occasionally, until starting to turn golden.

2 Pour the cream into the pan and stir until well combined. Allow to bubble gently for a few minutes.

3 Preheat the grill (broiler) to high. Transfer the creamy leeks to a shallow ovenproof dish and sprinkle with the cheese. Grill (broil) for 4–5 minutes, or until the cheese is golden brown and bubbling, and serve immediately.

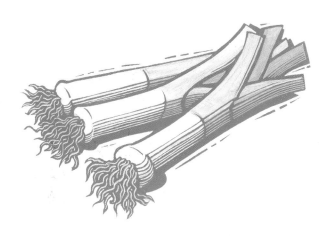

LEEK FRITTERS

These crispy fried morsels are best served at room temperature, with a good squeeze of lemon juice and a sprinkling of salt and freshly grated nutmeg. Matzo meal, a traditional Jewish ingredient, is used in these fritters: it is made from crumbled matzo, an unleavened bread, similar to water biscuits. Matzo meal is used in a similar way to breadcrumbs, which can also be used to make these fritters.

SERVES 4

INGREDIENTS
4 large leeks, total weight about 1kg/2¼lb, thickly sliced
150ml/¼ pint/⅔ cup coarse matzo meal
2 eggs, lightly beaten
olive or vegetable oil, for shallow frying

1 Cook the leeks in salted boiling water for 5 minutes, or until just tender. Drain well and leave to cool.

2 Chop the leeks coarsely. Put in a bowl and combine with the matzo meal, eggs, and salt and freshly ground black pepper.

3 Heat 5mm/¼in oil in a frying pan. Using two tablespoons, carefully spoon the leek mixture into the hot oil. Cook over a medium-high heat until golden brown on the underside, then turn and cook the second side. Drain on kitchen paper. Add more oil if needed and heat before cooking more mixture.

CAULIFLOWER WITH GARLIC

This simple dish makes a great accompaniment to any meat or fish dish. When buying cauliflower look for creamy white florets with the inner green leaves curled round the flower. Discard any with discoloured patches or yellow leaves. As an alternative, use broccoli in place of cauliflower. Broccoli should have a fresh appearance: avoid yellowing specimens and those that feel soft or are wilting.

SERVES 4–6

INGREDIENTS
1 large cauliflower, cut into bitesize florets
7 tbsp olive or vegetable oil
130g/4½oz/2¼ cups dry white or wholemeal (whole-wheat) breadcrumbs
5 garlic cloves, thinly sliced or chopped

1 Steam the cauliflower or cook in lightly salted boiling water until just tender. Drain and leave to cool.

2 Heat 60ml/4 tbsp of the oil in a large frying pan, add the breadcrumbs and cook over a medium heat, tossing and turning, until browned and crisp. Add the garlic, turn once or twice, then remove from the pan and set aside.

3 Heat the remaining oil in the pan, then add the cauliflower, mashing and breaking it up a little as it lightly browns in the oil. (Do not overcook but just cook until the cauliflower is lightly browned.)

4 Add the garlic breadcrumbs to the pan and cook, stirring, until well combined, with some of the cauliflower still holding its shape. Season to taste with salt and freshly ground black pepper and serve hot or warm.

COOK'S TIP
Serve this wonderful, garlicky cauliflower dish as they do in Italy, with cooked pasta, such as spaghetti or rigatoni.

Minty Broad Beans
with Lemon

Young, tender broad beans have a sweet, mild taste that combines surprisingly well with lemon and mint. Take advantage of them when they're in season and make them into this fresh, zesty dish. Green peas – either fresh or frozen – are also delicious served in the same way, but you don't need to peel off their already tender skins.

SERVES 4

INGREDIENTS
450g/1lb broad (fava) beans, thawed if frozen
30ml/2 tbsp garlic-infused olive oil
grated rind and juice of 1 unwaxed lemon
1 small bunch of fresh mint, roughly chopped

1 Using your fingers, slip the grey skins off the broad beans and discard – this takes a little time but the result is well worthwhile. Cook the beans in salted boiling water for 3–4 minutes, or until just tender.

2 Drain well and toss with the oil, lemon rind and juice, and mint. Season with more salt, if necessary, and freshly ground black pepper, and serve immediately.

COOK'S TIP
When using fresh broad beans, it is easier to cook them first, then run them under cold water before slipping off their skins. Quickly blanch the skinned beans in boiling water to reheat them.

FENNEL, POTATO & GARLIC MASH

This flavoursome mash goes well with practically all main dishes, whether fish,
poultry or meat. Floury varieties of potato such as Maris Piper, Pentland Squire,
King Edward or Marfona are the best ones to use for mashing as they produce
a light, fluffy result.

SERVES 4

INGREDIENTS
800g/1¾lb potatoes, cut into chunks
2 large fennel bulbs
90ml/6 tbsp garlic-infused olive oil
120–150ml/4–5fl oz/½–⅔ cup milk or single (light) cream

1 Boil the potatoes in salted water for 20 minutes, until tender.

2 Meanwhile, trim and coarsely chop the fennel, reserving any feathery tops. Chop the tops and set them aside. Heat 30ml/2 tbsp of the garlic-infused olive oil in a heavy pan. Add the fennel, cover and cook over a low heat for 20–30 minutes, until soft but not browned.

3 Drain and mash the potatoes. Purée the fennel in a food mill or blender and beat it into the potato with the remaining oil.

4 Warm the milk or cream and beat sufficient into the potato and fennel to make a creamy, light mixture. Season to taste with salt and freshly ground black pepper and reheat gently, then beat in any chopped fennel tops. Serve immediately.

STIR-FRIED BROCCOLI WITH SOY SAUCE & SESAME SEEDS

Purple sprouting broccoli has been used for this recipe, but when it is not available an ordinary variety of broccoli, such as calabrese, will also work very well. The soy sauce and sesame seeds give this dish an oriental flavour.

SERVES 2

INGREDIENTS
225g/8oz purple sprouting broccoli
15ml/1 tbsp olive oil
15ml/1 tbsp soy sauce
15ml/1 tbsp toasted sesame seeds

1 Using a sharp knife, cut off and discard any thick stems from the broccoli and cut the broccoli into long, thin florets.

2 Heat the oil in a wok or large frying pan and add the broccoli. Stir-fry for 3–4 minutes, or until tender, adding a splash of water if the pan becomes too dry.

3 Add the soy sauce to the broccoli, then season with salt and ground black pepper to taste. Add the sesame seeds, toss to combine and serve immediately.

COOK'S TIP
When buying broccoli, avoid any that looks wilted or has damaged flowerheads or leaves. Purple sprouting broccoli is less readily available than calabrese, but can often be found at farm stores.

Stir-fried Brussels Sprouts with Bacon & Caraway Seeds

This is a great way of cooking Brussels sprouts, helping to retain their sweet flavour and crunchy texture. Stir-frying guarantees that there will not be a single soggy sprout in sight, which is often what puts people off these fabulous vegetables.

Serves 4

Ingredients
450g/1lb Brussels sprouts, washed and trimmed
30ml/2 tbsp sunflower oil
2 streaky (fatty) bacon rashers (strips), finely chopped
10ml/2 tsp caraway seeds, lightly crushed

1 Using a sharp knife, cut the Brussels sprouts into fine shreds and set aside. Heat the sunflower oil in a wok or large frying pan and add the bacon. Cook for 1–2 minutes, or until the bacon is beginning to turn golden and crisp.

2 Add the shredded sprouts to the wok or pan and stir-fry for 1–2 minutes, or until lightly cooked but not soft.

3 Season the sprouts with salt and ground black pepper to taste and stir in the caraway seeds. Cook for a further 30 seconds, then serve immediately.

Mediterranean Tomato & Aubergine Gratin

This colourful dish makes the perfect partner to grilled, pan-fried or baked meat or poultry. If you prefer, thinly sliced courgettes (zucchini) can be used in this dish instead of the aubergines. Grill the courgettes for 10–15 minutes.

SERVES 4–6

INGREDIENTS
2 medium aubergines (eggplants), about 500g/1¼lb
90ml/6 tbsp olive oil
400g/14oz ripe tomatoes, sliced
40g/1½oz/½ cup freshly grated Parmesan cheese

1 Preheat the grill (broiler). Thinly slice the aubergines and arrange them in a single layer on a foil-lined grill rack. Brush the aubergine slices with some of the olive oil and grill (broil) for 15–20 minutes, turning once, until golden on both sides. Brush the second side with more olive oil after turning the slices.

2 Preheat the oven to 200°C/400°F/Gas 6. Toss the aubergine and tomato slices together in a bowl with a little seasoning, then pile them into a shallow, ovenproof dish. Drizzle with any remaining olive oil and sprinkle with the grated Parmesan cheese. Bake for 20 minutes, until the cheese is golden and the vegetables are hot. Serve the gratin immediately.

CREAMY POLENTA TOPPED WITH DOLCELATTE

Soft-cooked polenta is a tasty accompaniment to meat dishes as a change from the usual potatoes or rice, and cooking it with milk gives it a luxurious richness. It can also be enjoyed on its own as a hearty snack. Dolcelatte cheese is deliciously soft, with a luscious, sweet taste.

SERVES 4–6

INGREDIENTS
900ml/1½ pints/3¾ cups milk
115g/4oz/1 cup instant polenta
60ml/4 tbsp extra virgin olive oil
115g/4oz Dolcelatte cheese

1 Pour the milk into a large pan and bring to the boil, then add a good pinch of salt. Remove the pan from the heat and pour in the polenta in a slow, steady stream, stirring constantly to combine.

2 Return the pan to a low heat and simmer gently, stirring constantly, for 5 minutes. Remove the pan from the heat and stir in the olive oil.

3 Spoon the polenta into a serving dish and crumble the cheese over the top. Season with freshly ground black pepper and serve immediately.

Italian Deep-fried Golden Artichokes

In this Italian speciality the artichokes are baked, then pressed to open them and plunged into hot oil, where their leaves twist and brown, turning the artichokes into crispy flowers. This dish goes particularly well with lamb or pork steaks or can be served alone or with bread as an appetizer.

SERVES 4

INGREDIENTS
3 lemons, halved
8 small young globe artichokes
olive or vegetable oil, for deep-frying

1 Fill a large bowl with cold water and stir in the juice of one or two of the lemons. Trim and discard the stems of the artichokes, then trim off their tough ends and remove all the tough outer leaves until you reach the pale pointed centre. Carefully open the leaves of one of the artichokes by pressing it against the table or poking them open. Trim the tops if they are sharp.

2 If there is any choke inside the artichoke, remove it with a melon baller or small pointed spoon. Put the artichoke in the acidulated water and prepare the remaining artichokes in the same way.

3 Put the artichokes in a large pan and pour over water to cover. Bring to the boil, reduce the heat and simmer for 10–15 minutes, or until partly cooked. If they are small, cook them for only 10 minutes. Drain the artichokes and leave upside down until cool enough to handle. Press them open gently, being careful not to break them apart.

4 Fill a pan with oil to a depth of 7.5cm/3in and heat. Add one or two artichokes at a time, with the leaves uppermost, and press down with a spoon to open up the leaves. Fry for 5–8 minutes, turning, until golden and crisp. Remove from the pan, and drain on kitchen paper. Serve immediately, with the remaining lemon cut into wedges.

Squash & Baby New Potatoes in Warm Dill Sour Cream

Fresh vegetables and fragrant dill are delicious tossed in a simple sour cream or yogurt sauce. Choose small squash with bright skins that are free from blemishes and bruises. For a simpler salad, pour the dill sour cream over warm cooked potatoes. Serve either version of the potato salad with poached salmon or chargrilled chicken.

SERVES 4

INGREDIENTS

400g/14oz mixed squash, such as yellow and green courgettes (zucchini), and pale
 green patty pan
400g/14oz tiny, baby new potatoes
1 large handful mixed fresh dill and chives, finely chopped
300ml/½ pint/1¼ cups sour cream or Greek (US strained plain) yogurt

1 Cut the squash into pieces about the same size as the potatoes. Put the potatoes in a pan and add water to cover and a pinch of salt. Bring to the boil, then simmer for about 10 minutes, until almost tender. Add the squash and continue to cook until the vegetables are just tender, then drain.

2 Rinse the pan in cold water, return the vegetables to the pan and gently stir in the finely chopped fresh dill and chives.

3 Remove the pan from the heat and stir in the sour cream or yogurt. Return to the heat and heat gently until warm. Season and serve.

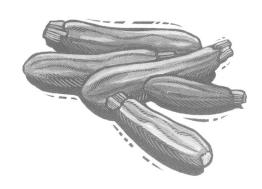

HOT DESSERTS

A hot dessert makes the perfect end to a meal and can take very little time to prepare. A few well-chosen ingredients can be turned into a sumptuous, mouthwatering treat with the minimum of effort. Among the recipes in this chapter you will find some traditional favourites with a new twist, such as Baked Apples with Figs & Marsala, Caramelized Upside-down Pear Pie, Portuguese Custard Tarts and Deep-fried Cherries in Batter.

Summer Berries in Sabayon Glaze

This luxurious combination of summer berries under a light and fluffy liqueur sauce is lightly grilled to form a crisp, caramelized topping. As well as berries, you can use larger fruits such as peaches or kiwi fruit, cut into chunks or slices.

SERVES 4

INGREDIENTS
450g/1lb/4 cups mixed summer berries, or other soft fruit
4 egg yolks
50g/2oz/¼ cup vanilla sugar or caster (superfine) sugar
120ml/4fl oz/½ cup liqueur, such as Cointreau or Kirsch, or a white dessert wine

1 Arrange the mixed summer berries or soft fruit in four individual flameproof dishes. Preheat the grill (broiler).

2 Whisk the yolks in a heatproof bowl with the sugar and liqueur or wine. Place over a pan of hot water and whisk constantly until the mixture is thick, fluffy and pale.

3 Pour equal quantities of the yolk mixture into each dish. Place under the grill for 1–2 minutes, until just turning brown. Add an extra splash of liqueur, if you like, and serve immediately.

Baked Apples with Figs & Marsala

The Marsala cooks down with the juice from the apples and the butter to make a rich, sticky sauce. For a really indulgent dessert, serve these delicious baked apples with a spoonful of extra-thick cream or fromage frais.

SERVES 6

INGREDIENTS
4 medium cooking apples
50g/2oz/¹⁄₃ cup ready-to-eat dried figs, chopped
50g/2oz/¹⁄₄ pint/²⁄₃ cup butter, softened
150ml/¹⁄₄ pint/²⁄₃ cup Marsala

1 Preheat the oven to 180°C/350°F/Gas 4. Using an apple corer, carefully remove the cores from the apples and discard them.

2 Place the cored apples in a small, shallow baking pan and stuff the chopped figs into the holes in the centre of each apple.

3 Top each apple with a quarter of the butter and pour over the Marsala. Cover the pan tightly with foil and bake for 30 minutes.

4 Remove the foil from the apples and bake for a further 10 minutes, or until the apples are tender and the juices have reduced slightly. Serve immediately with any remaining pan juices drizzled over the top.

Baked Bananas with Ice Cream & Toffee Sauce

Bananas make one of the easiest of all desserts, just as welcome as a comforting winter treat as they are to follow a barbecue. For an extra sweet finishing touch, grate some chocolate on the bananas just before serving. If cooking on a barbecue, turn the bananas occasionally to ensure even cooking.

SERVES 4

INGREDIENTS
4 large bananas
75g/3oz/scant ½ cup light muscovado (brown) sugar
75ml/5 tbsp double (heavy) cream
4 scoops good-quality vanilla ice cream

1 Preheat the oven to 180°C/350°F/Gas 4. Put the unpeeled bananas in an ovenproof dish and bake for 15–20 minutes, until the skins are very dark and the flesh feels soft when squeezed.

2 Meanwhile, heat the sugar in a small, heavy pan with 75ml/5 tbsp water until dissolved. Bring to the boil and add the double cream. Cook for 5 minutes, stirring occasionally until the sauce has thickened and is toffee-coloured. Remove from the heat.

3 Transfer the baked bananas in their skins to serving plates and split them lengthways to reveal the flesh. Pour some of the sauce over the bananas and top with scoops of vanilla ice cream. Serve the remaining sauce separately.

Deep-fried Cherries in Batter

Fresh fruit coated with a simple batter and then deep-fried is delicious and makes an unusual dessert. These succulent cherries are perfect sprinkled with sugar and cinnamon and served with a classic vanilla ice cream. They should be served immediately after deep-frying, while the batter is still nice and crisp.

SERVES 4–6

INGREDIENTS
450g/1lb ripe red cherries, on their stalks
225g/8oz batter mix
1 egg
vegetable oil, for deep-frying

1 Gently wash the cherries and pat dry with kitchen paper. Tie the stalks together with fine string to form clusters of four or five cherries.

2 Make up the batter mix according to the instructions on the packet, beating in the egg. Pour the vegetable oil into a deep-fat fryer or large, heavy pan and heat to 190°C/375°F.

3 Working in batches, half-dip each cherry cluster into the batter and then carefully drop the cluster into the hot oil. Fry for 3–4 minutes, or until golden. Remove the deep-fried cherries with a wire-mesh skimmer or slotted spoon, drain on a wire rack placed over crumpled kitchen paper, and serve immediately.

VARIATIONS
As an alternative to cherries, try deep-frying apple rings or chunks of banana in batter.

RASPBERRY BRÛLÉE

Cracking through the caramelized sugary top of a crème brûlée to reveal the creamy custard underneath is always so satisfying. These ones have the added bonus of a deliciously fruity custard packed with crushed raspberries. This is a really elegant dessert to serve at a dinner party and impress your guests.

SERVES 4

INGREDIENTS
115g/4oz fresh raspberries
300ml/½ pint/1¼ cups ready-made fresh custard
75g/3oz caster (superfine) sugar

1 Place the raspberries in a large bowl and crush with a fork. Add the custard and gently fold in until combined.

2 Divide the mixture between four 120ml/4fl oz/½ cup ramekin dishes. Cover with clear film (plastic wrap) and chill in the refrigerator for 2–3 hours.

3 Preheat the grill (broiler) to high. Remove the clear film from the ramekin dishes and place them on a baking sheet. Sprinkle the sugar over the custards and grill (broil) for 3–4 minutes, or until the sugar has caramelized.

4 Remove the custards from the grill and set aside for a few minutes to allow the sugar to harden, then serve.

COOK'S TIP
You can now buy little gas blow torches for use in the kitchen. They make quick work of caramelizing sugar on top of brûlées – and are fun to use!

BAKED RICOTTA CAKES

These honey-flavoured desserts take only minutes to make. The fragrant fruity sauce provides a contrast of both colour and flavour. The sauce can be made a day in advance and chilled until ready to use. Frozen fruit doesn't need extra water, as it usually yields its juice easily on thawing.

SERVES 4

INGREDIENTS
250g/9oz/generous 1 cup ricotta cheese
2 egg whites, beaten
60ml/4 tbsp scented honey, plus extra to taste
450g/1lb/4 cups mixed fresh or frozen fruit, such as strawberries, raspberries,
   blackberries and cherries

1 Preheat the oven to 180°C/350°F/Gas 4. Place the ricotta cheese in a bowl and break it up with a wooden spoon. Add the beaten egg whites and honey, and mix thoroughly until smooth and well combined.

2 Lightly grease four ramekins. Spoon the ricotta mixture into the prepared ramekins and level the tops using a metal spatula or the back of a spoon. Bake for 20 minutes, or until the ricotta cakes are risen and golden.

3 Meanwhile, make the fruit sauce. Reserve about one-quarter of the fruit for decoration. Place the rest of the fruit in a pan, with a little water if the fruit is fresh, and heat gently until softened. Leave to cool slightly and remove any stones (pits) if you are using cherries.

4 Press the fruit through a strainer, then taste and sweeten with a little honey if it is too tart. Serve the sauce, warm or cold, with the ricotta cakes. Decorate the tops with the reserved berries.

Hot Blackberry & Apple Soufflés

The deliciously tart flavours of blackberry and apple complement each other perfectly to make a light, mouthwatering and surprisingly low-fat, hot dessert. Running a table knife around the inside edge of the soufflé dishes before baking helps the soufflés to rise evenly without sticking to the rim of the dish.

Serves 6

Ingredients
350g/12oz/3 cups blackberries
1 large cooking apple, peeled and finely diced
150g/5oz/³⁄4 cup caster (superfine) sugar, plus extra caster or icing (confectioners')
*   sugar for dusting*
3 egg whites

1   Preheat the oven to 200°C/400°F/Gas 6. Put a baking sheet in the oven to heat. Cook the blackberries and apple in a pan for 10 minutes, or until the juice runs from the blackberries and the apple has pulped down well. Press through a strainer into a bowl. Stir in 50g/2oz/¼ cup of the caster sugar. Set aside to cool.

2   Put a spoonful of the fruit purée into each of six 150ml/¼ pint/²⁄3 cup greased and sugared individual soufflé dishes and smooth the surface. Set aside.

3   Whisk the egg whites in a large bowl until they form stiff peaks. Gradually whisk in the remaining caster sugar. Fold in the remaining fruit purée and spoon the flavoured meringue into the prepared dishes. Level the tops with a metal spatula and run a table knife around the edge of each dish.

4   Place the dishes on the hot baking sheet and bake for 10–15 minutes, until the soufflés have risen well and are lightly browned. Dust the tops with a little sugar and serve immediately before the soufflés have time to collapse.

Hot Chocolate Rum Soufflés

Melt-in-the-mouth soufflés are always impressive, yet they are often based on the simplest ingredients. Serve them as soon as they are cooked for a fantastic finale to a special dinner party. For an extra indulgent touch, serve the soufflés with whipped cream flavoured with dark rum and grated orange rind.

Serves 6

INGREDIENTS

50g/2oz/½ cup cocoa powder (unsweetened)
*65g/2½oz/5 tbsp caster (superfine) sugar, plus extra caster or icing (confectioners')
    sugar for dusting*
30ml/2 tbsp dark rum
6 egg whites

1 Preheat the oven to 190°C/375°F/Gas 3. Place a baking sheet in the oven to heat up.

2 Mix 15ml/1 tbsp of the cocoa with 15ml/1 tbsp of the sugar in a bowl. Grease six 250ml/8fl oz/1 cup ramekins. Pour the cocoa and sugar mixture into each of the dishes in turn, rotating them so that they are evenly coated.

3 Mix the remaining cocoa powder with the dark rum.

4 Whisk the egg whites in a clean, grease-free bowl until they form stiff peaks. Whisk in the remaining sugar. Stir a generous spoonful of the whites into the cocoa mixture to lighten it, then fold in the remaining whites.

5 Divide the mixture among the dishes. Place on the hot baking sheet, and bake for 13–15 minutes, or until well risen. Dust with caster or icing sugar.

GRILLED PEACHES WITH MERINGUES

Ripe peaches take on a fabulous scented fruitiness when grilled with brown sugar, and mini meringues are the perfect accompaniment. Serve with crème fraîche flavoured with a little grated orange rind. When buying peaches or nectarines, choose fruit with a rosy bloom, avoiding any that have a green-tinged skin or feel hard.

SERVES 6

INGREDIENTS
2 egg whites
115g/4oz/½ cup soft light brown sugar, plus extra for sprinkling
pinch of ground cinnamon
6 ripe peaches or nectarines

1 Preheat the oven to 140°C/275°F/Gas 1. Line two large baking sheets with baking parchment.

2 Whisk the egg whites until they form stiff peaks. Gradually whisk in the remaining sugar and the ground cinnamon until the mixture is stiff and glossy. Pipe 18 very small meringues on to the trays and bake for 40 minutes. Leave in the oven to cool.

3 Meanwhile, preheat the grill (broiler) to high. Halve and stone (pit) the peaches or nectarines, sprinkling each half with a little sugar as it is cut. Grill (broil) the fruit for 4–5 minutes, until it is just beginning to caramelize.

4 Arrange the grilled peaches on serving plates with the meringues. Top with a spoonful of cream or fromage frais, if you like. Serve immediately.

COOK'S TIPS
Use leftover egg whites to make these little cinnamon-flavoured meringues. The meringues can be stored in an airtight container for about 2 weeks. Serve them after dinner with coffee or with desserts such as mousse or fruit salad.

TANGY APRICOT & GINGER GRATIN

Made with flavoursome fresh apricots, this quick and easy dessert has a comforting,
baked cheesecake-like flavour. For an even easier version of this delicious gratin,
use 400g/14oz canned apricots in juice. Use the juice from the can to beat into
the cream cheese.

SERVES 4

INGREDIENTS
500g/1¼ lb apricots, halved and stoned (pitted)
75g/3oz/scant ½ cup caster (superfine) sugar
200g/7oz/scant 1 cup cream cheese
75g/3oz gingernut biscuits (gingersnaps) crushed to crumbs

1 Put the apricots in a pan with the sugar. Pour in 75ml/5 tbsp water and heat until barely simmering. Cover and cook very gently for 8–10 minutes, until they are tender but still holding their shape.

2 Preheat the oven to 200°C/400°F/Gas 6. Drain the apricots, reserving the syrup, and place in a large dish or divide among four individual ovenproof dishes. Set aside 90ml/6 tbsp of the syrup and spoon the remainder over the fruit.

3 Beat the cream cheese until softened, then gradually beat in the reserved syrup until smooth. Spoon the cheese mixture over the apricots. Sprinkle the biscuit crumbs over the cream cheese and juice mixture. Bake for 10 minutes, until the crumb topping is beginning to darken and the filling has warmed through. Serve immediately.

Blueberry & Almond Tart

This is a cheat's version of a sweet almond tart. Whisked egg whites and grated marzipan cook to form a light sponge under a topping of contrasting blueberries. Before whisking the egg whites for the filling, ensure that no traces of yolk remain.

SERVES 6

INGREDIENTS
250g/9oz shortcrust pastry (unsweetened)
175g/6oz/generous 1 cup white marzipan
4 large (US extra large) egg whites
130g/4½oz/generous 1 cup blueberries

1 Preheat the oven to 200°C/400°F/Gas 6. Roll out the pastry and use to line a 23cm/9in round, loose-based flan tin (quiche pan). Line with greaseproof (waxed) paper and fill with baking beans, then bake for 15 minutes. Remove the beans and greaseproof paper and bake for a further 5 minutes. Reduce the oven temperature to 180°C/350°F/Gas 4.

2 Grate the marzipan. Whisk the egg whites until stiff. Sprinkle half the marzipan over them and fold in. Then fold in the rest.

3 Turn the mixture into the pastry case (pie shell) and spread it evenly. Sprinkle the blueberries over the top and bake for 20–25 minutes, until golden and just set. Leave to cool for 10 minutes before serving.

COOK'S TIP
The best blueberries are those you pick yourself. If you buy them, look for plump berries of similar size, rejecting any shrivelled ones. Unwashed blueberries will keep for a week in the bottom of the refrigerator.

PORTUGUESE CUSTARD TARTS

Called pastis de nata *"cream pastries" in Portugal, these tarts are traditionally served with a small strong coffee as a sweet breakfast dish, but they are equally delicious served as a pastry or dessert. You can use ready-made custard or make your own.*

MAKES 12

INGREDIENTS
225g/8oz ready-made puff pastry, thawed if frozen
175ml/6fl oz/¾ cup custard
30ml/2 tbsp icing (confectioners') sugar

1 Preheat the oven to 200°C/400°F/Gas 6. Roll out the pastry and cut out twelve 13cm/5in rounds. Line a 12-hole muffin tin (pan) with the pastry rounds. Line each pastry round with a circle of baking parchment and some baking beans or uncooked rice.

2 Bake the tarts for 10–15 minutes, or until the pastry is cooked through and golden. Remove the paper and baking beans or rice and set aside to cool.

3 Spoon the custard into the pastry cases and dust with the icing sugar. Place the tarts under a preheated hot grill (broiler) and cook until the sugar caramelizes. Remove from the heat and leave to cool slightly before serving.

TREACLE TART

The best chilled commercial shortcrust pastry makes light work of this old-fashioned favourite, with its sticky filling and twisted lattice topping. Smooth creamy custard is the classic accompaniment, but it is also delicious served with cream, ice cream or crème fraîche. For a more textured filling, use wholemeal (whole-wheat) breadcrumbs or crushed cornflakes instead of the white breadcrumbs.

SERVES 4–6

INGREDIENTS
350g/12oz shortcrust pastry (unsweetened)
260g/9½oz/generous ¾ cup golden (light corn) syrup
1 lemon
75g/3oz/1½ cups fresh white breadcrumbs

1 On a lightly floured surface, roll out three-quarters of the pastry to a thickness of about 3mm/⅛in. Transfer to a 20cm/8in fluted flan tin (quiche pan) and trim off the overhanging pastry. Chill the pastry case (pie shell) in the refrigerator for 20 minutes. Reserve the pastry trimmings.

2 Put a baking sheet in the oven and preheat the oven to 200°C/400°F/Gas 6. To make the filling, warm the syrup in a pan until it melts. Grate the lemon rind and squeeze the juice.

3 Remove the syrup from the heat and stir in the breadcrumbs and lemon rind. Leave the mixture to stand for 10 minutes, then add more crumbs if it is too thin and moist. Stir in 30ml/2 tbsp of the lemon juice, then spread the mixture evenly in the pastry case, using a metal spatula.

4 Roll out the reserved pastry and cut into 10–12 thin strips. Twist the strips into spirals, then lay half of them on the filling. Arrange the remaining strips at right angles to form a lattice. Press the ends on to the rim.

5 Place the tart on the hot baking sheet and bake for 10 minutes. Lower the oven temperature to 190°C/375°F/Gas 5. Bake for 15 minutes more, until golden. Serve warm, topped with cream, ice cream or crème fraîche.

PEACH PIE

Fruit pies do not have to be restricted to the chunky, deep-dish variety. Here, juicy, ripe peaches are encased in crisp pastry to make a glorious puffed dome – simple but delicious. For a really crispy crust, glaze the pie with beaten egg yolk thinned with a little water before sprinkling with sugar. Serve the pie with good quality vanilla ice cream, clotted cream or crème fraîche.

SERVES 8

INGREDIENTS
6 large, firm, ripe peaches
40g/1½oz/3 tbsp butter
75g/3oz/6 tbsp caster (superfine) sugar, plus extra for glazing
450g/1lb puff pastry

1 Blanch the peaches in boiling water for 30 seconds. Drain, refresh in cold water, then peel. Halve, stone (pit) and slice the peaches.

2 Melt the butter in a large frying pan. Add the peach slices, then sprinkle with 15ml/1 tbsp water and the caster sugar. Cook for about 4 minutes, shaking the pan frequently to stop them sticking, until the sugar has dissolved and the peaches are tender. Set the pan aside to cool.

3 Cut the pastry into two pieces, one slightly larger than the other. Roll out on a lightly floured surface and, using plates as a guide, cut a 30cm/12in round and a 28cm/11in round. Place the pastry rounds on baking sheets lined with baking parchment, cover with clear film (plastic wrap) and chill for 30 minutes.

4 Preheat the oven to 200°C/400°F/Gas 6. Remove the clear film. Spoon the peaches into the middle of the larger round and spread them out to within 5cm/2in of the edge. Place the smaller pastry round on top. Brush the edge of the larger pastry round with water, then fold this over the top round and press to seal. Twist the edges together.

5 Lightly brush the pastry with water and sprinkle evenly with a little sugar. Make five or six small crescent-shaped slashes on the top of the pastry. Bake the pie for about 45 minutes, until golden, and serve warm.

Caramelized Upside-down Pear Pie

In this gloriously sticky dessert, which is almost like the French classic tarte tatin, the pastry is baked on top of the fruit, which gives it a crisp and flaky texture. When inverted, the pie looks wonderful. Look for good-quality chilled pastry that you can freeze for future use. Serve with whipped cream, ice cream or crème fraîche.

Serves 8

Ingredients
5–6 firm, ripe pears
175g/6oz/scant 1 cup caster (superfine) sugar
115g/4oz/½ cup butter
225g/8oz shortcrust pastry (unsweetened)

Variations
- *To make caramelized upside-down apple pie, replace the pears with eight or nine firm, full-flavoured eating apples – Cox's Orange Pippins would be a good choice. You will need more apples than pears, as they shrink during cooking.*
- *Nectarines, peaches or rhubarb also work well. Rhubarb is tart, so add more sugar. if necessary.*

1 Peel, quarter and core the pears. Toss them with some of the sugar in a bowl.

2 Melt the butter in a 27cm/10½in heavy, ovenproof omelette pan. Add the remaining sugar. When it changes colour, arrange the pears in the pan.

3 Continue cooking, uncovered, for 20 minutes, or until the fruit has completely caramelized. Leave the fruit to cool in the pan.

4 Preheat the oven to 200°C/400°F/Gas 6. Meanwhile, on a lightly floured surface, roll out the pastry to a round slightly larger than the diameter of the pan. Lay the pastry on top of the pears and then carefully tuck it in around the edge.

5 Bake for 15 minutes, then lower the oven temperature to 180°C/350°F/Gas 4. Continue to bake for a further 15 minutes, or until the pastry is golden.

6 Let the pie cool in the pan for a few minutes. To unmould, run a knife around the pan's edge, then, using oven gloves, invert a plate over the pan and quickly turn the two over together.

7 If any pears stick to the pan, remove them gently with a metal spatula and replace them on the pie. The pie is best served warm.

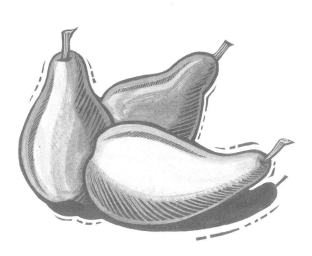

COLD &
FROZEN DESSERTS

Ice creams and other cold desserts make a perfect, refreshing end to a meal. Home-made ices, whether a lightly perfumed Strawberry & Lavender Sorbet, spicy Kulfi or a rich and creamy Soft Fruit & Meringue Gâteau, are surprisingly easy to make and a wonderful treat. Or impress your family and friends with Passion Fruit Creams, Chocolate Banana Fools or Fresh Fig Compote.

Oranges in Syrup

This recipe works well with most citrus fruits, as long as the peel is firm enough for paring – for example, try pink grapefruit or sweet, juicy clementines, which have been peeled but left whole. Serve the oranges with 300ml/½ pint/1¼ cups whipped cream flavoured with 5ml/1 tsp ground cinnamon or 5ml/1 tsp grated nutmeg, or with creamy yogurt.

Serves 6

Ingredients
6 medium oranges
200g/7oz/1 cup sugar
100ml/3½fl oz/scant ½ cup fresh strong brewed coffee
50g/2oz/½ cup pistachio nuts, chopped (optional)

1 Finely pare, shred and reserve the rind from one orange. Peel the remaining oranges. Cut each one crossways into slices, then re-form them, with a cocktail stick (toothpick) through the centre.

2 Put the sugar in a heavy pan and add 50ml/2fl oz/¼cup water. Heat gently until the sugar dissolves, bring to the boil and cook until the syrup turns pale gold.

3 Remove from the heat and carefully pour 100ml/3½fl oz/scant ½ cup freshly boiling water into the pan. Return to the heat until the syrup has dissolved in the water. Stir in the coffee.

4 Add the oranges and the rind to the coffee syrup. Simmer for 15–20 minutes, turning the oranges once during cooking. Leave to cool, then chill. Serve sprinkled with pistachio nuts, if using.

Cook's Tip
Choose a pan in which the oranges will just fit in a single layer – a deep frying pan may be best.

PASSION FRUIT CREAMS

These delicately perfumed creams are light with a fresh flavour. Ripe passion fruit should look purple and wrinkled – choose fruits that are heavy for their size. When halved, the fragrant, juicy flesh with small edible black seeds is revealed. These creams can be decorated with mint or geranium leaves and served with cream.

SERVES 6

INGREDIENTS
600ml/1 pint/2½ cups double (heavy) cream, or a mixture of single (light) and double (heavy) cream
6 passion fruits
30–45ml/2–3 tbsp vanilla sugar
5 eggs

1 Preheat the oven to 180°C/350°F/Gas 4. Line the bases of six 120ml/4fl oz/½cup ramekins with rounds of baking parchment and place in a roasting pan.

2 Heat the cream to just below boiling point, then remove the pan from the heat. Strain the flesh of four passion fruits and beat together with the sugar, to taste, and eggs. Whisk in the hot cream and then ladle into the ramekins.

3 Half fill the roasting pan with boiling water. Bake the creams for 25–30 minutes, or until set, then leave to cool before chilling.

4 Run a knife around the insides of the ramekins to loosen the creams, then invert them on to serving plates, tapping the bases firmly. Carefully peel off the baking parchment and keep the creams in the refrigerator until ready to serve. Spoon on a little passion fruit flesh just before serving.

CHOCOLATE BANANA FOOLS

This deluxe version of banana custard looks great served in glasses. You can use ready-made custard or make it yourself. The bananas should be ripe but still firm. This dessert can be made a few hours in advance and chilled until ready to serve, so is ideal for entertaining. If you like, top the banana fools with some extra grated chocolate. This sumptuous dessert is just the thing for chocolate lovers.

SERVES 4

INGREDIENTS
115g/4oz plain (semisweet) chocolate, chopped
300ml/½ pint/1¼ cups fresh custard
2 bananas

1 Put the chocolate in a heatproof bowl and melt in the microwave on high power for 1–2 minutes. Stir, then set aside to cool.

2 Pour the custard into a large bowl and gently fold in the melted chocolate to make a rippled effect.

3 Peel and slice the bananas and stir these into the chocolate and custard mixture. Spoon into four glasses and chill for 30 minutes–1 hour before serving.

COOK'S TIP
As an alternative to using the microwave, put the chocolate in a heatproof bowl and place it over a pan of gently simmering water. Leave until melted, not touching the water.

BLACKBERRIES IN PORT

Pour this rich fruit compote over ice cream or serve it with a spoonful of clotted cream to create an attractive, rich dessert. It's unbelievably quick and easy to make and is the perfect end to a special dinner party. Blackberries can be found growing wild on hedgerows in late summer and there's nothing better than going out and picking them yourself to make this lovely dessert.

SERVES 4

INGREDIENTS
300ml/½ pint/1¼ cups ruby port
75g/3oz/6 tbsp caster (superfine) sugar
450g/1lb/4 cups blackberries

1 Pour the port into a pan and add the sugar and 150ml/¼ pint/⅔ cup water. Stir over a gentle heat with a wooden spoon until the sugar has dissolved.

2 Remove the pan from the heat and stir in the blackberries. Set aside to cool, then pour into a bowl and cover with clear film (plastic wrap). Chill in the refrigerator until ready to serve.

Fresh Fig Compote

A vanilla and coffee syrup brings out the wonderful flavour of figs – serve thick yogurt or vanilla ice cream with the poached fruit. Using a good-quality, aromatic honey makes all the difference in this recipe – orange blossom honey works particularly well.

Serves 4–6

Ingredients
400ml/14fl oz/1⅔ cups fresh brewed coffee
115g/4oz/½ cup clear honey
1 vanilla pod (bean)
12 slightly under-ripe fresh figs

1 Choose a frying pan with a lid, large enough to hold the figs in a single layer. Pour in the coffee and add the honey.

2 Split the vanilla pod lengthways and scrape the seeds into the pan. Add the vanilla pod, then bring to a rapid boil and cook, uncovered, until the liquid has reduced to about 175ml/6fl oz/¾ cup.

3 Wash the figs and pierce the skins several times with a sharp skewer. Cut in half and add to the syrup. Reduce the heat, cover and simmer for 5 minutes. Remove the figs from the syrup with a slotted spoon and set aside to cool.

4 Strain the syrup over the figs. Allow to stand at room temperature for 1 hour before serving. Serve with yogurt or vanilla ice cream.

Cook's Tip
Figs come in three main varieties – red, white and black – and all three are suitable for cooking. They are sweet and succulent, and complement the stronger, more pervasive flavours of coffee and vanilla very well.

EGG CUSTARD WITH BURNT SUGAR

This delicious egg custard or crème brûlée is a rich, indulgent dessert that can be prepared well in advance, so is ideal for entertaining. You can buy vanilla sugar or make your own by placing a split vanilla pod (bean) in a jar of caster (superfine) sugar – the sugar will be ready to use after a couple of days.

SERVES 6

INGREDIENTS
1 litre/1³/4 pints/4 cups double (heavy) cream
6 egg yolks
90g/3¹/2oz/¹/2 cup vanilla sugar
75g/3oz/¹/3 cup soft light brown sugar

1 Preheat the oven to 150°C/300°F/Gas 2. Place six 120ml/4fl oz/¹/2 cup ramekins in a roasting pan or ovenproof dish and set aside.

2 Prepare the vanilla custard. Heat the double cream in a heavy pan over a gentle heat until it is very hot, but not boiling.

3 In a bowl, whisk the egg yolks and vanilla sugar until well blended. Whisk in the hot cream and strain into a large jug (pitcher). Divide the custard equally among the six ramekins.

4 Pour enough boiling water into the roasting pan to come about halfway up the sides of the ramekins. Cover the pan with foil and bake for about 30 minutes, until the custards are just set. (Push the point of a knife into the centre of one; if it comes out clean, the custards are cooked.) Remove from the pan, cool, then chill.

5 Preheat the grill (broiler). Sprinkle the brown sugar over the surface of the custards and grill (broil) for 30–60 seconds, until the sugar melts and caramelizes, taking care not to let it burn. Place in the refrigerator to chill and set the crust.

BAKED CARAMEL CUSTARD

Many countries have their own version of this classic dessert. Known as crème caramel *in France and* flan *in Spain, this chilled baked custard has a rich caramel flavour. By cooking the custard in a* bain-marie *or as here in a roasting pan with water, the mixture is cooked gently and the eggs are prevented from becoming tough or curdling. It is delicious served with fresh strawberries and thick cream.*

SERVES 6–8

INGREDIENTS
250g/9oz/1¼ cups vanilla sugar
5 large (US extra large) eggs, plus 2 extra yolks
450ml/¾ pint/scant 2 cups double (heavy) cream

> **VARIATION**
> For a special occasion, make individual baked custards in ramekin dishes. Coat six to eight ramekins with the caramel and divide the custard mixture among them. Bake, in a roasting pan of water, for 25–30 minutes or until set. If serving with strawberries, slice them thinly and marinate in a little sugar and a liqueur or dessert wine, such as Amaretto or Muscat wine.

1 Put 175g/6oz/generous ¾ cup of the sugar in a small heavy pan with just enough water to moisten the sugar. Bring to the boil over a high heat, swirling the pan until the sugar has dissolved completely. Boil the syrup for about 5 minutes, without stirring, until it turns a rich, dark caramel colour.

2 Working quickly, pour the caramel into a 1 litre/1¾ pint/4 cup soufflé dish. Holding the dish with oven gloves, carefully swirl it to coat the base and sides with the hot caramel mixture. Set aside to cool.

3 Preheat the oven to 160°C/325°F/Gas 3. In a bowl, whisk the eggs and egg yolks with the remaining sugar for 2–3 minutes, until smooth and creamy.

4 Heat the cream in a heavy pan until hot, but not boiling. Whisk the hot cream into the egg mixture and carefully strain the mixture into the caramel-lined dish. Cover tightly with foil.

5 Place the dish in a roasting pan and pour in just enough boiling water to come halfway up the side of the dish. Bake the custard for 40–45 minutes, until just set. To test whether the custard is set, insert a knife about 5cm/2in from the edge; if the blade comes out clean, the custard should be ready.

6 Remove the soufflé dish from the roasting pan and leave to cool for at least 30 minutes, then place in the refrigerator and chill overnight.

7 To turn out, carefully run a sharp knife around the edge of the dish to loosen the custard. Cover the dish with a serving plate and, holding them both together very tightly, invert the dish and plate, allowing the custard to drop down on to the plate.

8 Gently lift one edge of the dish, allowing the caramel to run down over the sides and on to the plate, then carefully lift off the dish. Serve immediately.

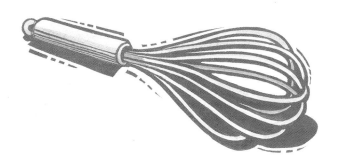

Chocolate & Espresso Mousse

Heady, strong espresso coffee adds a distinctive flavour to this smooth, rich mousse. Serving the mousse in chocolate cups makes for a really impressive dessert, but for a quicker version you could just serve it in dishes and decorate with sprigs of mint.

SERVES 4

INGREDIENTS
450g/1lb plain (semisweet) chocolate
45ml/3 tbsp freshly brewed espresso
25g/1oz/2 tbsp unsalted (sweet) butter
4 eggs, separated

1 For each chocolate cup, cut a double thickness 15cm/6in square of foil. Mould it around a small orange, leaving the edges and corners loose to make a cup shape. Remove the orange and press the bottom of the foil case gently on a surface to make a flat base. Repeat to make four foil cups.

2 Break half the chocolate into small pieces and place in a bowl set over a pan of very hot water. Stir occasionally until the chocolate has completely melted.

3 Spoon the chocolate into the foil cups, spreading it up the sides with the back of a spoon to give a ragged edge. Chill in the refrigerator for 30 minutes, or until set hard. Gently peel away the foil, starting at the top edge.

4 To make the chocolate mousse, put the remaining chocolate and espresso into a bowl set over a pan of hot water and melt as before, until smooth and liquid. Stir in the butter, a little at a time. Remove the pan from the heat and then stir in the egg yolks.

5 Whisk the egg whites in a bowl until stiff, but not dry, then fold them into the chocolate mixture. Pour into a bowl and chill for at least 3 hours, or until it is set. Scoop the chilled mousse into the chocolate cups just before serving.

Baby Summer Puddings

This classic English dessert is always a favourite, and serving it in individual portions with spoonfuls of clotted cream makes it extra special. White bread that is more than a day old actually works better than fresh bread.

SERVES 4

INGREDIENTS
6 white bread slices, crusts removed
450g/1lb/4 cups mixed summer fruits, such as strawberries, raspberries, redcurrants
   and blackcurrants
75g/3oz/6 tbsp caster (superfine) sugar

1 Cut out four rounds from the bread slices, large enough to fit in the bottom of four 175ml/6fl oz/³⁄4 cup dariole moulds.

2 Line the moulds with clear film (plastic wrap) and place a bread round in the base of each mould. Reserve two slices of bread and use the remaining slices to line the sides of the moulds, cutting and pressing to fit.

3 Put the summer fruits in a pan with the sugar and heat gently until the sugar has dissolved. Bring to the boil, then simmer gently for 2–3 minutes. Remove from the heat and leave to cool slightly, then spoon into the moulds.

4 Cut four rounds out of the remaining slices of bread to fit the top of the dariole moulds. Place the bread rounds on the fruit and push down to fit. Cover each dariole mould loosely with clear film and place a small weight on top.

5 Chill the desserts overnight, then turn out on to serving plates. Remove the clear film lining and serve immediately.

COOK'S TIP
You can enjoy this lovely dessert even in the winter. Use frozen summer fruits, which are available in supermarkets all year round. Simply thaw the fruits, then cook briefly.

Meringue Pyramid with Chocolate Mascarpone

This impressive cake makes a perfect centrepiece for a celebration buffet. Dust the pyramid with a little sifted icing (confectioners') sugar and sprinkle with just a few rose petals for simple but stunning presentation.

SERVES ABOUT 10

INGREDIENTS
200g/7oz plain (semisweet) chocolate
4 egg whites
150g/5oz/³⁄₄ cup caster (superfine) sugar
115g/4oz/½ cup mascarpone cheese

COOK'S TIP
The meringues for this dessert can be made up to a week in advance and stored in a cool, dry place in an airtight container.

1 Preheat the oven to 150°C/300°F/Gas 2. Line two large baking sheets with baking parchment or greaseproof (waxed) paper. Grate 75g/3oz of the chocolate, reserving the remainder.

2 Whisk the egg whites in a clean, grease-free bowl until they form stiff peaks. Gradually whisk in half the sugar, then add the rest and whisk until the meringue is very stiff and glossy. Add the grated chocolate and whisk lightly to mix.

3 Draw a 20cm/8in circle on the lining paper on one of the baking sheets, turn it upside down, and spread the marked circle evenly with about half the meringue. Spoon the remaining meringue in 28–30 teaspoonfuls on both baking sheets. Bake the meringue for 1–1½ hours, or until crisp and completely dried out.

4 Make the filling. Melt the remaining chocolate in a heatproof bowl over hot water. Cool slightly, then stir in the mascarpone. Cool the mixture until firm.

5 Spoon the chocolate mixture into a large piping (pastry) bag and use to sandwich the meringues together in pairs, reserving a small amount of filling for the pyramid.

6 Place the large round on a serving platter. Pile the sandwiched pairs on top in a pyramid, keeping them in position with a few well-placed dabs of the reserved filling.

Classic Chocolate Roulade

This rich, squidgy chocolate roll should be made at least eight hours before serving to allow it to soften. Expect the roulade to crack a little when you roll it up – sprinkle with a little grated chocolate, if you like, as a final decoration.

SERVES 8

INGREDIENTS
200g/7oz plain (semisweet) chocolate
200g/7oz/1 cup caster (superfine) sugar, plus extra caster or icing (confectioners')
  sugar to dust
7 eggs, separated
300ml/½ pint/1¼ cups double (heavy) cream

> COOK'S TIP
> *For a special dessert, decorate the roulade with swirls of whipped cream and chocolate coffee beans or with clusters of raspberries and mint leaves.*

1 Preheat the oven to 180°C/350°F/Gas 4. Grease and line a 33 × 23cm/13 × 9in Swiss roll tin (jelly roll pan) with baking parchment

2 Break the chocolate into squares and melt in a bowl over a pan of barely simmering water. Remove from the heat and leave to cool for about 5 minutes.

3 In a large bowl, whisk the sugar and egg yolks until light and fluffy. Stir in the melted chocolate.

4 Whisk the egg whites until stiff, but not dry, and then gently fold into the chocolate mixture.

5 Pour the chocolate mixture into the tin, spreading it level with a metal spatula. Bake for about 25 minutes, or until firm. Leave the cake in the tin and cover with a cooling rack, making sure it does not touch the cake.

6 Cover the rack with a damp dishtowel, then wrap in clear film (plastic wrap). Leave in a cool place for at least 8 hours.

7 Dust a sheet of greaseproof (waxed) paper with caster or icing sugar and turn out the roulade on to it. Peel off the lining paper.

8 To make the filling, whip the double cream until soft peaks form. Spread the cream over the roulade. Starting from one of the short ends, carefully roll it up, using the paper to help.

9 Place the roulade, seam side down, on a serving plate and dust generously with more caster or icing sugar before serving.

WHITE CHOCOLATE CASTLES

With a little ingenuity, good-quality bought ice cream can masquerade as a culinary masterpiece – it's down to perfect presentation. For a professional finish, dust the castles and plates with a hint of cocoa powder. A mixture of berries, such as blueberries and raspberries or redcurrants, will make the desserts extra colourful.

SERVES 6

INGREDIENTS
225g/8oz white chocolate, broken into pieces
250ml/8fl oz/1 cup white chocolate ice cream
250ml/8fl oz/1 cup dark chocolate ice cream
115g/4oz/1 cup berries

COOK'S TIP
Chocolate can also be melted in the microwave oven. Put the chocolate into a heatproof bowl and heat on high power for 1–2 minutes.

1 Put the white chocolate in a heatproof bowl, set it over a pan of gently simmering water and leave until melted. Line a baking sheet with baking parchment. Cut out six 30 × 13cm/12 × 5in strips of baking parchment, then fold each in half lengthways.

2 Stand a 7.5cm/3in pastry (cookie) cutter on the baking sheet. Roll one strip of paper into a circle and fit inside the cutter with the folded edge on the base paper. Stick the edges together with tape.

3 Remove the cutter and shape more paper collars in the same way, leaving the pastry cutter in place around the final collar.

4 Spoon a little of the melted chocolate into the base of the collar supported by the cutter. Using a teaspoon, spread the chocolate over the base and up the sides of the collar, making the top edge uneven. Carefully lift away the cutter.

5 Make five more chocolate cases in the same way, using the cutter for extra support each time. Leave the cases in a cool place or in the refrigerator to set.

6 Carefully peel away the paper from the sides of the chocolate cases, then lift the cases off the base. Transfer to serving plates.

7 Using a large melon baller or teaspoon, scoop the white and dark chocolate ice creams into the cases and decorate with berries. Serve immediately.

White Chocolate & Brownie Torte

This delicious and totally indulgent dessert is easy to make and guaranteed to appeal to just about everyone, particularly those who love chocolate. For extra decoration, put a few fresh summer berries such as strawberries or raspberries around the edge or on the centre of the torte.

SERVES 10

INGREDIENTS
300g/11oz white chocolate, broken into pieces
600ml/1 pint/2½ cups double (heavy) cream
250g/9oz rich chocolate brownies
cocoa powder (unsweetened), for dusting

1 Dampen the sides of a 20cm/8in springform tin (pan) and line with a strip of greaseproof (waxed) paper. Put the chocolate in a small pan. Add 150ml/¼ pint/⅔ cup of the cream and heat very gently until the chocolate has melted. Stir until smooth, then pour into a bowl and leave to cool.

2 Break the chocolate brownies into chunky pieces and sprinkle these over the base of the tin. Pack them down lightly to make a fairly dense base.

3 Whip the remaining cream until it forms peaks, then fold in the white chocolate mixture. Spoon into the tin to cover the layer of brownies, then tap the tin gently on the work surface to level the mixture. Cover and freeze overnight.

4 Transfer the torte to the refrigerator about 45 minutes before serving to soften slightly. Decorate with a light dusting of cocoa powder just before serving.

COOK'S TIP
If you can't buy good quality brownies, use a moist chocolate sponge or make your own.

Soft Fruit & Meringue Gâteau

This recipe takes only five minutes to prepare but looks and tastes as though a lot of preparation went into it. The trick is to use really good vanilla ice cream. For a dinner party, slice the gâteau and place on individual plates, spoon ready-made strawberry or raspberry coulis around each slice and garnish with whole fruits.

Serves 6

Ingredients

400g/14oz/3½ cups mixed small strawberries, raspberries and/or redcurrants
30ml/2 tbsp icing (confectioners') sugar
750ml/1¼ pints/3 cups vanilla ice cream
6 meringue nests or 115g/4oz meringue

1 Dampen a 900g/2lb loaf tin (pan) and line it with clear film (plastic wrap). If using strawberries, chop them into small pieces. Put them in a bowl and add the raspberries or redcurrants and icing sugar. Toss until the fruit is beginning to break up, but do not let it become mushy.

2 Put the ice cream in a bowl and break it up with a fork. Crumble the meringues into the bowl and add the soft fruit mixture.

3 Fold all the ingredients together until evenly combined and lightly marbled. Pack into the prepared tin and press down gently to level. Cover and freeze overnight. To serve, invert on to a plate and peel away the clear film. Serve in slices.

KULFI

This favourite Indian ice cream is traditionally made by carefully boiling milk until it has reduced to about one-third of its original quantity. Although you can save time by using condensed milk, nothing beats the luscious result achieved by using the authentic method. When they are available, rose petals are a stylish decoration in addition to the pistachio nuts.

SERVES 4

INGREDIENTS
1.5 litres/2½ pints/6¼ cups full-fat (whole) milk
3 cardamom pods
25g/1oz/2 tbsp caster (superfine) sugar
50g/2oz/½ cup pistachio nuts, skinned

1 Pour the milk into a large, heavy pan. Bring to the boil, reduce the heat and simmer gently for 1 hour, stirring occasionally.

2 Put the cardamom pods in a mortar and crush them with a pestle. Add the pods and the seeds to the milk and continue to simmer, stirring frequently, for 1–1½ hours, or until the milk has reduced to about 475ml/16fl oz/2 cups. Strain the milk into a jug (pitcher), stir in the sugar and leave to cool.

3 Grind half the pistachios in a blender or nut grinder. Cut the remaining pistachios into thin slivers and set them aside for decoration. Stir the ground nuts into the milk mixture.

4 Pour the milk and pistachio mixture into four kulfi or lolly (popsicle) moulds. Freeze the mixture overnight or until firm.

5 To unmould the kulfi, half fill a plastic container or bowl with very hot water, stand the moulds in the water and count to ten. Immediately lift out the moulds and invert them on a baking sheet. Transfer the ice creams to individual plates and sprinkle sliced pistachios over the top.

CARAMEL & PECAN TERRINE

Frozen or long-life cream is a useful ingredient to keep in the freezer or store cupboard for making impressive desserts without involving a special shopping trip. Caramel and nuts transform cream to parfait in this recipe. Take care that the syrup does not become too dark, or the ice cream will taste bitter.

SERVES 6

INGREDIENTS
115g/4oz/generous ½ cup sugar
450ml/¾ pint/scant 2 cups double (heavy) cream
30ml/2 tbsp icing (confectioners') sugar
75g/3oz/¾ cup pecan nuts, toasted

1 Heat the sugar and 75ml/5 tbsp water in a small, heavy pan until the sugar dissolves. Boil rapidly until the sugar has turned pale golden. Remove the pan from the heat and leave to stand until the syrup turns a rich brown colour.

2 Pour 90ml/6 tbsp of the cream over the caramel. Heat to make a smooth sauce. Leave to cool.

3 Rinse a 450g/1lb loaf tin (pan), then line the base and sides with clear film (plastic wrap). Whip a further 150ml/¼pint/⅔cup of the cream with the icing sugar until it forms soft peaks. Whip the remaining cream separately and stir in the caramel sauce and the toasted pecan nuts.

4 Spoon one-third of the caramel cream into the prepared tin and spread with half the plain whipped cream. Spread half of the remaining caramel cream over the top, then top with the last of the plain cream. Finally, add the remaining caramel cream and level the surface. Freeze for 6 hours.

5 To serve, dip the tin in very hot water for 2 seconds, invert it on to a serving plate and peel away the film. Serve sliced.

MINIATURE CHOC-ICES

These little chocolate-coated ice creams make a fun alternative to the more familiar after-dinner chocolates, especially on hot summer evenings – although they need to be eaten quickly. Serve the choc-ices in fluted paper cases. If you can, buy gold cases as they will contrast very prettily with the dark chocolate coating.

MAKES ABOUT 25

INGREDIENTS
750ml/1¼ pints/3 cups vanilla, chocolate or coffee ice cream
200g/7oz plain (semisweet) chocolate, broken into pieces
25g/1oz milk chocolate, broken into pieces
25g/1oz/¼ cup chopped hazelnuts, lightly toasted

1 Put a large baking sheet in the freezer for 10 minutes. Using a melon baller, scoop balls of ice cream and place these on the baking sheet. Freeze for at least 1 hour or until firm.

2 Line a second baking sheet with baking parchment and place in the freezer for 15 minutes. Melt the plain chocolate in a heatproof bowl set over a pan of gently simmering water. Melt the milk chocolate in a separate bowl.

3 Using a metal spatula, transfer the ice cream scoops to the parchment-lined sheet. Spoon a little plain chocolate over one scoop so that most of it is coated.

4 Sprinkle immediately with chopped nuts, before the chocolate sets. Coat half the remaining scoops in the same way, sprinkling each one with nuts before the chocolate sets. Spoon the remaining plain chocolate over all the remaining scoops.

5 Using a teaspoon, drizzle the milk chocolate over the choc-ices that are not topped with nuts. Freeze again until ready to serve.

BLACKBERRY ICE CREAM

This delicious, vibrant ice cream is simple to make and ideal as a prepare-ahead dessert. It's extra special if you use blackberries that you've picked – or you can make it using raspberries, blackcurrants, redcurrants or blueberries, if these are plentiful. Add a little extra sugar if the fruit is very tart.

SERVES 4–6

INGREDIENTS
500g/1¼lb/5 cups blackberries, hulled, plus extra to decorate
75g/3oz/6 tbsp caster (superfine) sugar
300ml/½ pint/1¼ cups whipping cream
crisp dessert biscuits (cookies), to serve

1 Put the blackberries into a pan, add 30ml/2 tbsp water and the sugar. Cover and simmer for 5 minutes, until just soft.

2 Pour the fruit into a strainer placed over a bowl and press it through the mesh, using a wooden spoon. Leave to cool, then chill.

3 Whip the cream until it is just thick but still soft enough to fall from a spoon, then mix it with the chilled fruit purée. Pour the mixture into a freezerproof container and freeze for 2 hours, or until it is part frozen.

4 Mash the mixture with a fork or process it in a food processor to break up the ice crystals. Return it to the freezer for 4 hours more, mashing or processing the mixture again after 2 hours.

5 Scoop the ice cream into dishes and decorate with extra blackberries. Serve with crisp dessert biscuits.

COOK'S TIP
Frozen blackberries can be used instead of fresh. There's no need to thaw them – just cook from frozen.

COFFEE ICE CREAM

This classic ice cream is always a favourite and, despite its simplicity, has an air of elegance about it. If you have an ice cream maker, simply pour the mixture into it and churn until firm. You can use ready-made custard or make your own.

SERVES 8

INGREDIENTS
600ml/1 pint/2½ cups custard
150ml/¼ pint/⅔ cup strong black coffee
300ml/½pint/1¼cups double (heavy) cream

1 Put the custard in a large bowl and stir in the coffee. In a separate bowl, whip the cream until soft but not stiff and fold evenly into the custard mixture.

2 Pour the mixture into a freezerproof container, cover with a tight-fitting lid or clear film (plastic wrap) and freeze for about 2 hours.

3 Remove the coffee ice cream from the freezer and beat well with a fork to break up the ice crystals.

4 Return the ice cream to the freezer, freeze it for a further 2 hours, then beat it again. Return it to the freezer until completely frozen, then serve.

WATERMELON ICE

This simple, refreshing dessert is absolutely perfect for serving after a hot, spicy main coursee. Kaffir lime leaves are used extensively in South-east Asian cooking. Their aromatic citrus flavour goes beautifully with watermelon.

SERVES 4–6

INGREDIENTS
90ml/6 tbsp caster (superfine) sugar
4 kaffir lime leaves, torn into small pieces
500g/1¼lb watermelon

1 Put the sugar and lime leaves in a pan with 105ml/7 tbsp water. Heat gently until the sugar has dissolved, then pour into a large bowl and set aside to cool.

2 Cut the watermelon into wedges with a large knife. Cut the flesh from the rind, remove the seeds and chop the flesh. Place the flesh in a food processor and process to a slush, then mix in the sugar syrup. Chill for 3–4 hours.

3 Strain the chilled mixture into a freezerproof container and freeze for 2 hours, then beat with a fork to break up the ice crystals. Return to the freezer and freeze for 3 hours more, beating at half-hourly intervals, then freeze until firm. Transfer the ice to the refrigerator about 30 minutes before serving.

COOK'S TIP
Melons should feel heavy for their size and give off a pleasant, sweet aroma: they should not smell too musky, as this is a sign that they are overripe. Ripe melons are best kept in a cool, airy place.

COCONUT ICE

The creamy taste and texture of this ice cream comes from the natural fat content of coconut, as the mixture contains neither cream nor egg and is very refreshing. The lime adds a delicious tangy flavour as well as pretty green specks to the finished ice. Decorate with toasted coconut shavings or toasted desiccated (dry unsweetened shredded) coconut (this browns very quickly, so watch it constantly).

SERVES 4–6

INGREDIENTS
115g/4oz/generous ½ cup caster (superfine) sugar
2 limes
400ml/14fl oz can coconut milk
toasted coconut shavings or desiccated (dry unsweetened shredded) coconut, to decorate (optional)

1 Pour 150ml/¼ pint/⅔ cup water into a small pan. Add the caster sugar and bring to the boil, stirring constantly until the sugar has completely dissolved. Remove the pan from the heat and leave the syrup to cool, then chill well.

2 Grate the rind from the limes finely, taking care to avoid the bitter pith. Squeeze out their juice and add to the pan of syrup with the rind. Add the coconut milk.

3 Pour the mixture into a freezerproof container and freeze for 5–6 hours, or until firm. Beat twice, at 2-hourly intervals with a fork or electric whisk, or process in a food processor to break up the crystals. Scoop into dishes and decorate with toasted coconut shavings, or desiccated coconut if you like.

COOK'S TIP
To make toasted coconut shavings, rinse the flesh from a coconut under cold water. Shave slices using a vegetable peeler, then toast under a medium grill (broiler) until they are curled and the edges have turned golden.

DAMSON WATER ICE

Damsons have a strong, sharp taste that makes them more suitable for cooking than for eating raw. Their robust flavour is ideal for making a water ice. If you can't find good, really ripe damsons, use another deep-red variety of plum or extra-juicy Victoria plums. To add an extra, nutty flavour to this mouthwatering ice, serve sprinkled with finely chopped toasted almonds.

SERVES 6

INGREDIENTS
500g/1¼lb ripe damsons
150g/5oz/¾ cup caster (superfine) sugar

1 Put the damsons into a pan and add 150ml/¼ pint/⅔ cup water. Cover and simmer gently for 10 minutes, or until the damsons are tender.

2 Pour 300ml/½ pint/1¼ cups water into a second pan. Add the sugar and bring to the boil, stirring until the sugar has completely dissolved. Pour the syrup into a bowl, leave to cool, then chill.

3 Break up the cooked damsons in the pan with a wooden spoon and scoop out any free stones (pits). Pour the fruit and juices into a large strainer set over a bowl. Press the fruit through the strainer and discard the skins and any remaining stones.

4 Pour the damson purée into a shallow plastic container. Stir in the syrup and freeze for 6 hours, beating once or twice to break up the ice crystals.

5 Spoon into tall serving glasses or dishes and serve the water ice with wafers.

Peach & Cardamom Yogurt Ice

Make the most of spices that are familiar in savoury cooking by discovering their potential for sweet dishes. Cardamom, often used in Indian cooking, has a warm, pungent aroma and a subtle lemony flavour. This ice, made with yoghurt has a luxurious velvety texture and it is more healthy than ice-cream.

Serves 4

Ingredients
8 cardamom pods
6 peaches, total weight about 500g/1¼lb, halved and stoned (pitted)
75g/3oz/6 tbsp caster (superfine) sugar
200ml/7fl oz/scant 1 cup natural (plain) yogurt

1 Put the cardamom pods on a board and crush them with the base of a ramekin, or place in a mortar and crush with a pestle.

2 Chop the peaches coarsely and put them in a pan. Add the crushed cardamom pods, with their black seeds, the sugar and 30ml/2 tbsp water. Cover and simmer for 10 minutes, or until the fruit is tender. Leave to cool.

3 Process the peach mixture in a food processor or blender until smooth, then press through a strainer placed over a bowl.

4 Mix the yogurt into the purée and pour into a freezerproof container. Freeze for 5–6 hours, until firm, beating once or twice with a fork, electric whisk, or in a processor to break up the ice crystals.

5 Scoop the ice cream on to a large platter and serve.

Variations
Yogurt ice cream can be made with other fruits and different flavourings. Try strawberries with lemon balm or apricots with ginger.

LEMON SORBET

This is probably the most classic sorbet of all. Refreshingly tangy and yet deliciously smooth, it quite literally melts in the mouth and cleans the palate. Try to buy unwaxed lemons for recipes such as this one where the lemon rind is used. The wax coating can adversely affect the flavour of the rind.

SERVES 6

INGREDIENTS
200g/7oz/1 cup caster (superfine) sugar, plus extra for coating rind to decorate
4 lemons, well scrubbed
1 egg white

1 Put the sugar in a pan and pour in 300ml/½ pint/1¼ cups water. Bring to the boil, stirring occasionally until the sugar has just dissolved.

2 Using a swivel vegetable peeler, pare the rind thinly from two of the lemons so that it falls straight into the pan.

3 Simmer for 2 minutes without stirring, then take the pan off the heat. Leave to cool, then chill in the refrigerator.

4 Squeeze the juice from all the lemons and add it to the syrup. Strain the syrup into a shallow freezerproof container, reserving the rind for decoration. Freeze the mixture for 4 hours, until it is mushy.

5 Process the sorbet (sherbet) in a food processor until it is smooth. Lightly whisk the egg white with a fork until it is just frothy. Replace the sorbet in the container, beat in the egg white and return the mixture to the freezer for 4 hours, or until it is firm.

6 Cut the reserved lemon rind into fine shreds and cook them in boiling water for 5 minutes, or until tender. Drain, then place on a plate and sprinkle generously with caster sugar. Scoop the sorbet into bowls or glasses and decorate with the sugared lemon rind.

STRAWBERRY & LAVENDER SORBET

A hint of lavender transforms a familiar strawberry sorbet into a perfumed dinner-party dessert. When buying strawberries look for plump, shiny fruit without any signs of leakage at the bottom of the punnet. To hull strawberries, prise out the leafy top with a sharp knife or a specially designed strawberry huller.

SERVES 6

INGREDIENTS
150g/5oz/³⁄4 cup caster (superfine) sugar
6 fresh lavender flowerheads, plus extra to decorate
500g/1¼lb/5 cups strawberries, hulled
1 egg white

1 Place the sugar in a pan and pour in 300ml/½ pint/1¼ cups water. Bring to the boil, stirring until the sugar has dissolved.

2 Take the pan off the heat, add the lavender flowers and leave to stand for 1 hour. If time permits, chill the syrup in the refrigerator before using.

3 Process the strawberries in a food processor or in batches in a blender, then press the purée through a large strainer into a bowl.

4 Pour the purée into a freezerproof container, strain in the syrup and freeze for 4 hours, or until mushy. Transfer to a food processor and process until smooth. Whisk the egg white until frothy, and stir into the sorbet (sherbet). Spoon the sorbet back into the container and freeze until firm.

5 Serve in scoops, piled into tall glasses, and decorate with lavender flowers.

BLACKCURRANT SORBET

Wonderfully sharp and bursting with flavour, blackcurrants make a really fabulous sorbet. Blackcurrants are more acidic than white or redcurrants and are very rarely eaten raw. Taste the mixture after adding the syrup, and if you find it too tart, add a little more sugar before freezing.

SERVES 6

INGREDIENTS

500g/1¼lb/5 cups blackcurrants, trimmed, plus extra sprigs to decorate
150g/5oz/¾ cup caster (superfine) sugar
1 egg white

1 Put the blackcurrants in a pan and add 150ml/¼ pint/⅔ cup water. Cover the pan and simmer for 5 minutes, or until the fruit is soft. Cool, then process to a purée in a food processor or blender.

2 Set a large strainer over a bowl, pour the purée into the strainer, then press it through the mesh with the back of a spoon to form a smooth liquid.

3 Pour 200ml/7fl oz/scant 1 cup water into a clean pan. Add the sugar and bring to the boil, stirring until the sugar has dissolved. Pour the syrup into a bowl. Cool, then chill in the refrigerator.

4 Mix the blackcurrant purée and sugar syrup together. Spoon into a freezerproof container and freeze until mushy. Lightly whisk the egg white until just frothy. Process the sorbet (sherbet) in a food processor until smooth, then return it to the container and stir in the egg white. Freeze for 4 hours, or until firm.

5 Transfer the sorbet to the refrigerator about 15 minutes before serving. Serve in scoops, decorated with the blackcurrant sprigs.

CAKES, COOKIES & BREAD

Home-baked cakes and sweet snacks are the ultimate indulgence but are viewed by many as taking too much time and effort. However, with just a few basic ingredients, you can whip up fabulous cakes and cookies in moments. Try delicious treats such as Cherry Chocolate Brownies, Chewy Flapjacks or Quick & Easy Teabread. The aroma and taste of home-baked bread is unbeatable so try baking a Granary Cob or a Cottage Loaf.

CHEWY FLAPJACKS

Flapjacks are popular with adults and children alike and they are so quick and easy to make. They are ideal for packed lunches, picnics, or served with afternoon tea. Store them in an airtight container – if they are not eaten immediately.

MAKES 12

INGREDIENTS
175g/6oz/³⁄4 cup unsalted (sweet) butter
50g/2oz/¹⁄4 cup caster (superfine) sugar
150g/5oz/scant ²⁄3 cup golden (light corn) syrup
250g/9oz/1¹⁄2 cups rolled oats

1 Preheat the oven to 180°C/350°F/Gas 4. Line the base and sides of a 20cm/8in square cake tin (pan) with baking parchment.

2 Mix the butter, sugar and syrup in a pan and heat gently until the butter has melted. Add the oats and stir until all the ingredients are combined. Turn the mixture into the tin and level the surface.

3 Bake the flapjacks for 15–20 minutes, until just beginning to turn golden. Leave to cool slightly, then cut into fingers and remove from the tin.

VARIATIONS
- *For alternative versions of the basic recipe, stir in 50g/2oz/¹⁄4 cup finely chopped ready-to-eat dried apricots or sultanas (golden raisins).*
- *To make a really decadent treat, you can dip the cooled flapjack fingers into melted chocolate.*

QUICK & EASY TEABREAD

This succulent, fruity teabread can be served just as it is, or spread with a little butter. The loaf can be stored, tightly wrapped in foil or in an airtight container, for up to five days. This is a great way to get children to eat some healthy dried fruit.

SERVES 8

INGREDIENTS
350g/12oz/2 cups luxury mixed dried fruit
75g/3oz/scant ⅓ cup demerara (raw) sugar, plus 15ml/1 tbsp
1 large (US extra large) egg
175g/6oz/1½ cups self-raising (self-rising) flour

1 Put the fruit in a bowl. Add 150ml/¼ pint/⅔ cup boiling water and leave to stand for 30 minutes.

2 Preheat the oven to 180°C/350°F/Gas 4. Grease and line the base and long sides of a 450g/1lb loaf tin (pan).

3 Beat the main quantity of sugar and the egg into the fruit. Sift the flour into the bowl and stir until combined. Turn into the prepared tin and level the surface. Sprinkle with the remaining sugar.

4 Bake the teabread for about 50 minutes, until risen and firm to the touch. When the bread is cooked, a skewer inserted into the centre will come out without any sticky mixture on it. Leave the loaf in the tin for 10 minutes before turning out on to a wire rack to cool.

ORANGE & PECAN SCONES

Serve these nutty orange scones with satiny orange or lemon curd or, for a simple, unsweetened snack, fresh and warm with unsalted (sweet) butter. Scones are best served on the day they are made, but can be frozen. To freeze, place in an airtight container. Thaw at room temperature for an hour.

MAKES 10

INGREDIENTS
225g/8oz/2 cups self-raising (self-rising) flour
50g/2oz/¼ cup unsalted (sweet) butter, chilled and diced
grated rind and juice of 1 orange
115g/4oz/1 cup pecan nuts, coarsely chopped

1 Preheat the oven to 220°C/425°F/Gas 7. Grease a baking sheet. Put the flour in a food processor with a pinch of salt and add the butter. Process the mixture until it resembles coarse breadcrumbs.

2 Add the orange rind. Reserve 30ml/2 tbsp of the orange juice and make the remainder up to 120ml/4fl oz/½ cup with water. Add the nuts and the juice mixture to the processor, process very briefly to a firm dough, adding a little water if the dough feels dry.

3 Turn the dough out on to a lightly floured surface and roll out to 2cm/¾in thick. Cut out scones using a round cutter and transfer them to the baking sheet. Re-roll the trimmings and cut more scones. Brush the scones with the reserved juice and bake for 15–20 minutes, until golden. Cool on a wire rack.

GOLDEN GINGER MACAROONS

Macaroons are classic no-fuss buscuits – easy to whisk up in minutes from the minimum ingredients and always acceptable. A hint of ginger makes this recipe that bit different. Bake these biscuits on non-stick baking trays or on a baking tray lined with baking parchment to prevent them from sticking

MAKES 18–20

INGREDIENTS
1 egg white
75g/3oz/scant ½ cup soft light brown sugar
115g/4oz/1 cup ground almonds
5ml/1tsp ground ginger

1 Preheat the oven to 180°C/350°F/Gas 4. In a large, grease-free bowl, whisk the egg white until stiff and standing in peaks, but not dry and crumbly, then whisk in the brown sugar.

2 Sprinkle the ground almonds and ginger over the whisked egg white and gently fold them together.

3 Using two teaspoons, place spoonfuls of the mixture on baking trays, leaving plenty of space between each. Bake for about 20 minutes, until pale golden brown and just turning crisp.

4 Leave to cool slightly on the baking trays before transferring to a wire rack to cool completely.

VARIATION
Other ground nuts, such as hazelnuts or walnuts, are good alternatives to the almonds. Ground cinnamon or mixed spice can be used instead of the ginger, if you like.

RICH CHOCOLATE BROWNIES

These brownies are packed with both milk and plain chocolate instead of adding sugar to the mixture. Serve them in small squares as they are very rich. They would be very popular for children's parties – or with anyone who loves chocolate.

MAKES 16

INGREDIENTS
300g/11oz each plain (semisweet) and milk chocolate
175g/6oz/³⁄4 cup unsalted (sweet) butter
75g/3oz/²⁄3 cup self-raising (self-rising) flour
3 large (US extra large) eggs, beaten

1 Preheat the oven to 180°C/350°F/Gas 4. Line the base and sides of a 20cm/8in square cake tin (pan) with baking parchment.

2 Break the plain chocolate and 90g/3½oz of the milk chocolate into pieces and put in a heatproof bowl with the butter. Melt over a pan of barely simmering water, stirring frequently.

3 Chop the remaining milk chocolate into chunky pieces. Stir the flour and eggs into the melted chocolate until evenly combined. Stir in half the chopped milk chocolate and turn the mixture into the prepared tin, spreading it into the corners. Sprinkle with the remaining chopped chocolate.

4 Bake the brownies for 30–35 minutes, until risen and just firm to the touch. Leave to cool in the tin, then cut the cake into squares. Store the brownies in an airtight container.

COOK'S TIP
When buying plain chocolate, bear in mind that the higher the percentage of cocoa solids, the higher the quality of the chocolate, and the less sugar it has. The best quality has 70 per cent cocoa solids.

RICH CHOCOLATE BISCUIT SLICE

This dark chocolate refrigerator cake contains crisp biscuit pieces and chunks of white chocolate for colour and flavour contrast. The slice is perfect served with strong coffee, either as a teatime treat or in place of dessert.

SERVES 8–10

INGREDIENTS
275g/10oz fruit and nut plain (semisweet) chocolate
130g/4½oz/9 tbsp unsalted (sweet) butter
90g/3½oz digestive biscuits (graham crackers)
90g/3½oz white chocolate

1 Grease and line the base and sides of a 450g/1lb loaf tin (pan) with baking parchment. Break the fruit and nut chocolate into pieces and place in a heatproof bowl with the butter. Place the bowl over a pan of barely simmering water and stir the chocolate gently until it is melted and smooth. Remove the bowl from the pan and leave to cool for 20 minutes.

2 Break the biscuits into small pieces. Chop the white chocolate into chunks. Stir the biscuits and white chocolate into the melted mixture until evenly combined. Turn the mixture into the prepared tin and pack down gently. Chill for about 2 hours, or until set. Cut the cake into slices.

CHERRY CHOCOLATE BROWNIES

This is a modern version of the classic Black Forest gâteau. Choose really good-quality bottled fruits because this will make all the difference to the end result. Look out for bottled fruits at Christmas-time, in particular, when supermarket shelves are packed with different varieties. Other types of fruit will work equally well.

SERVES 4

INGREDIENTS
4 chocolate brownies
300ml/½ pint/1¼ cups double (heavy) cream
20–24 bottled cherries in Kirsch

1 Using a sharp knife, carefully cut each brownie in half crossways to make two thin slices. Place one brownie square on each of four serving plates.

2 Pour the cream into a large bowl and whip until soft but not stiff, then divide half the whipped cream between the four brownie squares.

3 Divide half the cherries among the cream-topped brownies, then place the remaining brownie halves on top of the cherries. Press down lightly.

4 Spoon the remaining cream on top of the brownies, then top each one with more cherries and serve immediately.

CINNAMON PINWHEELS

These sweet pastries go well with tea or coffee or as an accompaniment to ice cream and creamy desserts. Cinnamon is one of the most popular spices, sometimes used in savoury cooking but most commonly in cakes and all kinds of sweet recipes. Its warm, slightly woody flavour makes these simple pinwheels really special.

MAKES 20–24

INGREDIENTS
50g/2oz/¼ cup caster (superfine) sugar, plus a little extra for sprinkling
10ml/2 tsp ground cinnamon
250g/9oz puff pastry
beaten egg, to glaze

1 Preheat the oven to 220°C/425°F/Gas 7. Grease a large baking sheet. Mix the sugar with the cinnamon in a small bowl.

2 Roll out the pastry on a lightly floured surface to a 20cm/8in square and sprinkle with half the sugar mixture. Roll out the pastry to a 25cm/10in square so that the sugar is pressed into it.

3 Brush with the beaten egg and then sprinkle with the remaining sugar mixture. Loosely roll up the pastry into a log, brushing the end of the pastry with a little more egg to secure the edge in place.

4 Using a sharp knife, cut the log into thin slices and transfer them to the prepared baking sheet. Bake for 10 minutes, until golden and crisp. Sprinkle with more sugar and transfer to a wire rack to cool.

COOK'S TIP
If you find the cinnamon pinwheeels turn soft during storage, re-crisp them briefly in the oven.

Almond Cigars

These simple, Moroccan-inspired pastries can be prepared in minutes. They are perfect served with strong black coffee or black tea, or as an after-dinner treat. They are also delicious served with traditional sweet Moroccan mint tea.

Makes 8–12

Ingredients
250g/9oz marzipan
1 egg, lightly beaten
8–12 sheets filo pastry
melted butter, for brushing

1 Knead the marzipan until soft and pliable, then put it in a mixing bowl and mix in the lightly beaten egg. Chill in the refrigerator for 1–2 hours.

2 Preheat the oven to 190°C/375°F/Gas 5. Lightly grease a baking sheet. Place a sheet of filo pastry on a piece of greaseproof (waxed) paper, keeping the remaining pastry covered with a damp cloth, and brush with melted butter.

3 Shape 30–45ml/2–3 tbsp of the almond paste into a cylinder and place at one end of the pastry. Fold the pastry over to enclose the ends of the paste, then roll up to form a cigar shape. Place on the baking sheet and make 7–11 more cigars in the same way.

4 Bake the pastries in the preheated oven for about 15 minutes, or until golden brown. Transfer to a wire rack to cool before serving.

ALL BUTTER COOKIES

Crisp, buttery cookies are perfect with strawberries and cream or any creamy dessert or fruit compote. These biscuits or cookies are known as refrigerator biscuits as the mixture is chilled until it is firm enough to cut neatly into thin biscuits.

MAKES 28–30

INGREDIENTS
275g/10oz/2½ cups plain (all-purpose) flour
200g/7oz/scant 1 cup unsalted (sweet) butter
90g/3½oz/scant 1 cup icing (confectioners') sugar, plus extra for dusting
10ml/2 tsp vanilla essence (extract)

1 Put the flour in a food processor. Add the butter and process until the mixture resembles coarse breadcrumbs. Add the icing sugar and vanilla, and process until the mixture comes together to form a dough. Knead lightly and shape into a thick sausage, 30cm/12in long and 5cm/2in in diameter. Wrap in clear film (plastic wrap) and chill for at least 1 hour, until firm.

2 Preheat the oven to 200°C/400°F/Gas 6. Grease two baking sheets. Using a sharp knife, cut 5mm/¼in thick slices from the dough and space them slightly apart on the baking sheet.

3 Bake for 8–10 minutes, alternating the position of the baking sheets in the oven halfway through cooking, if necessary, until the biscuits are cooked evenly and have just turned pale golden around the edges. Leave on the baking sheet for 5 minutes, then transfer to a wire rack to cool. Serve dusted with icing sugar.

COOK'S TIP
The cookie dough can be frozen and when thawed enough to slice, can be freshly baked, but do allow a little extra cooking time.

ALMOND COOKIES

These short, light cookies have a melt-in-the-mouth texture. Their simplicity means they are endlessly versatile – irresistible with tea or coffee with special desserts. If you like, you can dust the cookies with cocoa powder or a mixture of sugar and cinnamon.

MAKES ABOUT 24

INGREDIENTS

115g/4oz/1 cup plain (all-purpose) flour
175g/6oz/1½ cups icing (confectioners') sugar, plus extra for dusting
50g/2oz/½ cup chopped almonds, plus halved almonds to decorate
115g/4oz/½ cup unsalted (sweet) butter, softened

1 Preheat the oven to 180°C/350°F/Gas 4. Combine the flour, sugar and chopped almonds in a bowl.

2 Put the softened unsalted butter in the centre of the flour and nut mixture and use a rounded knife or your fingertips to draw the dry ingredients into the butter until a dough is formed. Shape the dough into a ball.

3 Place the dough on a lightly floured surface and roll it out to a thickness of about 3mm/⅛in. Using a 7.5cm/3in cookie cutter, cut out about 24 rounds, re-rolling the dough as necessary. Place the cookie rounds on baking sheets, leaving a little space between them. Press an almond half lightly on to the top of each, and bake the cookies for about 25 minutes, until pale golden.

4 Leave the cookies on the baking sheet for 10 minutes, then transfer to wire racks to cool. Dust thickly with sifted icing sugar before serving.

CHOCOLATE TRUFFLES

These rich chocolates are the ultimate indulgence. You can replace the coffee liqueur with whisky, brandy or your own favourite liqueur. For an even simpler version, roll the truffles in cocoa powder instead of dipping in melted chocolate.

MAKES 24

INGREDIENTS
350g/12oz plain (semisweet) chocolate
75ml/5 tbsp double (heavy) cream
30ml/2 tbsp coffee liqueur, such as Tia Maria, Kahlúa or Toussaint
225g/8oz good-quality white or milk dessert chocolate

1 Melt 225g/8oz of the plain chocolate in a heatproof bowl set over a pan of barely simmering water. Stir in the cream and liqueur, then leave to cool and chill for 4 hours, until firm.

2 Divide the mixture into 24 equal pieces and quickly roll each into a ball. Chill for about 1 hour, or until the truffles are firm again. Line a board or tray with foil or baking parchment.

3 Melt the remaining plain, white or milk chocolate in separate small bowls. Using two forks, carefully dip eight of the truffles, one at a time, into the melted plain chocolate, then place them on the prepared board or tray.

4 Repeat to cover the remaining 16 truffles with the melted white or milk chocolate. Leave to set before placing in individual mini paper cases or transferring to a serving dish.

VARIATIONS
Add one of the following to the mixture:
- *Hazelnuts: Roll each ball of chilled truffle mixture around a whole skinned hazelnut*
- *50g/2oz/⅓ cup finely chopped candied fruit, such as pineapple and orange.*

STUFFED PRUNES

Prunes and plain chocolate are delectable partners, especially when the dried fruit is soaked in Armagnac. Serve these sophisticated sweetmeats dusted with cocoa powder as a special dinner-party treat with coffee.

MAKES ABOUT 30

INGREDIENTS
225g/8oz/1 cup unpitted prunes
50ml/2fl oz/¼ cup Armagnac
150ml/¼ pint/⅔ cup double (heavy) cream
350g/12oz plain (semisweet) chocolate, broken into squares

> COOK'S TIP
> *Armagnac is a type of French brandy produced in the Pays de Gascogne in the south-west of the country. It has a pale colour and a biscuity aroma. Other types of brandy can be used in this recipe.*

1 Put the prunes in a bowl and pour the Armagnac over. Stir, then cover with clear film (plastic wrap) and set aside for 2 hours, or until the prunes have absorbed the liquid.

2 Make a slit along each prune and remove the stone (pit), making a hollow for the filling, but leaving the fruit intact.

3 Heat the cream in a pan almost to boiling point. Put 115g/4oz of the chocolate in a bowl and pour over the hot cream.

4 Stir until the chocolate has melted and the mixture is smooth. Leave to cool, until it has the consistency of softened butter.

5 Fill a piping (pastry) bag with a small plain nozzle with the chocolate mixture. Pipe into the cavities of the prunes. Chill for about 20 minutes.

6 Melt the remaining chocolate in a heatproof bowl set over a pan of barely simmering water. Using a fork, dip the prunes, one at a time, into the chocolate to coat them generously. Place on a tray lined with baking parchment and leave to set.

CHOCOLATE CRISPY COOKIES

These simple little chocolate-coated cornflake cookies are always a great hit with children and they are a lot of fun to make. Roll the edges of the cookies in icing (confectioners') sugar before serving.

MAKES 10

INGREDIENTS
90g/3½oz milk chocolate, broken into squares
15ml/1 tbsp golden (light corn) syrup
90g/3½oz/4½ cups cornflakes

1 Line a large baking sheet with baking parchment. Put the chocolate and syrup in a heatproof bowl placed over a pan of simmering water and stir until melted.

2 Put the cornflakes in a plastic bag and, using a rolling pin, lightly crush them. Remove the chocolate mixture from the heat and add the cornflakes. Mix until thoroughly combined.

3 Place a 6cm/2½in round cutter on the baking parchment and put a spoonful of the chocolate mixture in the centre. Pack down firmly with the spoon to make a thick cookie. Ease away the cutter, using the spoon to keep the mixture in place. Continue making cookies in this way until all the mixture has been used up. Cover and chill for at least 1 hour before serving.

MERINGUE SQUIGGLES

These delightful meringue wands are easy to make, taste delicious and look fantastic. They're popular with children and adults alike and are great as a teatime treat or as a simple dessert with ice cream.

MAKES 14–16

INGREDIENTS
2 egg whites
90g/3½oz/½ cup caster (superfine) sugar
multi-coloured sugar sprinkles, to decorate

1 Preheat the oven to 150°C/300°F/Gas 2. Line a large baking sheet with baking parchment. Put the egg whites in a large bowl, reserving about 15ml/1 tbsp for decoration, and whisk until they form firm peaks. Add a spoonful of caster sugar and whisk briefly to combine. Add another spoonful and whisk again. Continue in this way until all the sugar has been incorporated.

2 Spoon the meringue mixture into a large piping (pastry) bag fitted with a large plain nozzle. Pipe wavy lines of meringue, about 13cm/5in long, on to the baking sheet and bake for about 1 hour, or until dry and crisp.

3 Carefully peel the meringues off the paper and transfer to a wire rack to cool. Using a fine pastry brush, brush the tops of the meringues with the reserved egg white, then scatter over the multi-coloured sugar sprinkles to decorate.

COOK'S TIP
If you prefer not to use raw egg white to decorate the meringue squiggles, use a sugar paste instead. Put 45ml/3 tbsp icing (confectioners') sugar in a small bowl and add a few drops of water. Stir well to make a paste, then brush on to the meringues.

Chocolate & Prune Bars

Wickedly self-indulgent and very easy to make, these fruity chocolate bars will keep for 2–3 days in the refrigerator – that is if they don't all get eaten as soon as they are ready.

MAKES 12 BARS

INGREDIENTS
250g/9oz good-quality milk chocolate
50g/2oz/¼ cup unsalted (sweet) butter
115g/4oz digestive biscuits (graham crackers)
115g/4oz/½ cup ready-to-eat prunes

1 Break the chocolate into small pieces and place in a heatproof bowl. Add the butter and melt in the microwave on high for 1–2 minutes. Stir to mix and set aside. (Alternatively, place the bowl over a pan of gently simmering water and leave until melted, stirring frequently.)

2 Put the biscuits in a plastic bag and seal, then break into small pieces with a rolling pin. Roughly chop the prunes and stir into the melted chocolate with the biscuits.

3 Spoon the chocolate and prune mixture into a 20cm/8in square cake tin (pan) and chill for 1–2 hours until set. Remove the cake from the refrigerator and, using a sharp knife, cut into 12 bars and serve.

BLUEBERRY CAKE

Baking a cake no longer has to be a chore as cake mixes are available from most supermarkets, making life very easy. Dust with icing (confectioners') sugar and serve for a simple and fuss-free dessert.

SERVES 6–8

INGREDIENTS
220g/8oz packet sponge cake mix
1 egg, if needed
115g/4oz/1 cup blueberries

1 Preheat the oven to 190°C/375°F/Gas 5. Grease a 20cm/8in cake tin (pan). Make up the sponge cake mix according to the instructions on the packet, using the egg if required. Spoon the mixture into the prepared cake tin.

2 Bake the cake according to the instructions on the packet. Ten minutes before the end of the cooking time, sprinkle the blueberries over the top of the cake. (Work quickly so that the cake is out of the oven for as short a time as possible, otherwise it may sink in the middle.)

3 Leave the cake to cool in the tin for 2–3 minutes, then carefully remove from the tin and transfer to a wire rack. Leave to cool completely before serving.

STRAWBERRY SHORTBREADS

Make these pretty desserts in summer, when strawberries are at their best. Serve them as soon as they are ready because the shortbread cookies will lose their lovely crisp texture if left to stand for too long.

SERVES 4

INGREDIENTS
150g/5oz strawberries
450ml/³/4 pint/scant 2 cups double (heavy) cream
6 round shortbread biscuits (cookies)

1 Reserve three strawberries for decoration. Hull the remaining strawberries and cut them in half.

2 Put the halved strawberries in a bowl and gently crush using the back of a fork. (Only crush the berries lightly; they should not be reduced to a purée.)

3 Put the cream in a large, clean bowl and whip to form soft peaks. Add the crushed strawberries and gently fold in to combine. (Do not overmix.)

4 Halve the reserved strawberries, then spoon the strawberry and cream mixture on top of the shortbread cookies. Decorate each one with half a strawberry and serve immediately.

Rhubarb & Ginger Trifles

Choose a good-quality jar of rhubarb compote for this tasty recipe; try to find one with large, chunky pieces of fruit to make the trifles even more delicious and to make each mouthful a succulent treat.

SERVES 4

INGREDIENTS
12 gingernut biscuits (gingersnaps)
50ml/2fl oz/¼ cup rhubarb compote
450ml/¾ pint/scant 2 cups extra thick double (heavy) cream

1 Put the ginger biscuits in a plastic bag and seal. Bash the biscuits with a rolling pin until roughly crushed.

2 Set aside two tablespoons of the crushed biscuits and divide the rest among four glasses.

3 Spoon the rhubarb compote on top of the crushed biscuits, then top with the cream. Place in the refrigerator and chill for about 30 minutes.

4 Sprinkle the reserved crushed biscuits over the trifles and serve immediately.

VARIATIONS
You can use different fruit compotes, either bought or home-made. (Gently stew the fruit in a little water, with sugar to taste, until soft.) Try using pears, or a mixture of summer berries or dried fruit.

GRANARY COB

Mixing and shaping a simple round loaf can be one of the most satisfying kitchen activities and the result is incomparably excellent. This healthy bread is made with fresh yeast – it is a similar colour and texture to putty and should crumble easily when broken. For the best results, buy fresh yeast in small quantities as required: it will keep for up to one month in the refrigerator.

MAKES 1 ROUND LOAF

INGREDIENTS
450g/1lb/4 cups Granary (multigrain) or malthouse flour
12.5ml/2½ tsp salt
15g/½oz fresh yeast
wheat flakes or cracked wheat, for sprinkling

> COOK'S TIP
> *You can buy fresh yeast from bakers, health food stores and from most supermarkets that have an in-store bakery.*

1 Lightly flour a baking sheet. Mix the flour and 10ml/2 tsp of the salt together in a large bowl and make a well in the centre. Place in a very low oven for 5 minutes to warm.

2 Measure 300ml/½ pint/1¼ cups lukewarm water. Mix the yeast with a little of the water, then blend in the rest. Pour the yeast mixture into the centre of the flour and mix to a dough.

3 Turn out on to a lightly floured surface and knead for about 10 minutes, until smooth and elastic. Place in a lightly oiled bowl, cover with lightly oiled clear film (plastic wrap) and leave to rise in a warm place for 1¼ hours, or until doubled in bulk.

4 Turn the dough out on to a lightly floured surface and knock back (punch down). Knead for 2–3 minutes, then roll into a ball. Place in the centre of the prepared baking sheet. Cover with an inverted bowl and leave to rise in a warm place for 30–45 minutes, until doubled in size again.

5 Preheat the oven to 230°C/450°F/Gas 8 towards the end of the rising time. Mix 30ml/2 tbsp water with the remaining salt and brush evenly over the bread. Sprinkle the loaf with wheat flakes or cracked wheat.

6 Bake the bread for 15 minutes, then reduce the oven temperature to 200°C/400°F/Gas 6 and bake for a further 20 minutes, or until the loaf is firm to the touch and sounds hollow when tapped on the base. Cool on a wire rack.

GRANT LOAVES

This quick and easy recipe was created by a baker called Doris Grant and was published in the 1940s. It is a dream for busy cooks as the dough requires no kneading and takes only a minute to mix. Nowadays we can make the recipe even quicker by using easy-blend yeast, which is added directly to the dry ingredients.

MAKES THREE LOAVES

INGREDIENTS
1.3kg/3lb/12 cups wholemeal (whole-wheat) bread flour
15ml/1 tbsp salt
15ml/1 tbsp easy-blend (rapid-rise) dried yeast
15ml/1 tbsp muscovado (molasses) sugar

1 Thoroughly grease three loaf tins (pans), each 21 × 11 × 6cm/8½ × 4½ × 2½in and set aside in a warm place. Sift the flour and salt together in a large bowl and warm slightly.

2 Sprinkle the dried yeast over 150ml/¼ pint/⅔ cup lukewarm water. After a couple of minutes, stir in the muscovado sugar. Leave for 10 minutes.

3 Make a well in the centre of the flour. Pour in the yeast mixture and add a further 900ml/1½ pints/3¾ cups lukewarm water. Stir to form a slippery dough. Mix for about 1 minute, working the dry ingredients from the sides into the middle.

4 Divide among the prepared tins, cover with oiled clear film (plastic wrap) and leave to rise in a warm place for 30 minutes, or until the dough has risen by about one-third to within 1cm/½ in of the top of the tins.

5 Meanwhile, preheat the oven to 200°C/400°F/Gas 6. Bake for 40 minutes, or until the loaves are crisp and sound hollow when tapped on the base. Turn out on to a wire rack to cool.

PITTA BREAD

This light bread can be eaten in a variety of ways, such as filled with salad or little chunks of meat cooked on the barbecue, or it can be torn into pieces and dipped in savoury dips such as hummus or tzatziki. Chop any leftover bread and incorporate into the Lebanese salad fattoush with parsley, mint, tomatoes and cucumber.

SERVES 4

INGREDIENTS
15ml/1 tbsp dried active yeast
350g/12oz/3 cups plain (all-purpose) flour
5ml/1 tsp salt
50g/2oz/¼ cup butter, melted, or 60ml/4 tbsp vegetable oil

1 Measure 500ml/17fl oz/generous 2 cups lukewarm water. In a bowl, dissolve the dried yeast in about 75ml/5 tbsp of the water. Leave in a warm place for about 10 minutes, or until frothy.

2 Stir the remaining water, the flour, salt and melted butter or vegetable oil into the yeast mixture and mix until it forms a smooth batter. Cover with a clean dishtowel, then leave in a warm place for about 1 hour, until doubled in size.

3 Stir the batter and, if it seems too thick to ladle out, add a little water. Cover and leave to stand in a warm place for about 1 hour.

4 Cook the flat breads in a non-stick frying pan. Ladle 45–60ml/ 3–4 tbsp of batter (or less for smaller breads) into the pan and cook over a low heat until the top is bubbling and the colour has changed. (Traditionally these breads are cooked on only one side, but they can be turned over and the second side cooked for just a moment, if you like.)

5 Remove the cooked flat bread from the frying pan with a spatula and keep warm in a clean dishtowel, if you are going to eat it immediately. Continue cooking until you have used up all the remaining batter.

TRADITIONAL IRISH SODA BREAD

Irish soda bread contains no yeast and therefore does not need to be left to rise, so it is quick and easy to make. It is best eaten on the day that it is made, preferably while still warm. You can bake a loaf in the morning, ready to take on a picnic.

SERVES 4–6

INGREDIENTS

450g/1lb/ 4 cups plain wholemeal (all-purpose whole-wheat) flour
10ml/2 tsp bicarbonate of soda (baking soda)
400ml/14fl oz/1⅔ cups buttermilk
5ml/1 tsp salt

1 Lightly grease a baking sheet. Preheat the oven to 200°C/400°F/Gas 6. Place the flour in a large bowl and stir in the bicarbonate of soda and salt. Make a well in the centre.

2 Gradually pour the buttermilk into the well, beating in the flour from around the edges to form a soft, not sticky, dough.

3 Turn the dough out on to a lightly floured surface and knead for 5 minutes, until smooth. Shape into a 20cm/8in round and place on the prepared baking sheet.

4 Using a sharp knife, cut a deep cross on the top of the dough and bake for 30–35 minutes, or until slightly risen and cooked through. Cool slightly on a wire rack before serving.

Spring Onion Flatbreads

Use these flatbreads to wrap around barbecue-cooked meat and chunky vegetable salads, or serve with tasty dips such as hummus. They taste at their very best as soon as they're cooked so don't leave it too long before you eat them.

Makes 16

Ingredients
450g/1lb/4 cups strong white bread flour, plus extra for dusting
5ml/1 tsp salt
7g/¼ oz easy-blend (rapid-rise) dried yeast
4 spring onions (scallions), finely chopped

1 Place the flour in a large mixing bowl and stir in the salt, yeast and spring onions. Make a well in the centre and pour in 300ml/½ pint/1¼ cups hand-hot water. Mix to form a soft, but not sticky, dough.

2 Turn out the dough on to a floured work surface and knead for about 5 minutes, until smooth. Put the dough back in the bowl, cover with a damp dishtowel and leave in a warm place until doubled in size.

3 Knock back (punch down) the dough to get rid of any excess air and turn out on to a floured work surface. Divide the dough into 16 pieces and roll each piece into a smooth ball. Roll out each ball to a 13cm/5in round.

4 Heat a large frying pan until hot. Dust off any excess flour from one dough round and place in the frying pan. Cook for about 1 minute, until golden, then flip over and cook for a further 30 seconds. Repeat with the remaining dough rounds.

Variation
To make garlic flatbreads, use 2 finely chopped garlic cloves in place of the chopped spring onions. To add extra bite, mix in 1 finely chopped fresh red chilli as well.

COTTAGE LOAF

Create a culinary masterpiece from a few basic ingredients and experience the satisfaction of traditional baking. Serve this classic-shaped loaf with creamy butter to accompany a delicious home-made soup.

MAKES 1 LARGE ROUND LOAF

INGREDIENTS
675g/1½lb/6 cups unbleached strong white bread flour
10ml/2 tsp salt
20g/¾oz fresh yeast

COOK'S TIPS
- To ensure a good-shaped cottage loaf the dough needs to be firm enough to support the weight of the top ball.
- Do not over-prove the dough on the second rising or the loaf may topple over – but even if it does it will still taste good.

---

1 Lightly grease two baking sheets. Sift the flour and salt together into a large bowl and make a well in the centre.

2 Mix the yeast in 150ml/¼ pint/⅔ cup lukewarm water until dissolved. Pour into the centre of the flour and add a further 250ml/8fl oz/1 cup lukewarm water, then mix to a firm dough.

3 Knead the dough on a lightly floured surface for 10 minutes, until it is smooth and elastic. Place in a lightly oiled bowl, cover with lightly oiled clear film (plastic wrap) and leave to rise in a warm place for about 1 hour.

4 Turn out on to a lightly floured surface and knock back (punch down). Knead for 2–3 minutes, then divide the dough into two-thirds and one-third and shape each piece into a ball. Place the balls of dough on the prepared baking sheets. Cover with inverted bowls and leave to rise in a warm place for 30 minutes.

5 Gently flatten the top of the larger round of dough and cut a cross in the centre, about 4cm/1½in across. Brush with a little water and place the smaller round on top. Carefully press a hole through the middle of the top ball, down into the lower part, using your thumb and first two fingers. Cover with lightly oiled clear film and leave to rest in a warm place for about 10 minutes.

6 Preheat the oven to 220°C/425°F/Gas 7 and place the bread on the lower shelf of the oven. Bake for 35–40 minutes, or until it is a rich golden brown colour and the base sounds hollow when tapped. Cool on a wire rack before serving.

POPPY-SEEDED BLOOMER

This long, crusty loaf gets its fabulous flavour from poppy seeds. Cut into thick slices, the bread is perfect for mopping up the cooking juices of hearty stews, or for absorbing good dressing on summery salads.

MAKES 1 LARGE LOAF

INGREDIENTS
675g/1½lb/6 cups unbleached strong white bread flour
12.5ml/2½ tsp salt
15g/½oz fresh yeast
poppy seeds, for sprinkling

COOK'S TIP
The traditional cracked, crusty appearance of this satisfying white loaf is difficult to achieve in a domestic oven. However, you can get a similar result by spraying the oven with water before baking. If the underneath of the loaf is not very crusty at the end of baking, turn it over on the baking sheet, switch off the heat and leave it in the oven for a further 5–10 minutes.

1 Lightly grease a baking sheet. Sift the flour and 10ml/2 tsp salt together into a large bowl and make a well in the centre.

2 Measure 450ml/¾ pint/scant 2 cups lukewarm water and stir about a third of it into the yeast in a bowl. Stir in the remaining water and pour into the centre of the flour. Mix, gradually incorporating the surrounding flour, to a firm dough.

3 Turn out on to a lightly floured surface and knead the dough well, for at least 10 minutes, until smooth and elastic. Place the dough in a lightly oiled bowl, cover with lightly oiled clear film (plastic wrap) and leave to rise, at cool room temperature (about 15–18°C/60–65°F), for 5–6 hours, or until doubled in bulk.

4 Knock back (punch down) the dough, turn out on to a lightly floured surface and knead it thoroughly for about 5 minutes. Return the dough to the bowl and re-cover. Leave to rise, at cool room temperature, for a further 2 hours or slightly longer.

5 Knock back again and repeat the thorough kneading. Leave the dough to rest for 5 minutes, then roll out on a lightly floured surface into a rectangle 2.5cm/1in thick. Roll the dough up from one long side and shape it into a square-ended, thick baton shape about 33 × 13cm/13 × 5in.

6 Place the loaf, seam side up, on a lightly floured baking sheet. Cover with lightly oiled clear film and leave to rest for 15 minutes. Turn the loaf over and place on the greased baking sheet. Plump the loaf up by tucking the dough under the sides and ends. Using a sharp knife, cut six diagonal slashes on the top.

7 Leave to rest, covered, in a warm place, for 10 minutes. Meanwhile, preheat the oven to 230°C/450°F/Gas 8.

8 Mix the remaining salt with 30ml/2 tbsp water and brush this glaze over the bread. Sprinkle with poppy seeds.

9 Spray the oven with water, bake the bread immediately for 20 minutes, then reduce the oven temperature to 200°C/400°F/Gas 6. Bake for 25 minutes more, or until golden and sounds hollow when tapped on the base. Transfer to a wire rack to cool.

SPLIT TIN

The deep centre split down this loaf gives it its name. The split tin loaf slices well for making delicious thick-cut sandwiches. It is also wonderful for serving hearty chunks of bread to accompany robust cheese or to dip in a piping hot soup.

MAKES 1 LOAF

INGREDIENTS
500g/1¼lb/5 cups unbleached strong white bread flour, plus extra for dusting
10ml/2 tsp salt
15g/½oz fresh yeast
60ml/4 tbsp lukewarm milk

COOK'S TIP
Insead of making the cut, you can form the dough into two pieces, placed side by side lengthways in the tin – they will join to make one loaf

1 Grease a 900g/2lb loaf tin (pan). Sift the flour and salt into a bowl and make a well in the centre. Mix the yeast with 150ml/¼ pint/⅔ cup lukewarm water. Stir in another 150ml/¼ pint/⅔ cup lukewarm water. Pour the yeast mixture into the centre of the flour and using your fingers, mix in a little flour to form a smooth batter.

2 Sprinkle a little more flour from around the edge over the batter and leave in a warm place for about 20 minutes to "sponge". Add the milk and remaining flour; mix to a firm dough.

3 Place on a lightly floured surface and knead for about 10 minutes, until smooth and elastic. Place in a lightly oiled bowl, cover with lightly oiled clear film (plastic wrap) and leave to rise in a warm place for 1–1¼ hours, or until nearly doubled in bulk.

4 Knock back (punch down) the dough and turn out on to a lightly floured surface. Shape it into a rectangle, the length of the prepared tin. Roll the dough up lengthways, tuck the ends under and place, seam side down, in the tin. Cover the loaf and leave to rise in a warm place for about 20–30 minutes, or until nearly doubled in bulk again.

5 Using a sharp knife, make one deep central slash. Dust the top of the loaf with a little sifted flour. Leave for 10–15 minutes. Meanwhile, preheat the oven to 230°C/450°F/Gas 8. Bake for 15 minutes, then reduce the oven temperature to 200°C/400°F/Gas 6. Bake for 20–25 minutes, until it is golden and sounds hollow when tapped on the base. Cool on a wire rack.

FRENCH BAGUETTE

Fine French flour is available from French delicatessens and superior supermarkets. If you cannot find any, try ordinary plain flour instead. Baguettes have a wide variety of uses: split horizontally and fill with meats, cheeses and salads; slice diagonally and toast the slices to serve with soup; or simply cut into chunks, spread with butter and serve with French cheeses.

MAKES 3 LOAVES

INGREDIENTS
500g/1¼lb/5 cups unbleached strong white bread flour
115g/4oz/1 cup fine French plain (all-purpose) flour
10ml/2 tsp salt
15g/½oz fresh yeast

COOK'S TIP
Baguettes are difficult to reproduce at home as they require a very hot oven and steam. However, by using less yeast and a triple fermentation you can produce a bread with a superior taste and far better texture than mass-produced baguettes.

1 Sift the flours and salt into a bowl. Add the yeast to 550ml/18fl oz/2½ cups lukewarm water in another bowl and stir. Gradually beat in half the flour mixture to form a batter. Cover with clear film (plastic wrap) and leave in a warm place for about 3 hours, or until nearly trebled in size.

2 Add the remaining flour a little at a time, beating with your hand. Turn out on to a lightly floured surface and knead for 8–10 minutes to form a moist dough. Place in a lightly oiled bowl, cover with lightly oiled clear film and leave to rise, in a warm place, for about 1 hour, until doubled in size.

3 Knock back (punch down) the dough, turn out on to a lightly floured surface and divide into three equal pieces. Shape each into a ball and then into a 15 × 7.5cm/6 × 3in rectangle. Fold the bottom third up lengthways and the top third down and press down. Seal the edges. Repeat two or three more times until each loaf is an oblong. Leave to rest in between folding for a few minutes.

4 Gently stretch each piece of dough into a 33–35cm/13–14in long loaf. Pleat a floured dishtowel on a baking sheet to make three moulds for the loaves. Place the loaves between the pleats, cover with lightly oiled clear film and leave to rise in a warm place for 45–60 minutes, until doubled in size.

5 Preheat the oven to maximum, at least 230°C/450°F/Gas 8. Roll the loaves on to a baking sheet, spaced well apart. Slash the top of each loaf diagonally several times. Place at the top of the oven, spray the inside of the oven with water and bake for 20–25 minutes, until the loaves are golden brown and sound hollow when tapped on the base. Cool on a wire rack.

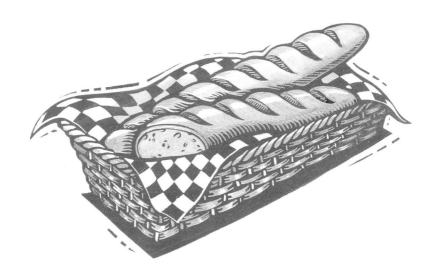

INDEX

A

almonds: almond cigars, 288

almond cookies, 290

blueberry & almond tart, 240

Spanish salted almonds, 84

anchovies: anchovy & pepper salad, 205

marinated anchovies, 98

apples: baked apples with figs & Marsala, 231

hot blackberry & apple soufflés, 236

apricots: apricot turnovers, 58

tangy apricot & ginger gratin, 239

artichokes: artichoke & cumin dip, 89

globe artichokes with green beans & garlic dressing, 196

Italian deep-fried golden artichokes, 226

Asian-style crab cakes, 128

asparagus, bacon & leaf salad, 206

aubergines: aubergines with cheese sauce, 160

Mediterranean tomato & aubergine gratin, 224

pink grapefruit & avocado salad, 200

B

bacon: asparagus, bacon & leaf salad, 206

bacon-rolled mushrooms, 102

Scotch pancakes, 63

stir-fried brussels sprouts with bacon & caraway seeds, 223

bananas: baked bananas with ice cream & toffee sauce, 232

chocolate banana fools, 250

basil: Gruyère and basil tortillas, 85

marinated lamb with oregano &, 136

tomato, bean & fried basil salad, 199

warm pasta with crushed tomatoes &, 182

beans: 41

mixed bean & tomato chilli, 170

tomato, bean & fried basil salad, 199

Tuscan bean soup, 75

beef: beef cooked in red wine, 134

beef patties with onions & peppers, 133

Sicilian meatballs in tomato sauce, 132

steak with tomato salsa, 135

beetroot with fresh mint, 194

black pudding: roast chicken with black pudding & sage, 152

blackberries: blackberries in port, 251

blackberry ice cream, 269

hot blackberry & apple soufflés, 236

blackcurrant sorbet, 277

blueberries: blueberry cake, 297

blueberry & almond tart, 240

borlotti beans: rosemary risotto with, 188

bread: 53

cottage loaf, 306–7

eggy bread, 62

French baguette, 312–13

granary cob, 300–1

Grant loaves, 302

pitta bread, 303

poppy-seeded bloomer, 308–9

quick & easy teabread, 281

split tin, 310–11

spring onion flatbreads, 305

toasted sourdough with goat's cheese, 164

traditional Irish soda bread, 304

brioche sandwiches, chocolate, 57

broad beans: minty broad beans with lemon, 220

pancetta and broad bean risotto, 189

broccoli: stir-fried with soy sauce & sesame seeds, 222

brownies: cherry chocolate brownies, 286

rich chocolate brownies, 284

white chocolate & brownie
torte, 264
brûlée, raspberry, 234
bruschetta, walnut & goat's
cheese, 96
brussels sprouts: stir-fried with
bacon & caraway
seeds, 223
butter beans: butter bean,
sun-dried tomato & pesto
soup, 76
butter bean, tomato & red
onion salad, 198

C

cabbage: bubble &
squeak, 212–13
cannellini beans: Tuscan bean
soup, 75
capers: pan-fried skate wings
with, 125
cappelletti in chicken broth
with Parmesan, 77
caramel: baked caramel
custard, 254–5
caramel & pecan
terrine, 267
caramelized upside-down pear
pie, 244–5
carrots: spicy Moroccan carrot
salad with coriander, 201
cauliflower: cauliflower with
garlic, 219
curried cauliflower soup, 71
cavalo nero: Tuscan bean
soup, 75
cheese: 22–3
aubergines with cheese
sauce, 160
baked leek & potato
gratin, 175

baked ricotta cakes, 235
baked sweet potatoes with
leeks & Gorgonzola, 173
cappelletti in chicken broth
with Parmesan, 77
cheese & tomato
soufflés, 161
cheesy creamy leeks, 217
classic Margherita
pizza, 162
creamy polenta topped with
Dolcelatte, 225
croque-monsieur, 60
goat's cheese pastries, 163
Gruyère & basil tortillas, 85
halloumi & grape salad with
fresh herbs, 197
Israeli cheese with olives, 94
Mediterranean tomato &
aubergine gratin, 224
Parmesan tuiles, 87
spaghetti with raw tomato
& ricotta sauce, 184
Stilton & watercress
soup, 79
tangy apricot & ginger
gratin, 239
tomato & tapenade tarts
with mascarpone
topping, 165
walnut & goat's cheese
bruschetta, 96
yogurt cheese in olive oil, 95
chermoula paste, mackerel
in, 116
cherries: cherry chocolate
brownies, 286
deep-fried cherries in
batter, 233
chicken: chilli-spiced chicken
wings, 103

chicken escalopes with
lemon & serrano
ham, 154
honey mustard chicken, 149
quick-and-easy tandoori
chicken, 151
roast chicken with black
pudding & sage, 152
soy-marinated chicken with
asparagus, 153
stir-fried chicken with Thai
basil, 150
chickpeas: hummus, 90
spicy chickpea samosas, 168
chillies: chilli prawn
skewers, 99
chilli-spiced chicken
wings, 103
grilled hake with lemon &
chilli, 121
jalapeno-style soup, 80
mixed bean & tomato
chilli, 170
Chinese crab wontons, 100
Chinese spiced pork
chops, 141
chocolate: chocolate &
espresso mousse, 256
chocolate & prune bars, 296
chocolate banana fools, 250
chocolate brioche
sandwiches, 57
chocolate crispy
cookies, 294
chocolate truffles, 291
classic chocolate
roulade, 260–1
hot chocolate rum
soufflés, 237
meringue pyramid
with chocolate

mascarpone, 258–9

New York egg cream, 65

rich chocolate biscuit
   slice, 285

rich chocolate brownies, 284

stuffed prunes, 292–3

white chocolate & brownie
   torte, 264

white chocolate
   castles, 262–3

chorizo: chorizo sausage &
   spring onion hash, 146

warm chorizo & spinach
   salad, 207

cider, pan-fried gammon
   with, 148

cinnamon pinwheels, 287

coconut: 37

   coconut ice, 272

   creamed coconut
      macaroons, 283

cod: cod & spinach
   parcels, 112

   roast cod wrapped in
      prosciutto, 111

   salt cod & potato
      fritters, 113

coffee: chocolate & espresso
   mousse, 256

   coffee ice cream, 270

cookies: all butter
   cookies, 289

   almond cookies, 290

   chocolate crispy
      cookies, 294

coriander: marinated smoked
   salmon with lime and, 124

   spicy Moroccan carrot salad
      with, 201

courgettes: linguine with
   courgettes and mint, 180

couscous, 17, 40

crab: Asian-style crab
   cakes, 128

   Chinese crab wontons, 100

   crab & cucumber
      wraps, 127

   crab risotto, 191

creams: flavoured, 49

croque-monsieur, 60

cucumber: crab & cucumber
   wraps, 127

   sour cucumber with dill, 195

cumin: artichoke & cumin
   dip, 89

curries: curried cauliflower
   soup, 71

   curried lamb samosas, 105

custard: chocolate banana
   fools, 250

   Portuguese custard
      tarts, 241

D

damson water ice, 273

dill: sour cucumber
   with, 195

   squash & baby new
      potatoes in warm dill
      sour cream, 227

Dolcelatte: creamy polenta
   topped with, 225

duck with plum sauce, 157

E

eggs: baked caramel
   custard, 254–5

   baked eggs with leeks, 93

   chopped egg & onions, 92

   egg custard with burnt
      sugar, 253

   eggs Benedict, 61

eggs mimosa, 91

eggy bread, 62

hot blackberry & apple
   soufflés, 236

hot chocolate rum
   soufflés, 237

potato & onion
   tortilla, 174

F

farfalle with tuna, 186

fennel: fennel, potato &
   garlic mash, 221

   haddock with fennel butter
      & lemon, 114

fettucine all'Alfredo, 178

figs: baked apples with figs
   & Marsala, 231

   fresh fig compote, 252

fish: 15–16, 24–5

   baked whole fish with
      tomato & pine nuts, 109

   filo-wrapped fish with
      tomato sauce, 110

   poached fish in spicy
      tomato sauce, 108

flapjacks, chewy, 280

flavourings, 34–7

flour, 38

frozen desserts: blackcurrant
   sorbet, 277

   damson water ice, 273

   lemon sorbet, 275

   strawberry & lavender
      sorbet, 276

   watermelon ice, 271

   see also ice cream

fruit: 18–19

   preserved, 37

   see also individual types
      of fruit

G

gammon, pan-fried with cider, 148

garlic: cauliflower with garlic, 219

fennel, potato & garlic mash, 221

globe artichokes with green beans & garlic dressing, 196

pea soup with, 70

potato & garlic broth, 73

roast shoulder of lamb with whole garlic cloves, 139

spaghettini with roasted garlic, 183

ginger: fragrant lemon grass & ginger pork patties, 147

gnocchi: home-made potato gnocchi, 187

goat's cheese: goat's cheese pastries, 163

pasta with roast tomatoes &, 181

toasted sourdough with, 164

walnut & goat's cheese bruschetta, 96

goose fat, potatoes roasted in, 211

gorgonzola: baked sweet potatoes with leeks & Gorgonzola, 173

granary cob, 300–1

Grant loaves, 302

grapefruit: pink grapefruit & avocado salad, 200

grapes: halloumi & grape salad with fresh herbs, 197

green beans: globe artichokes with green beans & garlic dressing, 196

Gruyère and basil tortillas, 85

H

haddock: haddock with fennel butter and lemon, 114

smoked haddock fillets with quick parsley sauce, 115

hake: grilled hake with lemon & chilli, 121

herbs: 28–9

halloumi & grape salad with fresh herbs, 197

honey: honey & watermelon tonic, 64

honey mustard chicken, 149

hummus: 90

roasted pepper & hummus wrap, 172

I

ice cream: baked bananas with ice cream & toffee sauce, 232

blackberry ice cream, 269

coconut ice, 272

coffee ice cream, 270

kulfi, 266

miniature choc-ices, 268

peach & cardamom yogurt ice, 274

soft fruit & meringue gâteau, 265

Israeli cheese with olives, 94

Italian deep-fried golden artichokes, 226

J

jalapeno-style soup, 80

juniper berries, pork with, 142

K

kebabs: pork, 144

tofu & pepper, 169

kulfi, 266

L

lamb: curried lamb samosas, 105

lamb steaks with redcurrant glaze, 138

marinated lamb with oregano & basil, 136

North African lamb with prunes, 137

roast shoulder of lamb with whole garlic cloves, 139

leeks: baked eggs with, 93

baked leek & potato gratin, 175

baked sweet potatoes with leeks & Gorgonzola, 173

cheesy creamy leeks, 217

leek fritters, 218

lemon: chicken escalopes with lemon & serrano ham, 154

grilled hake with lemon & chilli, 121

haddock with fennel butter &, 114

lemon sorbet, 275

minty broad beans with, 220

lemon grass & ginger pork patties, 147

lentils: 41

spiced lentils, 171

limes: marinated smoked salmon with lime and coriander, 124

sea bass with parsley & lime butter, 120

thyme & lime-flavoured
turkey patties, 155
linguine: linguine with
courgettes and mint, 180
linguine with rocket &
Parmesan, 185

M

mackerel in chermoula
paste, 116
marinades, 45
Marsala, baked apples with
figs and, 231
mascarpone: meringue
pyramid with chocolate
mascarpone, 258–9
tomato & tapenade tarts
with mascarpone
topping, 165
meatballs: Sicilian meatballs in
tomato sauce, 132
Mediterranean tomato &
aubergine gratin, 224
meringue: grilled peaches
with, 238
meringue pyramid
with chocolate
mascarpone, 258–9
meringue squiggles, 295
soft fruit & meringue
gâteau, 265
mint: beetroot with fresh
mint, 194
linguine with courgettes
&, 180
minty broad beans
with lemon, 220
Moroccan carrot salad with
coriander, spicy, 201
mushrooms: bacon-rolled
mushrooms, 102

mushroom polenta, 166
mushroom stroganoff, 167
mussels: mussel risotto, 190
mussels in white wine, 129

N

New York egg cream, 65
North African lamb with
prunes, 137

O

oats: chewy flapjacks, 280
crunchy oat cereal, 56
oils, 38–9, 44
olive oil: yogurt cheese in, 95
olives: Israeli cheese with
olives, 94
potato & olive salad, 204
red onion & olive
pissaladière, 97
onions: beef patties with
onions & peppers, 133
butter bean, tomato & red
onion salad, 198
Caribbean roasted sweet
potatoes, onions and
beetroot, 261
cheese & onion
quiche, 148–9
chopped egg & onions, 92
French onion soup, 76
grilled onion & aubergine
salad with tahini, 272
onion & sausage tart
tatin, 145
potato & onion
tortilla, 174
red onion & olive
pissaladière, 97
red onion tart with a polenta
crust, 234–5

shallot and garlic tarte
tatin, 232–3
simple cream of onion
soup, 68–9
oranges: orange & pecan
scones, 282
oranges in syrup, 248
oregano: marinated lamb with
oregano & basil, 136

P

pancakes: Scotch pancakes, 63
warm pancakes with
pears, 59
pancetta & broad bean
risotto, 189
Parmesan: cappelletti in
chicken broth with, 77
linguine with rocket
&, 185
Parmesan tuiles, 87
passion fruit creams, 249
pasta: 39
pasta with roast tomatoes &
goat's cheese, 181
tiny pasta in broth, 78
warm pasta with crushed
tomatoes & basil, 182
peaches: grilled peaches with
meringues, 238
peach & cardamom yogurt
ice, 274
peach pie, 243
pears: caramelized upside-
down pear pie, 244–5
warm pancakes with, 59
peas: pea soup with garlic, 70
tonno con piselli, 117
pecan nuts: caramel & pecan
terrine, 267
orange & pecan scones, 282

peppers: anchovy & pepper salad, 205
  beef patties with onions & peppers, 133
  pepperonata, 88
  roasted pepper & hummus wrap, 172
  tofu & pepper kebabs, 169
pesto: butter bean, sun-dried tomato & pesto soup, 76
pheasant cooked in port, 156
pine nuts, baked whole fish with tomato and, 109
pissaladière, red onion & olive, 97
pitta bread, 303
pizzas: classic Margherita, 162
  red onion & olive pissaladière, 97
plums: duck with plum sauce, 157
polenta: 40, 52–3
  creamy polenta topped with Dolcelatte, 225
  mushroom polenta, 166
  polenta chips, 86
pork: Chinese spiced pork chops, 141
  fragrant lemon grass & ginger pork patties, 147
  paprika pork, 143
  pork & juniper berries, 142
  pork kebabs, 144
  sticky glazed pork ribs, 140
port: blackberries in, 251
  pheasant cooked in, 156
Portuguese custard tarts, 241
potatoes: 50
  baked leek & potato gratin, 175
  bubble & squeak, 212–13

chorizo sausage & spring onion hash, 146
fennel, potato & garlic mash, 221
home-made potato gnocchi, 187
potato & garlic broth, 73
potato & olive salad, 204
potato & onion tortilla, 174
potato, caraway seed & parsley salad, 203
potatoes roasted in goose fat, 211
prawn & new potato stew, 126
salt cod & potato fritters, 113
sauté potatoes, 214
spicy potato wedges, 210
squash & baby new potatoes in warm dill sour cream, 227
straw potato cake, 215
prawns: chilli prawn skewers, 99
  prawn & new potato stew, 126
prosciutto, roast cod wrapped in, 111
prunes: chocolate & prune bars, 296
  North African lamb with, 137
  stuffed prunes, 292–3

R

raspberry brûlée, 234
red onion & olive pissaladière, 97
redcurrant glaze, lamb steaks with, 138
rhubarb & ginger trifles, 299
rice: 17, 40–1, 51
  see also risotto
ricotta: baked ricotta cakes, 235
  spaghetti with raw tomato & ricotta sauce, 184
risotto: crab risotto, 191
  mussel risotto, 190
  pancetta and broad bean risotto, 189
  rosemary risotto with borlotti beans, 188
rocket: linguine with rocket and Parmesan, 185
rosemary risotto with borlotti beans, 188

S

sage, roast chicken with black pudding and, 152
salmon: marinated smoked salmon with lime & coriander, 124
  salmon & green sauce, 123
  teriyaki salmon, 122
samosas: curried lamb, 105
  spicy chickpea samosas, 168
sausages: onion & sausage tarte tatin, 145
scones, orange & pecan, 282
Scotch pancakes, 63
sea bass: sea bass with parsley & lime butter, 120
  sea bass in a salt crust, 119
serrano ham, chicken escalopes with lemon &, 154
shellfish, 25

Sicilian meatballs in tomato sauce, 132

skate: pan-fried skate wings with capers, 125

soft fruit: baby summer puddings, 257

soft fruit & meringue gateau, 265

summer berries in sabayon glaze, 230

soufflés: hot blackberry & apple, 236

hot chocolate rum soufflé, 237

spaghetti with raw tomato & ricotta sauce, 184

spaghettini with roasted garlic, 183

Spanish salted almonds, 84

spices and aromatics, 30–3

spinach: cod & spinach parcels, 112

warm chorizo & spinach salad, 207

spring onions: champ, 216

chopped egg & onions, 92

chorizo sausage & spring onion hash, 146

pork kebabs, 144

spring onion flatbreads, 305

spring rolls, Vietnamese, 104

squash: squash & baby new potatoes in warm dill sour cream, 227

squash soup with tomato salsa, 74

steak with tomato salsa, 135

Stilton and watercress soup, 79

stock, 44–5

straw potato cake, 215

strawberries: strawberry & lavender sorbet, 276

strawberry shortbreads, 298

stroganoff, mushroom, 167

sugars & sweet spreads, 34

summer puddings, baby, 257

sweet potatoes: baked sweet potatoes with leeks & Gorgonzola, 173

T

tagliatelle with vegetables, 179

tahini: hummus, 90

tandoori chicken, quick-and-easy, 151

tapenade: tomato & tapenade tarts with mascarpone topping, 165

tarte tatin, onion & sausage, 145

teabread, quick & easy, 281

teriyaki salmon, 122

Thai basil, stir-fried chicken with, 150

three-delicacy soup, 81

thyme and lime-flavoured turkey patties, 155

toffee sauce, baked bananas with ice cream and, 232

tofu & pepper kebabs, 169

tomato & tapenade tarts with mascarpone topping, 165

tomato, bean & fried basil salad, 199

tonic, honey & watermelon, 64

tonno con piselli, 117

tortillas: Gruyère and basil, 85

potato & onion, 174

treacle tart, 242

turkey patties, thyme and lime-flavoured, 155

turnips: raw turnip salad in sour cream, 202

Tuscan bean soup, 75

V

vegetables: 16–17, 20–1, 41, 53

tagliatelle with, 179

Vietnamese spring rolls, 104

W

walnut & goat's cheese bruschetta, 96

water chestnuts: Chinese crab wontons, 100

watercress: salmon with green sauce, 123

Stilton and watercress soup, 79

watermelon: honey & watermelon tonic, 64

watermelon ice, 271

wedges, spicy potato, 210

whitebait: crisp fried whitebait, 101

wine: beef cooked in red wine, 134

mussels in white wine, 129

wontons, Chinese crab, 10

Y

yogurt: peach & cardamom yogurt ice, 274

yogurt cheese in olive oil, 95